On the Current Situation in the Ukraine

On the

Current Situation
in the Ukraine

By Serhii Mazlakh and Vasyl' Shakhrai

Edited by Peter J. Potichnyj
Introduction by Michael M. Luther

Ann Arbor
The University of Michigan Press

Paperback ISBN: 978-0-472-75164-8

Introduction

By Michael M. Luther

On the Current Situation in the Ukraine is a cry of despair over a
revolution that was betraying a nation. It is also a confession by its
two authors of a loss of faith in their party as the embodiment of
that revolution. Their emotions when writing the book were no less
turbulent than the events in the Ukraine which they were describ-
ing, and these events were no less complex than the history of its
people. Few areas were ethnically, religiously, or culturally as diverse
as the Ukraine on the eve of the revolution. Divided into Russian
and Habsburg territories, the Ukraine was a patchwork quilt of
forest, steppe, and farmland—with several dense outcroppings of
modern industry to mar an otherwise Acadian scene—extending from
the Don and the Kuban rivers in European Russia northwestward
in an arc around the Black Sea to the San River in Austrian Poland
and to the Carpathian Mountains in Hungary. The Ukrainians,
who comprised the overwhelming majority of the population, were
also the territory's most numerous social class, the peasantry. By
religion, they were members of either the Orthodox or the Uniate
church, depending by and large on whether they lived on the
Eastern, Russian, side or the Western, Habsburg, side of the border.
This coincidence of occupation and religion with nationality not
only reinforced the separation of the Ukrainians from the other
nationalities in their midst—chiefly Russians, Poles, and Jews—but
served to aggravate whatever tensions already existed between them.
And in the Eastern Europe of the early twentieth century, with its
growing capitalism and its aristocratic politics, those tensions had
reached the bursting point.

The ingredients for the explosion, which was finally detonated
in 1917, had long been in preparation. In both the Habsburg and
the Russian empires the Ukrainian population had been subjected
to policies of forced assimilation; in the former to the Poles; in the

latter, to the Russians. In both instances, the motive was the same—
to prolong the existence of a decrepit monarchy and a decaying
social system. In Russia an imperial ukase of 1876 had prohibited
the use of the Ukrainian language in all manner and form, including theatrical and musical performances, with the exception of belles
lettres and historical documents. Academic institutions were either
closed down or purged of "disruptive elements"; increasing numbers
of Ukrainian intellectuals sought refuge in purely literary activity or
emigrated to the more liberal environment of Lviv (Lvov) in Austrian Galicia. However, although the Ukrainians fared better under
Austrian rule, they were still subject to pressures. In the latter part of
the nineteenth century the Austrians had given the Polish gentry
free rein over the Ukrainian population of that province. By thus
placating the Poles, Vienna—which abhorred turmoil—could relax,
safe in the assurance that there would be no new Polish uprisings.
But while the Polish Conservatives kept the peace, their agreement
with Vienna did not prevent them from dreaming of an independent
Poland restored to its early eighteenth-century borders. Such a Poland
was unthinkable without the Galician Ukraine and the Ukraine as
a component province was inconceivable unless the Ukrainian population were "reassimilated" to the Polish language and culture. But
the Ukrainians, who comprised approximately two-fifths of the population of the entire province, but formed a solid majority in its eastern
portion, proved unwilling candidates for citizenship in the projected
state. In fighting off the attempts at Polonization, the Ukrainian
political parties looked more and more to the mass of Ukrainians in
Russia as partners in a new national movement whose aim by 1917
would be nothing less than statehood.

It was not surprising, therefore, that when World War I broke
out, the Austrian authorities, under Polish urging, began treating
the Galician Ukrainians as enemies of the state; a rein of terror was
unleashed against the population by the military authorities which
merely reinforced the Ukrainians in their cause of national liberation. Meanwhile, anti-Ukrainian measures also were in force across
the border. When Russia entered the war, the few remaining Ukrainian organizations and activities were suppressed, a policy that was
extended to Galicia with exceptional vigor by Russian occupation
troops in 1915. Yet the autocracy's repressive policies, far from
putting an end to Ukrainian national development, had merely
guaranteed its growth and radicalization, for the Ukrainian national
movement had long since ceased to be an affair of poets and professors and had taken hold of the Ukrainian village and town.

"National differences and antagonisms between peoples are
daily more and more vanishing," declared Marx's *Communist Mani-*
festo, "owing to the development of the bourgeoisie, to freedom of
commerce, to the world's market, to uniformity in the mode of production and in the conditions of life corresponding thereto." Yet
the Czechs and the South Slavs—the *völkerabfälle*—whose absorption
by more powerful capitalist neighbors Marx and Engels had foretold
in 1849, had shown no disposition to assimilation. The "nonhistoric"
Ukrainian nation had likewise refused to disappear. On the contrary,
the development of capitalist agriculture and the simultaneous
growth of new industries in the latter part of the nineteenth century
in both Austrian and Russian Ukraine not only strengthened Ukrainian national consciousness, but by juxtaposing class antagonisms
onto already existing national tensions, spurred the growth of a
radical movement for national and social liberation.

St. Petersburg and Vienna had never succeeded in divesting the
Ukrainian of his national identity although much of his speech had
become Polonized or Russified and he could speak Polish (chiefly in
Galicia) or Russian with the landowners, government officials, and
merchants. While membership in the official (Orthodox) church
helped bind him in the Russian Empire to the tsar and his government, still here as well as in Galicia, the Ukrainian peasant retained
his national styles in clothing and in the applied and decorative arts,
observed his national rituals and customs, and expressed his inner-
most feelings in folk poetry and song. His pejoratives for the Russian
(*katsap*), the Pole (*liakh*), and the Jew (*zhyd*) * in his midst and
his denigration of them in his maxims bore witness to his feeling of
ethnic separation but also of a marked antagonism toward them.

The buying and selling of land throughout both major portions
of the Ukraine in the latter part of the nineteenth century, stimulated by the serf emancipation (in Russia) and by the sharp decline
in world grain prices had resulted, on the one hand, in the accumu-
lation of real estate by both the large landowners and an emerging
group of prosperous peasant proprietors, and in the creation, on the
other hand, of a multitude of impoverished peasants owning too
little, if any, land to afford even a subsistence level of existence.
Outlets for the rural poor were provided by tenant farming or through
employment as agricultural labor on the large estates and as unskilled factory labor, usually in the winter months, in the new

---

* The term *zhyd* in Ukrainian was both the formal term and a
pejorative.

industries. With the Ukrainian peasants, whether prosperous or poor, demanding land from the wealthy Russian and Polish estate owner (who often chose to live in the district town in order to enjoy better police protection) and the peasant-turned-worker demanding improved working and living conditions from the Russian and Polish factory owner or manager, a line was drawn in the popular mind between the Ukrainian village, economically and nationally oppressed, and the non-Ukrainian town as the agent of oppression.

As national and class tensions increased, each feeding on the other, the barometer of popular moods registered a particularly stormy spell for the Jews, who faced a rising tide of economically inspired popular hostility which Russian and Polish officials were only too happy to inflame into ethnoreligious violence. However, the waves of anti-Jewish pogroms which with varying intensity rolled over the Ukraine from the 1880's on through the revolution of 1905 and into World War I provided an embittered Ukrainian population with little more than an emotional release. The debts and the slums remained.

The impoverishment of the Ukrainian peasantry in Russia in the postreform period had drawn a new young generation of Ukrainian intelligentsia—students, doctors, teachers, journalists, lawyers—to the Populist movement of the late 1870's and the 1880's. Prepared as it was to abandon the university and the literary salon for the village, it was also agreed on the need to submerge its national feeling for the sake of a common revolutionary struggle against the autocracy. Russian liberal and revolutionary circles were now maintaining that Ukrainian national feeling existed only on the other side of the border, in Lviv (Lvov) : "Our Ukrainians" are perfectly content to be part of a single Russia. It fell to a succeeding generation of Ukrainian intelligentsia to try to convince them otherwise.

In spite of the rather contemptuous treatment which the founders of "scientific socialism" accorded the "nonhistoric" Slavs (except the Poles) soon after the suppression of the revolutions of 1848, at the turn of the century a new generation of Ukrainian intelligentsia began to abandon Populism for Marxism. Viewing Populism as essentially a Russian movement concerned primarily with the Russian village and showing little regard for industrialization, let alone for its impact on Ukrainian society, these Marxists turned their attention to the plight of the Ukrainian peasantry, especially of the agricultural laborers, as well as to the conditions of the Ukrainian proletariat. The latter interested them not only as a socioeconomic, but more significantly, as an ethnocultural problem.

Arriving at the mines and factories as unskilled labor, the Ukrainians encountered Russians who were skilled workers, technicians, and administrators recruited from the provinces to the north. For these, the national and industrial wealth of the Ukraine were an extension and a vital part of the Russian economy, without which Russia's cities could not be fed, nor its industries operate. The Ukraine for them and particularly its heavily industrialized eastern portion was "South Russia" and they viewed their own language and culture not as barriers, but as instruments to bind the Ukraine's economy and population to the rest of the country. Their thinking was reciprocated by many of the Ukrainian workers for whom the Russian language and culture symbolized superior professional status. The Ukrainian language was being discarded along with the peasant blouse; assimilationists of whatever political persuasion felt vindicated in disparaging Ukrainian national consciousness; the Marx and Engels of 1849 appeared to be correct in their prognosis.

The Ukrainian Marxists had to give priority in their activities to the problem of russification in the factories. Their entire program in the nationality question, calling for Ukrainian statehood, rested on the claim that a Ukrainian proletariat was emerging which would lead the revolutionary struggle of the Ukrainian toilers for socialism. They argued that the russification process was temporary and that the Russian workers would be Ukrainianized once Ukrainians came to dominate the labor force. The Ukrainian Marxists were also concerned about their nation's economic losses. The taxes which the state levied on the Ukrainian peasantry to help finance its industrialization schemes were employed less for the benefit of the Ukraine than for the rest of the empire. Between 1868 and 1892 the Ukraine received back only 60.2 percent of the revenues which it contributed to the state treasury. By 1910 only 45.7 percent of these revenues were returned.* The antipathy of the Ukrainian peasant for the non-Ukrainian city was now translated by the revolutionary intelligentsia into an opposition to Russia. Industrialization helped forge a link between the Ukrainian workers and peasants and their intelligentsia.

Between 1900 and 1914, in spite of internal dissension among the Ukrainian Marxists, their influence grew rapidly among both Ukrainian peasants and workers. Ukrainian Social Democratic literature first gained wide circulation in the countryside at the time of the peasant disturbances in Kharkov and Poltava provinces in 1902.

* Cited in V. Levinskii, *Tsarskaia Rossiia i Ukrainskii vopros* (Geneva, 1917), p. 33.

Their publications, both scholarly and agitational, increased in circulation steadily up to World War I in spite of the government's repressive policies. When in February, 1917, the monarchy collapsed, the Ukrainian Marxists, organized into the Ukrainian Social Democratic Labor Party, became, along with a newly organized Ukrainian Party of Socialist Revolutionaries, the leaders of a movement for national autonomy and the mainstay of the Ukrainian Central Rada, an embryonic autonomous government.

The emergence in April, 1917, of the Central Rada bore witness to the mobilization of broad sectors of the Ukrainian population in European Russia behind the national movement. The failure of the successive Provisional Governments in Petrograd to come to terms with the Rada on the question of Ukrainian autonomy merely forfeited its support when in early November the Provisional Government had to face a Bolshevik assault against its authority. In the meantime the Rada proceeded to proclaim the Ukraine's autonomy in a first and second "Universal" in June and July respectively. But the Bolsheviks, having subsequently overthrown the Provisonal Government in Petrograd, were to fare no better in their relations with the Ukrainian national movement.

In late November 1917, as local Bolshevik organizations undertook the conquest of power town by town throughout the Ukraine, the General Secretariat as the executive organ of the Central Rada sought but failed to get the support of the anti-Bolshevik forces then organizing their own campaign against Petrograd. When in the following January and February the Bolshevik Central Committee dispatched Russian troops to the Ukraine to overthrow the Central Rada, the latter was compelled to turn to the Central Powers for assistance. In the middle of February, 1918, German and Austro-Hungarian troops entered the Ukraine to protect the Rada, in return for large-scale shipments of grain, coal, wool, iron ore, and other raw materials to buttress the faltering economies of the Central Powers. The Bolsheviks were forced to retreat, having failed to gain the support of the local Ukrainian population for its cause. But the Central Rada was not saved. The German occupation forces, furious over the Central Rada's inability or refusal to coax grain out of a recalcitrant peasantry, ousted their host in late April and installed the more cooperative government of Hetman Paul Skoropadski. A former estate owner in Chernyhiv (Chernigov) and Poltava provinces and a general in the Imperial Russian Army, the hetman traded on the name of his illustrious forbears in order to ingratiate himself with the liberal and conservative Russians who now flocked to the Ukraine. As the ultraconservative League of Landowners and the Union of Industry, Commerce, Finance, and Agriculture grew in influence in the socioeconomic realm, and as members of the Octobrist and the Constitutional Democratic parties, which were strongly opposed to Ukrainian separatism, filled more and more positions in the new government, opposition to the hetman began to grow. By acquiescing in the forced requisition of grain by the occupation troops and then by forcing the peasantry to return the lands seized during the revolution to their former owners, the hetmanate succeeded in triggering widespread peasant discontent against both itself and the occupation authorities. By May the cities, too, were in open defiance of authority. Unemployment was increasing as all but essential war production ceased; strikes were spreading and being repressed with ever-greater severity.

By the autumn much of the Ukraine was in turmoil. On November 9, 1918, with uprisings breaking out throughout Germany, the Kaiser fled and a republic was proclaimed. In the Ukraine the German occupation forces began to establish councils of soldiers' deputies, which proceeded to make contact with the Bolshevik soviets in the underground. Skoropadski realized that he could no longer rely on the support of the occupation forces. He, therefore, turned for support to the White Army forces under General Anton Denikin. The price for an alliance was the hetman's abandonment of the principle of an independent Ukraine, which he had earlier upheld. The country was to become federated with a new anti-Bolshevik Russia. The maneuver, however, failed to save him.

With the German and Austro-Hungarian troops evacuating the Ukraine following the collapse of their respective governments, and with insurrection erupting in the wake of the withdrawal, a vacuum of power in the Ukraine was created. The Directory, the "pseudonym of the Central Rada" as Shakhrai and Mazlakh dubbed it in *On the Current Situation in the Ukraine,* was the first of several groups to attempt to impose its rule on the territory. Under the leadership of Volodymyr Vynnychenko and Simon Petliura, who had been chairman and secretary for war, respectively, in the government of the Central Rada, a hastily mobilized army now began to occupy one town and district after another. Skoropadski fled to exile in Germany, and Ukrainian independence was once again proclaimed by the nationalist forces. Now it was General Denikin's turn to intervene, especially since his aim of a reconstituted Great Russia was inconceivable without the Ukraine. Support came to him from the Entente's representatives in Russia. Vynnychenko responded by turning to the Bolsheviks for an accommodation. The Central Committee's response was to order the Communist Party (of Bolsheviks) of the Ukraine, which came into existence the previous July, to create a new Provisional Workers' and Peasants' Government of the Ukraine to challenge the Directory. In January, 1919, following a growing number of clashes between the armed forces under Petliura and the Bolsheviks, the Directory declared war against Soviet Russia.

If the turbulent events of the preceding months had eroded the nationalist ideal of an independent Ukraine, they also bore witness to the failure of the Bolsheviks in the sphere of the nationality question. Even before the Revolution, and often in opposition to many of his Bolshevik colleagues, Lenin had come to recognize the importance of a program of concessions to national sentiment for the success of the Bolshevik Revolution. Without such a program, the support of large masses of non-Russian workers and peasants, let alone of the radical non-Russian intelligentsia, for the Bolshevik cause would have been doubtful.

Once the Bolsheviks had taken power in Petrograd and were responsible for feeding the Russian cities as well as preparing to defend themselves from attack by anti-Bolshevik forces, the Ukraine with its natural and industrial wealth became the key to their survival. If the Bolsheviks were to gain control of the territory, they would have to win the Ukrainian population away from the Rada. Lenin, who had been advocating regional autonomy as a concession to the "more advanced" national minorities of the Russian Empire, called for the creation in the Ukraine of a territorial Party organization and government. More than that, he was even willing to permit the establishment of a "federation" of Soviet Russia with the projected Soviet Ukrainian government, thereby coopting an early demand of the Ukrainian national movement. Formally, at least, the Bolsheviks in the Ukraine would have to begin thinking of themselves less as members of a single "All-Russian" polity than as the revolutionary vanguard of the workers and peasants of the Ukraine. But Lenin's appeal, instead of bringing into existence much needed unity among the heretofore disjointed local party organizations, forced into the open long smoldering conflicts over the Party's policies on the nationality question.

The debates on these policies began in December, 1917, at the First All-Ukrainian Consultative Conference of Party Organizations and at the First All-Ukrainian Congress of Soviets, which were convened to establish a territorial Party organization and a Soviet Ukrainian government "federated" to Soviet Russia, respectively. By the time of the Second All-Ukrainian Congress of Soviets, held in Katerynoslav (Ekaterinoslav) in mid-March, 1918, the Party had accepted for Soviet Russia alone the Central Powers' peace terms at

Brest Litovsk. Consequently, the Congress itself became the arena for a debate over the possibility and the desirability of the Ukraine serving as a springboard for revolution in Central Europe, now that Soviet Russia was enjoying its "breathing spell." The decisions of the Congress were to be challenged at a Consultative Conference held in April at the port city of Tahanrih (Taganrog) on the Sea of Azov, and at a First and then at a Second Congress of the Communist Party of Bolsheviks of the Ukraine (C.P. (b) U.) held in Moscow in early July and in the following October. The evacuation of the German and the Austro-Hungarian occupation troops from the Ukraine in November, 1918, put an end to this series of debates.

Four positions emerged at these meetings. The Left Wing Bolsheviks, who were well represented in the Party organizations of the Ukraine, arrived at the First Consultative Conference and the First All-Ukrainian Congress of Soviets prepared to oppose what they regarded as Lenin's concessions to the peasant-supported, petty-bourgeois nationalist movement as completely antithetical to the proletarian internationalism of the Bolshevik revolution. But their spokesmen, Iurii Piatakov and Eugenia Bosh of the Kievan Party organization, had to retreat from their inclination to reject Lenin's proposals when confronted with the spectacle of a Party having hardly any support among the Ukrainian working class and poor peasantry and therefore facing certain defeat at the hands of the Central Rada. From their point of view at any rate, the organizations which Lenin was proposing were territorial rather than national; the principle of internationalism would remain unsullied.

Then came Soviet Russia's signing of the Peace Treaty of Brest Litovsk with the Central Powers (March 3, 1918), which the Left-Wing Bolsheviks, including the Kievan Left, had vehemently opposed. The latter now formulated a new tactic which would allow for the organization of an uprising in the Ukraine as the spark for the long-awaited European revolution. So that the Central Powers should not use the uprising as a pretext to overthrow the Bolsheviks in Russia, the Kievan Left was prepared to seek the separation of the Ukraine from Soviet Russia, thereby divesting the latter from all responsibility for the insurrection. Lenin, however, was not prepared to risk a confrontation with the Central Powers. But in attempting to curb the revolutionary "adventurism" of the Kievan Left, he forced it to advocate the transformation of the territorial party and Soviet organizations in the Ukraine into fully independent bodies, if only in order to escape his control. The internationalist Left thus became the unwilling promoter of separatism.

Meanwhile, a so-called Right Wing* position developed among the Party organizations in the eastern portion of Russian Ukraine. Its proponents considered their territory—the Donets Basin, Kharkiv (Kharkov), Katerynoslav, and Kryvyi Rih (Krivoi Rog)—because of its heavy industry and large numbers of Russian workers, an intrinsic and therefore inseparable part of Soviet Russia. Emmanuel Kviring and Ia. Iakovlev-Epshtein, the leading spokesman for this, the "Katerynoslav" point of view,† were prepared to support Lenin's organizational plan, but on condition that their own territory of "South Russia" not be incorporated into a nationally and economically "alien" Ukraine. Lenin rejected the offer as tantamount to the dismemberment of the Ukraine and therefore certain to alienate Ukrainian national feeling. At the First All-Ukrainian Congress of Soviets he had to order the Right Wing Bolsheviks to accept the subordination of the eastern industrial region and therefore of their own party and soviet organizations to the jurisdiction of the "All-Ukrainian" party and Soviet government.

As with the Kievan Left, so now with the "Katerynoslavians," Lenin's position forced a change of tactics: the Right insisted that the Soviet Russian Party and government—to them the embodiment of the proletarian revolution—would have to exercise the strictest possible control over their "branch" organizations in the Ukraine. Otherwise, either the Kievan Left Bolsheviks would plunge Soviet Russia into a suicidal war or else the local party and government would fall victim to the influences of a petty-bourgeois peasant and nationalist environment.

The unity which Lenin thus sought to impose was disintegrating in the face of the clash of the "Kievan" and "Katerynoslav" points of view by the time of the Second All-Ukrainian Congress of Soviets in mid-March. Party unity had to be restored if only because the Central Rada, thanks in large measure to the military support which it was receiving from the Central Powers, was reestablishing its control over the Ukraine. Lenin had already dispatched the Ukrainian Mykola Skrypnyk, a long-time party functionary in St. Petersburg, to the Ukraine as chairman of the People's Secretariat—the administrative organ of the Soviet Ukrainian government. At the Second Congress, Skrypnyk was to represent a third, middle, position between the Kievan Left and the Katerynoslav Right on the status of the Ukraine. He called for the formal separation of the Ukraine from

---

* Not to be confused with the "Right Deviation" of a later period.
† Both were members of the Katerynoslav party organization.

Soviet Russia for the sole benefit of the Central Powers. In fact, however, the former party and governmental ties to Soviet Russia would remain. In fact, however, the former party and governmental ties to Soviet Russia would remain. A Bolshevik-instigated revolution in the Ukraine could not, therefore, invite retaliation by the Central Powers against a totally peaceful Soviet Russia. The Congress adopted the proposal: the "federative" bonds between the Soviet Russian and Soviet Ukrainian governments were "dissolved," the Ukraine was now "independent," and the Kievan Left, at least, was happy over the implicit recognition which the Congress thereby gave to its revolutionary orientation.

The Katerynoslavians, however, were not willing to permit even the myth of an independent Ukraine to stand. As Party members from all over the Ukraine, fleeing the approaching troops of the Central Powers and the Central Rada, converged on Tahanrih (Taganrog) in the middle of April, the Right Wing used the occasion of yet another consultative conference to seek support for its position. Now, however, it went down to an even more thorough defeat. The conference gave its support to the desire of both the Kievan Left and Skrypnyk for a mass uprising in the Ukraine; the bonds between the Soviet Ukrainian and the Soviet Russian party organizations were declared dissolved. Henceforth, relations between the two organizations would be conducted through the newly created "International Bureau for the Convening of the Third International." With both the Soviet Ukrainian party and government now freed from Lenin's interference, the final obstacle to organizing the revolution was removed.

Sharing in the victory of the Kievan Left and of Skrypnyk's center group was a fourth group of national Bolsheviks whose support came chiefly from the party organizations in Poltava and the other provinces of the Right Bank Ukraine* and whose chief spokesman was Vasyl' Shakhrai, the coauthor of *On the Current Situation in the Ukraine*.

Shakhrai had entered the party organization in Poltava soon after completing the local military academy† in February, 1917. From the first, his membership in the party proved beneficial to both himself and his comrades. For him the party represented the only militant

---

* That portion of Russian Ukraine lying to the west of the Dnepr River and embracing Volynia, Kiev, and Podolia provinces. Left Bank Ukraine lay to the east of the Dnieper and embraced Poltava, Kharkiv, and Chernyhiv provinces.

† The academy had been moved here from Vilnius during the war.

organization which could lead the Ukrainian workers and peasants in a social as well as a national revolution. The local Bolsheviks were getting in return a young activist who had shown his revolutionary mettle when, subsequently, as an academy instructor, he led the cadets in ousting the old administration following the collapse of the monarchy. Moreover, as one of the few Ukrainians among the Bolsheviks in Poltava, he could address the native population in a language which they understood and with which, at a moment of rising national passions, they could identify. The local Bolsheviks at the time were coexisting with the Mensheviks in a "unified" organization, and Shakhrai decided that the organization could not contain both groups. He was supported in his opposition to the Mensheviks by Serhii Mazlakh (Robsman), a seasoned Bolshevik of Jewish origin who had just emerged from six years of revolutionary activity in the underground and from four years of emigré life before that. By August, 1917, thanks to their actions, the Mensheviks were ousted. In the now purely Bolshevik organization, Shakhrai and Mazlakh were elected members of the editorial board of its weekly publication. In the meantime Shakhrai had begun to defend the Ukrainian national movement as such, much to the alarm of the predominantly Jewish Mensheviks, who regarded any encouragement of Ukrainian nationalism as an invitation to peasant antisemitism. Shakhrai's fellow Bolsheviks saw no reason to criticize him, at least not yet. On the contrary, with anti-Russian feeling running high among the local Ukrainians, Shakhrai's seemed the only position likely to gain their support. No doubt because of his ability to make Bolshevism palatable to his Ukrainian audiences, he was elected a delegate to both the First All-Ukrainian Consultative Party Conference and to the First All-Ukrainian Congress of Soviets and designated the People's Secretary for Military Affairs in the Soviet Ukrainian government. By virtue of his governmental position and also because of his impeccable national credentials, he was appointed a member of the Soviet Ukrainian delegation which accompanied Trotsky in late January to the peace negotiations at Brest Litovsk.

It was while a member of the government, in which he had to work closely with members of the Kievan and the Katerynoslavian points of view that his relations with the Party began to suffer. If the Left and the Right Wings were dismayed by the "bourgeois nationalist" in their midst, he in turn was increasingly angered by their blanket condemnation of the Ukrainian national movement and by their readiness to sacrifice the Ukraine to their own particular brands of revolutionary tactics.

If only for the sake of party harmony, at the First All-Ukrainian Consultative Conference Shakhrai had refrained from voicing what were then the objectives of the national Bolsheviks—a Ukrainian socialist state, separate and equal to Soviet Russia and with its own Bolshevik party and Soviet government. He joined, instead, with the Kievan Left Wing to support Lenin's call for a territorial party organization, but insisted that its central committee have jurisdiction over all affairs pertaining to the Ukraine and that its headquarters be located in Kiev, the center of Ukrainian national activity. At the First All-Ukrainian Congress of Soviets he voted for the creation of a Soviet Ukrainian government. At the Second All-Ukrainian Congress of Soviets and then at Tahanrih (Taganrog), he supported the proposals for the separation of the Soviet Ukraine and its party from Soviet Russia. But in suggesting the name "Ukrainian Communist Party" for the now independent organization, thereby imparting a national-territorial rather than a purely territorial (Communist Party of the Ukraine) connotation, he found himself once again in opposition to all except a group of fellow national Bolsheviks.

Defeated at every turn in his effort to gain the Party's support for Ukrainian nation statehood, Shakhrai withdrew from involvement in Party and government activity. When the conferees at Tahanrih (Taganrog) left for Moscow to prepare for the First Congress of what would become the Communist Party (of Bolsheviks) of the Ukraine, Shakhrai set off in the company of Mazlakh, now a supporter of the national Bolshevik position, for Saratov, the closest Bolshevik-controlled city to the Ukraine. Here they encountered new attacks in the Party press against their views by the spokesmen for the Kievan and Katerynoslavian factions. As evidenced by the reactions in *On the Current Situation in the Ukraine*, they took particular exception first, to the continued refusal of the Katerynoslavians to apply the term "Ukraine" to the Donets Basin-Kryvyi Rih (Krivoi Rog) area, and second, to the economic arguments which the spokesmen of both groups advanced for Russia's claim to the Ukraine. Their only satisfaction at this time came from an article in which the Ukrainian Bolshevik V. P. Zatonskii, an early defender of the Ukrainian national-liberation struggle, attacked the Party's failure to implement its oft-proclaimed support for the Ukrainian nation's right to self-determination.

But Zatonskii's defense of the national Bolshevik position was ineffective. The First Congress of the Communist Party (of Bolsheviks) of the Ukraine (C.P. (b.) U.) the name finally adopted for the territorial party, reversed the basic decisions of the Tahanrih conference. The Party organization was once again subordinated to the control of the Central Committee of the Russian Party. Even worse, from the point of view of the national Bolsheviks, was the adoption by the Congress of a resolution which the Katerynoslav spokesman, Kviring, had submitted, calling for "the revolutionary unification of the Ukraine and Russia on the basis of proletarian centralism within the boundaries of the Russian Soviet Socialist Republic. . . ."* Not a word about a Ukrainian government. Forgotten also was the federation.† Shakhrai and Mazlakh were to note later, in commenting on the work of the Congress, that the Katerynoslavans had thus prepared the way for each local soviet in the Ukraine to be tied directly to the All-Russian center. Under such conditions, no sense of territorial, let alone national, identity could be created.

That the emphasis on "proletarian centralism" reflected the views not only of the Katerynoslavians, that within the Central Committee of the Russian party certain individuals were encouraging the revival of what the national Bolsheviks regarded as the old Tsarist bureaucratic mentality, albeit expressed in Marxist terms, was a conclusion which Shakhrai at least had no doubt arrived at even before the first Congress of the C.P. (b.) U. The complete subordination, as far back as January, 1918, of the Soviet Ukrainian to the Soviet Russian government and party in all important matters concerning the Ukraine could not have occurred except with the permission if not the connivance of the Central Committee of the Russian party. The federation which Lenin had ordered into existence was merely a mask to conceal the old Russian centralism. The dispatch of Russian Bolshevik troops to the Ukraine (January and February, 1918) was a clear indication of this orientation. The Russian troops distinguished themselves in suppressing the national intelligentsia and in

* Komissiia po istorii Oktiabr'skoi revoliutsii i K.P. (b.)U. *Pervyi s"ezd Kommunisticheskoi partii (bol'shevikov) Ukrainy. Stat'i i protokoly s"ezda* (Kharkov, 1923), p. 136.

† In late January, 1919, a "Declaration of the Provisional Workers' and Peasants' Government of the Ukraine" will call for the "unification of the Ukrainian Soviet Republic with Soviet Russia on principles of a socialist federation, whose form will be established by mandated representatives at an All-Ukrainian Congress of Soviets." As finally established, these forms would result in the incorporation of the Soviet Ukrainian republic within the R.S.F.S.R. The ambiguity of the Soviet Ukraine's status led Stalin in 1922 to advocate the abolition of the "federation" while Lenin, in response to Stalin's plan for "autonomization," called instead for the creation of the U.S.S.R.

closing down the Ukrainian cultural organizations—all in the name of a struggle against "bourgeois nationalism."* Then the peace negotiations at Brest Litovsk demonstrated that the Central Rada was not alone in its willingness to offer up the Ukraine to German imperialism: in the course of negotiations the Soviet Ukrainian government, with the apparent knowledge of the Central Committee, offered to accede to all the demands which the representatives of the Central Powers were making on the Ukraine's natural resources, in return for being recognized by the Central Powers as the sole authority in the Ukraine. The offer was rejected and the Central Powers signed a separate treaty with the Central Rada. Nonetheless, Lenin's disregard for the Ukraine's integrity was obvious. Finally, in the middle of February Lenin consented to the creation of the Donets-Kryvyi Rih (Krivoi Rog) Soviet Republic, carved out of the industry-rich eastern part of the Ukraine. The intent of the separation was clear. The German and Austro-Hungarian troops, invited into the Ukraine by the terms of the treaty which the Central Powers had reached with the Central Rada, were about to occupy the area; its valuable natural and industrial wealth would be lost to Soviet Russia. Therefore, declare the area independent of the Ukraine and thus not subject to the terms of the treaty. The deception failed, but the question was whether the dismemberment of the Ukraine in order to aid Soviet Russia would have benefitted the proletarian revolution. Shakhrai did not consider the one as a prerequisite for the other, all the more so since the Katerynoslavans were laying claim to the territory for Russia in terms other than those of revolutionary tactics. That the Party's Central Committee shared the Katerynoslavian position in this respect became all too clear in July, during the negotiations for a peace treaty which Soviet Russia was obligated by the Central Powers to negotiate with the recently installed Ukrainian government of Hetman Paul Skoropadski. The bone of contention between the two sides was once again the Donets-Kryvyi Rih (Krivoi Rog) territory, now under German occupation. With Stalin, the chief Soviet negotiator claiming the area for Soviet Russia, Christian Rakovski, a member of the Soviet negotiating party, provided the rationale for the claim in terms that would make not only the Katerynoslavans but also the old Imperial bureaucracy feel quite at home:

* Lenin was quite aware of the harm done the Bolshevik cause in the Ukraine by these actions. He had to persuade the commander-in-chief of the troops, Antonov-Ovseenko, to use extreme tact in dealing with the Ukrainians. He also advised him to make wide use of his Ukrainian family name in order to ingratiate the Bolsheviks with the local population.

Russian capital and Russian labor had developed the area's resources and built its industries.

If further evidence was needed that the Bolsheviks had, indeed,
succeeded to the mentality of the Russian autocracy, Shakhrai found
it in a speech which Lenin delivered in late November, 1918—a little
more than a year since the creation of the dictatorship of the proletariat—to an audience of Party functionaries. Calling on them to
regard themselves as patriotic Russians, who were defending their
country against foreign domination, he likewise and in the same
patriotic vein asked them to welcome into their ranks the (Great
Russia-oriented) "petty-bourgeois" democrats. As Shakhrai and
Mazlakh were to point out in their pamphlet, both the March and
the November revolutions had had a decidedly Russian national
character insofar as one of their objectives was to extricate Russia
from a disastrous war. Now came the influx of the Russian petty
bourgeoisie to spread their nationalist poison among a Russian working class which was already suffering from the disease of a "one and
indivisible" Russia. Lenin had become the "tsar and God of Soviet
Russia."*

By December, 1918, Shakhrai's disillusionment with the Party
and its leaders was well-nigh complete. Publicly expressing the view
that the Ukraine must become independent drew threats of arrest by
organs of the Cheka on at least two occasions—the latter threat made
"jokingly" by Stalin.**

To Shakhrai, the armed struggle unfolding in the Ukraine at the
end of 1918 appeared to repeat the events of December, 1917, and
January, 1918—with many of the same actors and with most of the
same attitudes. As for himself, by this time, he was no longer willing
to mount the platform and defend the Bolshevik record before hostile Ukrainian audiences. Soon after the Consultative Conference in
Tahanrih (Taganrog) (April, 1918) and before settling in Saratov,
he had traveled to Moscow together with Mazlakh to plead with
Lenin for a separate Party organization for the Ukraine. While there
Shakhrai had turned to writing in order to publicize his views. A
pamphlet he wrote was never published although part of the text was
incorporated into *On the Current Situation in the Ukraine*.† A second pamphlet, *The Revolution in the Ukraine*, which he wrote

---

* *On the Current Situation in the Ukraine.*
** *On the Current Situation in the Ukraine.*
† Pp. 50–52 of the original Ukrainian text.

under the pseudonym of V. Skorovstans'kyi, appeared in Ukrainian in November, 1918.*

Addressing an audience of Bolsheviks who, in his opinion, had still failed to come to terms with the reality of the national-liberation struggle in the Ukraine, Shakhrai in this pamphlet depicts the Ukrainian movement as an objective historical process, at each stage of which a particular class with a particular program emerges as hegemon. By the time of the Bolshevik revolution the Ukrainian workers and poor peasants have taken over the leadership of the movement and pressed their demands for socialism within a separate, independent nation-state. The validity of these demands, Shakhrai contends, is to be found in the recognition which the two major antagonists, the bourgeois Central Rada and the Bolsheviks, gave to Ukrainian independence—the former by proclaiming a sovereign Ukrainian republic in the middle of January and the latter by proclaiming an independent Soviet republic at the Second All-Ukrainian Congress of Soviets in the middle of March, 1918. The occupation of the Ukraine by troops of the Central Powers represents, in the author's opinion, one more stage in the realization of the final goal. It unites the heretofore separate parts of Austrian (Galicia) and Russian Ukraine under a single rule.

Looking back on the events of the preceding months in the Ukraine, Shakhrai found that neither the local soviets, as essentially organizations of the Russian proletariat, nor the Bolsheviks, as the dominant political element in the soviets, could assume leadership of the national-liberation struggle if only because both were oriented toward Russia. Specifically, Shakhrai states, the Bolsheviks lost the Ukraine when they refused to acknowledge the sovereignty of a Soviet Ukrainian government which they themselves had created. To justify their conduct, they spoke of the need to unify the proletariat of all the nations. But what did this mean? Shakhrai maintained that they were unable to create more than an abstract unity. In fact, by their very refusal to grant real equality to the Ukrainian workers and peasants, they brought about the fragmentation of the revolutionary forces.

* The pamphlet appeared subsequently in two Russian language editions—in the middle of December, 1918, and in late January, 1919. The author indicates in the introduction as well as in his *On the Current Situation in the Ukraine* that he had originally hoped to write a study of the theory and practice of self-determination, but failing this, wrote the pamphlet instead.

A month later Shakhrai, joined by Mazlakh, was no longer willing to lay the blame for failure at the door of the Bolsheviks in general. Shakhrai had written in his earlier pamphlet that the reactionary policies of the hetmanate, by radicalizing the Ukrainian population, had provided the Bolsheviks with a second chance to assume the leadership of the Ukrainian national-liberation struggle. The moment of truth demanded that blame for past errors be duly apportioned among the Bolsheviks.

In their now open confrontation with the Party, Shakhrai and Mazlakh came to realize that their chief opponent was Lenin himself. They feared him because as the Party's leading advocate of a concrete program in the nationality question, he appeared to be what in fact he was not: the herald of an era of liberation for the non-Russian peoples of the former empire. The threat which he posed to the cause of the two authors was all the more serious because his tactics were far more sophisticated than those of either the Kievan Left or the Katerynoslavian Right wings.

Neither the Left nor the Right had bothered to conceal its antipathy for the Ukrainian national movement. Psychologically and ideologically they were predisposed to the preservation of the boundaries of the former Russian Empire. In the case of the Kievans, many were cosmopolitan intellectuals who felt equally at ease in Paris, Berlin, Vienna, or Petrograd. For them, an All-Russian solution to the proletarian revolution was a way station on the road to the internationalization of the revolution itself, and to the creation of that international or cosmopolitan society with which they identified themselves. The Katerynoslavians were likewise wedded to a future international society, although their preoccupation was less with what they regarded as a distant ideal than with the more immediate and realistic necessity for strong state power. Either because they could not conceive of any political organization that was not based on Russia as a nation and territory, or because they felt the need to identify with a powerful centralized state, they looked to Petrograd as the embodiment of their political existence. Drawing on their own limited, chiefly urban, experience in the Ukraine, they insisted as in an article by Rakovski, not only on the allegedly ethno-cultural similarity between the Ukrainian and the Russian peasant but on the "purely Russian origin" of the Ukrainian worker. Remove the Ukrainian nationalists, argued Rakovski, and the national movement would collapse.* Both the right and the left, in condemn-

* Kh. Rakovski, "Beznadezhnoe delo," *Izvestiia*, January 3, 1919, p. 1.

ing the aims of the Ukrainian national movement, found ready arguments in Marx's and Engels' pronouncements on the economic bases of national communities and on their distinction between "progressive" (industrial) and "inert" (peasant) nations. The Ukrainians, as a peasant nation, were in effect the Czechs and the Sorbs of the Russian Empire, doomed to absorption into a more energetic, industrial, and revolutionary Russia. Furthermore, if proof were needed that the Ukraine, a small nation, could not possibly exist as an independent state alongside powerful imperialist states, the two groups pointed to its occupation by German and Austro-Hungarian troops. Finally, they argued from the egalitarian character of socialism itself: once socialism is achieved, all nations will be equal. Therefore, the struggle for socialism alone is necessary. They viewed the separate demand for national equality as at best irrelevant and at worst as a divisive, and hence a destructive, weapon in the hands of the bourgeoisie against the international proletariat.

Lenin was in complete agreement with both the Left and the Right wings on the need for an All-Russian solution to the proletarian revolution, both in the interests of victory and as a prerequisite to the fusion of nations. But in seeking to appeal to the non-Russian peoples as the victims of past national oppression he clashed with the Kievans and the Katerynoslavians who were prepared to appeal to them solely as exploited classes. His task as he saw it was to devise policies in the nationality question which offered guarantees against national oppression as well, while not sacrificing any of the principles of Bolshevism whether in the form of ultimate ends or of the means for their realization. The manner in which he formulated and executed the demand for national self-determination was remarkable for substituting illusion for reality.

"The right of nations to self-determination up to and including state separation." Here was the right which Lenin offered to the non-Russian nations but in the exercise of which he attached two conditions. First, having ruled against the creation of a federation, the choice for the non-Russian peoples would be either in behalf of state association, by which Lenin meant association with the centralized state of the proletariat, or of independent statehood. Second, the exercise of the right to self-determination could have no validity except under the aegis of socialism, for only socialism made possible the fullest realization of democratic rights. Speaking more bluntly in 1916 with regard to elections to a future constituent assembly, Lenin stated, "The slogan of the 'constituent assembly' as an independent slogan is false, for the entire question is who will convoke it."* The transfer of this bit of political wisdom to the politics of national self-determination was not difficult to make. Therefore, the elections to the First All-Ukrainian Congress of Soviets, which were ordered by Lenin and which were to be regarded as the realization by the people of the Ukraine (and not by the Ukrainian people) of their right of determination as a nation took place for the most part in those villages and towns where the Bolsheviks were in control. Moreover, they were based on a weighted vote which favored the proletariat (much of it Russian) over the peasantry (almost totally Ukrainian). If, then, only some thirty-nine out of more than 2,126 cities, towns, and villages† were represented in the voting, no matter. For the creation of a Soviet Ukrainian government recognized by Soviet Russia was far more than what the Provisional Government, let alone the autocracy, had been willing to grant. Under these circumstances the Ukrainian people might actually welcome the seeming reality of national self-determination, especially since association with Bolshevik Russia, voted by the Congress, meant sharing the benefits of socialism. For the Bolsheviks it meant preservation of the All-Russian character of the state while hopefully not antagonizing the Ukrainian people.

As members of the proletarian state, the Ukrainian people, as pointed out earlier, would enjoy regional autonomy. Here, too, the Ukrainian people would be given an artfully contrived substitute for what had been sought. The Ukrainian nationalists, no less than many of the other non-Russian nationalists, had since the turn of the century voiced the demand for the transformation of the Russian Empire into a democratic federation of nations, with the non-Russian nations enjoying complete national autonomy. To Lenin the combination of federation and national autonomy meant purely and simply the preservation of the state (in a territorial sense) as a conglomeration of compact nationalities. This was precisely the aim of the non-Russian nationalists: autonomy to the nation as a distinct economic, political, and ethnocultural entity, with the power, derived from the federal structure of the state, to preserve and to strengthen the nation. To Lenin, however, the nationalists' program spelled defeat for the proletariat. Having seized power, the workers and poor peasants (under the direction of their party) could only preserve and extend their victory if they could transform Russia from an essentially agrarian into a modern industrial society. Industrialization demanded the movement of large masses of population

---

* V. I. Lenin, "Neskol'ko tezisov," *Sochineniia*, 2d ed., XVIII, p. 311.
† Of at least 2,000 inhabitants each.

from the countryside to the new industries, and therefore the disintegration of the nationally compact communities. Added to this was Lenin's own predilection for the assimilation of the non-Russian peoples to the Russian language and culture as the result of their intermingling in the new urban centers and their consequent need for a common idiom of communication. Herein lay Lenin's insistence on a centralized state, for only where power was centralized could the needs of industrialization take precedence over particularist (national) interests. From this consideration stemmed his willingness to offer not national but regional autonomy—autonomy to a particular region, regardless of the national composition of its population. The Ukrainian people, in accepting this brand of autonomy, renamed "federation" for their sake at the First All-Ukrainian Congress of Soviets, were in effect forfeiting their claim to nationhood. Yet here, too, Lenin was counting on the Ukrainian people to accept his offer, and for the same reasons that they would accept his brand of national self-determination.

Shakhrai and Mazlakh were no less wary of Lenin's *realpolitik* in the nationality question than they were of the internationalism of the Kievans or of the "proletarian" orientation of the Katerynoslavians. They could easily dispose of the arguments of the latter two groups. Assertions about ethnocultural similarities and the absence of a Ukrainian national consciousness were repudiated most eloquently, they felt, by the very existence of the Ukrainian national-liberation movement. Their opponents to the contrary, political unity as the necessary result of economic interdependence was difficult to demonstrate in a world where independent nation-states were bound together by an ever-expanding network of commercial interchange. And if, as the Kievans contended, Russia depended economically on the Ukraine, then Russia should be attached to the Ukraine and not vice versa. Finally, in agreeing that socialism brings with it national equality, the authors argued that statehood should therefore be granted to all nations and not just to Russia.

It is at this point that Shakhrai and Mazlakh attack Lenin. Along with the proponents of the Ukrainian national movement, they viewed Lenin's program for the nationality question as a subterfuge for the re-creation of a "one and indivisible" Russia and concluded that only independent statehood could guarantee the Ukrainian nation against economic exploitation and cultural oppression in the future. If the Kievans, the Katerynoslavians and Lenin were predisposed to disparage the ability of the Ukrainian workers and peasants to achieve socialism without the aid of the Russian proletariat, by way of denying them the right to their own state, the authors of *On the*

Current Situation in the Ukraine would have to demonstrate the opposite: that the Ukrainian people possessed all the prerequisites for conquering state power in their own right.

To begin with, the regional identities of the precapitalist countryside had given way among large sectors of the rural population to an awareness of the existence of national community, thanks to the development of a market economy and its concomitant of a modern transportation and communications system. The growth of a national consciousness, they maintain was likewise fostered by the movement into the towns and cities of large numbers of Ukrainian peasants looking for work in the new industries. On the basis of reason alone, state the authors, Lenin is correct in asserting that industrialization breeds assimilation (i.e., Russification) of heretofore compact agrarian nations. But history shows otherwise. At first the Ukrainian worker is drawn to the Russian cultural milieu. Then, however, he rebels against acculturation when he realizes the gulf that separates the more cultured cities from the ignorant, oppressed village. He returns to his own people in order to awaken in them an awareness of their own worth. It is this social consciousness which becomes the psychological condition for the creation of the modern national intelligentsia. As guardian of the spiritual needs of the people, the intelligentsia demands a nation that is educated. It therefore fosters and promotes a cultural revolution which in turn brings ever new recruits to its ranks. Instead of disappearing as a nation, the Ukrainian people begin to assert their identity. Shakhrai and Mazlakh drew support for their views about the nationality question not from the assimilationist Lenin but from Karl Kautsky, the Czech nationalist turned Social Democrat. The latter's description of the national rebirth of the Czechs and the South Slavs and of the subsequent politicization of their cultural movement provided the two authors with valuable insight into the Ukrainian experience. The Ukraine's colonial status in the Russian Empire gave rise to a revolutionary movement which, by virtue of its emphasis on national liberation, differed fundamentally from the revolutionary movement in Russia. The course of revolution in each country would likewise be different. Lenin had projected a proletarian revolution within the boundaries of the state, being guided by the experience of the revolutionary movements in the nation-states of Western Europe. Mazlakh and Shakhrai found the Western European models irrelevant to the developments in the Russian and Austrian multi-national empires. Here revolutions take place within the context of nations, giving rise in each case to a class (proletarian) dictatorship based on the nation. The proletariat of the oppressed nation begins its struggle for liberation at a time when the imperialist bour-geoisie seeks to extend the boundaries of the state to embrace as many nations as possible. To struggle for the nation-state, therefore, means to struggle against the bourgeoisie. The Ukrainian workers become the hegemon of the national struggle. Not national (cultural) de-velopment, but the development of the nation becomes the objective.

Shakhrai and Mazlakh end their criticism of the Party with a direct appeal to Lenin to heed the demands of the Ukrainian workers and peasants for statehood or stand convicted as a hypocrite along with Woodrow Wilson, who also advocated national self-determina-tion while supporting the (anti-Bolshevik) proponents of a recon-stituted Great Russia. They reject his proffer of concessions to the Ukrainian people—their right to use their own language and to de-velop their national culture; the use of native personnel in Party and government institutions—as self-debating. These policies will merely strengthen national consciousness, resulting in increased demands for independence.

Lenin, of course, realized the dangers confronting him in the nationality question. Recognizing the independence of the non-Rus-sian peoples risked the collapse of a unified, coordinated struggle against both the internal and foreign enemies of the revolution; re-jecting the demand for independence risked alienating large masses of non-Russians from the Bolsheviks. In December, 1919, the Party's Central Committee adopted the very tactic of concessions which Shakhrai and Mazlakh warned against. The left-wing Ukrainian in-telligentsia, growing increasingly disillusioned with the social policies first of the Central Rada and then of the Directory, and viewing with increasing alarm the growing power of the Entente-supported White armies, found themselves more and more attracted to the Bolsheviks. As increasing numbers of left-wing Ukrainian Social Democrats and Ukrainian Socialist Revolutionaries defected to the local Bolshevik and Soviet organizations, giving these a more "national" coloration, the services of a Shakhrai were no longer prized; his ideas were in any event deemed subversive. The Bolshevik censors in Saratov permitted the local bookshops to accept for sale only one hundred copies of *Revolution in the Ukraine* in the Ukrainian language edition; the sale of the Russian language edition was prohibited. *On the Current Situation in the Ukraine* brought its authors expulsion from the Party in June, 1919. Mazlakh was subsequently reinstated following his ap-peal to the Central Committee of the Russian Party.* Shakhrai made

* Mazlakh then went on to become a member of the Central Statistical Bureau of the Soviet Ukrainian republic, disappearing from public view at the time of the purges in the late 1930's.

no effort to regain his Party membership. Instead, he left Saratov for the Ukraine, which Denikin's Volunteer Army was then in the process of occupying. Working as the editor of several underground newspapers in the Kuban, he was seized by Denikin's forces in the autumn of 1919 and executed.

After his death, debate within the Party continued over his role in the revolution. A commission of the Soviet Ukrainian government, established in 1925 to commemorate the Bolsheviks of the Ukraine killed in the revolution and civil war, decided to include Shakhrai's name among those to be honored. At the same time, the Poltava province soviet named a street for him.

Although articles and books as late as the early 1930's continued to refer to him, he was to become a "former person" in the period of the Stalin purges before and after World War II. Since Khrushchev's denunciation of the Stalin "cult of personality," his name has begun to reappear, and while his *Revolution in the Ukraine* is available on request from the Lenin State Library in Moscow, the Party censors still consider *On the Current Situation* too dangerous for the Soviet scholars studying the history of the revolution in the Ukraine even to cite in their research. To this day, it is kept in the Library's "Closed Fund."

Lenin may have proven Shakhrai and Mazlakh wrong with regard to the alienation of the mass of Ukrainians from a Russian-oriented Bolshevik party. They in turn were to be proven correct in predicting continued dissatisfaction, particularly among the Ukrainian intelligentsia, with concessions in the nationality question which fell short of creating an independent Ukraine. At the time of Shakhrai's death a new "federalist" faction in the Communist Party (of Bolsheviks) of the Ukraine, under the leadership of George Lapchinskii, one of Shakhrai's early supporters, prepared a memorandum which in essence echoed his national-Bolshevik orientation, even repeating his demand for the creation of a "Ukrainian Communist Party (of Bolsheviks)," the name appearing on the title page of the original edition *On the Current Situation in the Ukraine.* The national-Bolshevik theme was to be repeated in the literature of the Ukrainian Communist Party (of borot'bists) * and of the Ukrainian Communist Party,† organized in late 1919 and

---

* On the U.C.P. (of borot'bists) see I. Majstrenko, *Borot'bism* (New York, 1954). The "Borot'bists," composed essentially of a left-wing group from the Ukrainian Party of Socialist Revolutionaries, were to fuse into the C.P.(b.)U. in March, 1920.

† The U.C.P. was organized by one of several left-wing splinter groups in the Ukrainian Social Democratic Party, and existed until its "self-liquidation" in 1924.

in 1920, respectively. A far greater threat to Bolshevik control in the Ukraine came from the Ukrainianized policies of
Alexander Shumskyi, the People's Commissar for Education in the
Soviet Ukraine from 1924 to 1926. By fostering the use of the Ukrainian language not only by Ukrainians but by the large non-Ukrainian
population in the republic, this former Borot'bist was in effect not
only reversing the earlier trend of Russification but subverting Lenin's program of regional autonomy. The implied insistence on a
Ukrainian national-territorial identity in Shumskyi's cultural policies
received reinforcement in the summons of the Ukrainian writer
Khvylovyi to turn "away from Moscow," to reject, in effect, the
forced association with Russia and seek moral inspiration from the
more advanced civilization of the West. "Shumskysm" and "Khvy-
lovysm," bred by the ambiguities in Lenin's nationality policies, in
turn evoked an attack against "bourgeois nationalism" among those
Party members who had never accepted even Lenin's limited concessions to national feeling. Nor did the purge of Shumskyi and
Khvylovyi end the agitation. Skrypnyk, who had been Lenin's chief
spokesman in the Ukraine in the period of Shakhrai's active membership in the Soviet Ukrainian government and who succeeded Shumskyi as People's Commissar for Education, was himself won over to
a policy of encouraging the growth of Ukrainian national consciousness. His suicide in 1933, occurring against an unfolding background
of purges of a whole generation of Ukrainian intellectuals, many of
whom had gone over to the Soviets in the period of the civil war,
put an end to the agitation first spurred by Shakhrai and Mazlakh.
But with the demise of Stalin, a new generation of Ukrainians in
the universities, the professions, the mass media, the arts and letters
and the administration was beginning to speak out with ever-greater
frankness over the creeping Russification which from the late 1930's
had been quietly but relentlessly eroding the cultural gains made
under Shumskyi and Skrypnyk. Most eloquent in his condemnation
of this process has been the literary critic Ivan Dzyuba, whose *Internationalism or Russification?*,* written in late 1965, was a response
to the arrest of a group of young Ukrainian intellectuals earlier that
year† by organs of the K.G.B.

Almost a half century separates Dzyuba's cry of anguish from *On
the Current Situation in the Ukraine*, an expanse of time and a
change of circumstance which explain the quite worshipful treat-

---

* Ivan Dzyuba, *Internationalism or Russification?* (London, 1968).
† The arrests took place about two weeks before the more publicized
arrests of Siniavskii and Daniel'.

ment of Lenin in the former and his denigration in the latter. But the intellectual and emotional bonds between the two works far outweigh their differing treatment of particulars: the wrath they feel over the contradiction between promise and performance in the nationality question; the faith they express in the "collective instinct" of the Ukrainian people for self-preservation. Not the national *per se*, but the international as the sum total of national components is their ultimate concern. Without the guidance, let alone the knowledge of what had been said earlier by the Shakhrais and Mazlakhs, the younger generation has arrived at conclusions about itself, its people, and its society which the older generation could easily recognize as its own. The search for identity, individual and national, has become part of the "permanent revolution" of the twentieth century.

Preface

By Peter J. Potichnyj

The pamphlet *Do Khvyli*, written by V. Shakhrai and S. Mazlakh in January 1919, is the first eloquent expression of national communism. It should thus prove to be of interest not only to students of Soviet history, but also to scholars concerned with international Communist movement and with nationalism as such. While the work appeared in the original Ukrainian in 1967 in New York, its present publication in English removes it and its authors from the oblivion to which they were consigned by some fifty years of official Soviet secrecy. The work has been kept in the Special Collection (*Otdel Spetskhraneniia*) of the Lenin and Saltykov-Shchedrin libraries (among others) and has been available only to a restricted number of readers who have received special permission to see it. Only recently have the names of the authors of this document reappeared—rather unexpectedly—in the Soviet Union, in publications devoted to the October Revolution in the Ukraine. A picture of Shakhrai was even printed in *Peremoha Velykoi Zhovtnevoi Sotsialistychnoi Revoliutsii na Ukraini* (Kiev, 1967, I, p. 267), but this partial rehabilitation of Shakhrai and Mazlakh does not extend to their work. Their powerful polemical tract, with its radical critique of Lenin's and other Bolshevik's ideas on nationality policy, is apparently still considered dangerous, for it remains behind closed doors in the USSR to this day.

Because of the historical importance of this document, considerable pains have been taken to translate it in a form that corresponds most closely to the Ukrainian text, consistent with the need to present a readable rendering of the original. The authors of the pamphlet were not especially good Ukrainian prose stylists, and they composed it in the heat of revolutionary passion. The document clearly deserves attention, less for its literary merit than for the ideas expressed in it. The translation, therefore, attempts to reproduce the latter as accurately as possible, sacrificing smoothness where necessary.

In order to facilitate understanding on the part of the reader, and to make the translation approximate the format of the original Ukrainian text, the editor has employed several devices.

In the text and notes the modified Library of Congress system of transliteration is followed.

Square brackets are used to indicate the authors' interjections in material quoted by them in the text. The editor's interpolations and the footnotes that should have been supplied by the authors or which are clearly implied by the text are also enclosed in brackets but are identified as the editor's.

Asterisk and dagger symbols are used for the original footnotes and explanatory material.

My editorial notes are numbered and appear in the Notes following the text.

The list of sources used by the authors and a list of abbreviations used either in the text or in the editor's notes are also included. The sources for the explanatory notes are too numerous to be cited except where specific references facilitate understanding. A selective list of general sources is included.

Finally, it is my pleasure to acknowledge my indebtedness to Professors F. C. Barghoorn, Z. K. Brzezinski, H. G. Skilling, G. S. N. Luckyj, and Grey Hodnett for their generous help from the very inception of this undertaking. The editorial advice of Lawrence E. Miller and Harris Coulter has been of enormous help in seeing the manuscript through to completion.

I am also grateful to McMaster University and to Canada Council for research grants that enabled me to prepare the manuscript for publication. To numerous individuals in the libraries of Columbia, Yale, and Toronto universities, in the New York Public Library, and especially to Mrs. M. Parker of McMaster University Library, I offer sincere thanks for their generous assistance. To Professor Michael M. Luther go my thanks for providing an illuminating Introduction. Mrs. S. Bell, of McMaster University, took on the onerous work of retyping parts of the manuscript.

To my wife, naturally, I owe a special debt that words can never adequately express.

Dundas, Ontario
April, 1969

Contents

Chapter 1

Pro Domo Nostra

Mindful of the well-known Russian saying, "Better late than never," we have decided to address ourselves to the workers and peasants of Russia and the Ukraine. We do this not because we consider ourselves highly educated persons who can teach others; on the contrary, we reckon ourselves the most ordinary of people. But just now we are passing through one of the most crucial moments in the gigantic struggle between labor and capital; between the old bourgeois society built on compulsion and oppression and a new society founded on the international solidarity of workers, a free family of free peoples, a socialist society. Every member should help a bit—in any way at all—no matter how little his strength, depending on how he understands and interprets this all-important movement. We are firmly convinced that the present is only a link in the chain of gigantic battles waged by the people to free themselves from the shackles of modern capitalism and imperialism, that it will be followed by new struggles whose intensity and tragedy will assume unprecedented proportions, and that the nature of future developments will depend on the turn taken by the events of today. Events have their own logic which almost invariably outweighs human logic. In revolutionary times the true nature of society and of its individual classes, groups, and persons reveals itself with blinding clarity; so-called historical necessity ceases to be the mere outcome of research into historical events and takes on the clarity of a phenomenon familiar to every citizen. But we also know that historical necessity results from the wills of classes, groups, and individuals; if some thought or idea spreads among the population, it captures a greater or lesser number of people and becomes a factor determining the thrust of historical necessity. History is the resultant of the actions of the masses; it is not the work of great personalities or heroes, it is not made in palaces, ministerial offices, or the salon cars of supreme commanders, but is forged in the perpetual daily struggle of the masses for their own interests. History yields examples of common men, who never dreamed of discovering America or of giving happiness to humanity, expressing a thought that "soared into the air," taking the pulse of the historical moment, and "becoming corporals" whose thinking became a factor in history. We are not trying to "become corporals," but if our modest voice finds a response in the masses and turns history even a little in the direction we desire, we will be satisfied, and our work will not have been in vain.

We take the liberty of addressing the workers and peasants of the Ukraine and Russia for yet another reason. We have been destined to observe with our own eyes the development of events in the Ukraine during the revolution, to participate to the extent we could in those events, and the historical experience we acquired in those times must, we think, be utilized not only for our personal profit but also to help all who are struggling for the happiness and fulfillment of the living, those to whom the fate of the Ukraine and Russia is not an abstraction, whom the fate of the Ukraine and Russia "keeps awake at night."

We love Russia and the Ukraine. We love them as children love their mother. The happiness and fate of Russia and the Ukraine are our happiness, our fate. In them we love all humankind. A new Russia and a new Ukraine, two sisters with equal rights, two free countries—separate and independent but united by common interests, respect, and consideration—are what we are yearning for. This is our appeal, and this is what justifies us in daring to call the attention of the workers and peasants to our thoughts, to our mind's cold observations and heart's sorrowful remarks.

"Better late than never." If late, the blame rests not only on us, but also on the fate which compels us to live in more or less splendid isolation, where news is late and fragmentary, and we have difficulty orienting ourselves in time.

We have done the best we could. If anyone can do better, let him try.

Chapter 11

War and Revolution

The days pass, the nights fly by
And the Ukraine is burning, as you know. . . .[1]

Not only the Ukraine is burning, but the whole world. It has been burning for five years. The world conflagration, the historically unprecedented war which flared up in 1914, is turning into a new revolutionary conflagration. Provoked by the imperialist war for the benefit of our own and foreign capitalists, large landowners, bankers—a war for new markets, a new division of the world, the partition of "small, oppressed nations"—the revolutionary conflagration is flaring up and spreading, "purifying" and burning out everything which remained after the ruin of 1914–18, turning to ashes the corpse of the old bourgeois society.

The Ukraine had the misfortune of being one of those countries, like Belgium, Poland, Serbia, Armenia, and others, where the bloody events of the present war took place, and the fate of the plunderers of the world was decided. The Ukraine paid dearly with the blood and toil of her sons for the honor of being the arena of these events, of witnessing them and standing at the forefront of the world movement. And there will be more to pay later—this will be seen to by the new conqueror of the world, the ruler of the imperialist bourgeoisie, the apostle of the "self-determination of small nations," the president of the United States, Woodrow Wilson.

The World War and the World Revolution are the two outstanding facts of the era in which we are living.

War and revolution represent a crisis of society, of the social community.

"Every crisis rejects the conventional, tears off the outer shell, casts out the antiquated, reveals deeper springs and forces."*

* [V. I.] N. Lenin, "Itogi diskussii o samoopredelenii," *Sbornik Sotsial-Demokrata*, No. 1 (October, 1916), p. 26.

What has this present crisis revealed? The World War has manifestly laid bare the contradictions of contemporary bourgeois, capitalist, imperialist society. This society is founded on the division between the producer and the means of production and exchange—land, factories, and railways—on the private ownership of the means and instruments of production and exchange, and on the expropriation and proletarization of the laboring masses; on an opposition between lifeless things and the living producer, between the forces of labor and the products of labor, between capital and labor; a society in which the primary motive of social production and social life is not the satisfaction of human, social needs, but the unending pursuit of gain, profit, and lucre; a society which discovers in every acquisition or conquest—whether of a country or a branch of social production—only a new boundary, and thereby arouses in itself a burning desire to dominate, seize, and appropriate all it surveys. This society has developed productive forces so gigantic as to be able, in a short time, to deluge the world with its products and capital. Yet at the same time it is unable to satisfy the needs of its own populations and free them from the threat and horror of famine, cold, poverty, and disease. The world is divided among the individual plunderers, the great powers, whereas each of them in fact needs a whole world for itself. Productive forces cannot be left to lie idle, capital must be invested and must bring profits—the rest is none of our business.

Vivat profitum, pereat mundus! Après nous le déluge!

"War is the continuation of politics by other means." This lofty saying of the German imperialist Clausewitz reveals the true meaning of the present imperialist war. What could not be accomplished through peaceful competition, peace treaties, customs, and policies, had to be gained through war.

The war erupted, with the necessity of natural law, from the jungle of contemporary society—and this is why no one can discover who started it or who is to blame for it.

It is the present social structure which is to blame for the war.

The war has manifestly demonstrated its inability to settle the questions which it was supposed to resolve. It should have abolished the contradition between the huge productive forces of society and social relations based on the ownership and exploitation by capital of a living labor force, on the insatiable desire for new markets and profits.

Not only did the war fail to abolish this contradiction, it aggravated it, leading society to the verge of generalized misery, savagery, and destruction. So as not to perish, society has made powerful efforts in a new direction, hastening to settle by other means the issue which the war could not resolve.

The revolution is the extension of politics and war—only by other means.

Like the Roman aristocrats who gorged themselves with fine food and then vomited so as to be able to begin gorging again, the previous politics and war were supposed to abolish the contradictions between social relations and their own forces of production through a "just" (i.e., on the principle that the "loser pays") [2] division and redivision of free lands and nations embodying the unscrupulous destruction and waste of human labor, finished products, and productive forces.

The revolution is an attempt to turn these productive forces to the satisfaction of human needs, to improve the life of the working masses, and to abolish the contradiction between labor and capital by destroying capital.

The revolution is a war against the old society for the sake of a new socialist society—to counterbalance the imperialist war within the old capitalist society which was supposed to prolong the life of that society.

The war among the imperialists of different nations gave birth to revolution—a war of the proletariat and peasantry against all imperialists, native and foreign.

And as the process continues, the anti-imperialist struggle is increasingly replaced by the revolutionary struggle against imperialists of all kinds, waged by the broad toiling masses led by the proletariat. The imperialist war has been replaced by a civil war.

This is the basic fact of the present era.

Chapter III

Two Revolutionary Eras

The Russian revolution of March, 1917, was a critical point in the transformation of the imperialist war into a social revolution, a civil war.

Before November, 1918, the Russian revolution was the only beacon—an island in the midst of the imperialist states, in the midst of the stormy sea of imperialist war. It took place against the background of the global hostility of the two imperialist camps: the Anglo-French-Italian-American alliance (Entente) and the quadruple union of the Central Powers headed by Germany.

In October–November, 1918, the international situation changed in two ways. On the one hand, Germany was defeated by the Entente on the western front, which evoked a revolutionary movement in Germany, and the citadel of Central European imperialism collapsed under the revolutionary surge. The Russian revolution was no longer a solitary island, but found a partner in revolutionary Germany. On the other hand, the total defeat of German imperialism and the victory of the German revolution destroyed one of the imperialist camps, leaving only one survivor. This survivor is being joined, every hour and every day, by fragments of the shattered Russian, German, and Austrian imperialism.

The solitary revolution had to defend itself against the rapacious intentions of the two imperialist camps—which neutralized each other and thus helped revolutionary Russia.

Now the revolutionary tide has spread to Central and Southeastern Europe. But the struggle in these countries has not yet ended in victory for the proletariat, and direct help from them is not to be expected; on the contrary, they themselves need assistance against their own imperialist bourgeoisie and against Anglo-American capital. However, it is no longer possible to maneuver between the hostile

6

imperialists, relying first on one and then on the other, since now there is only one imperialist camp.

Formerly, imperialist groups made great efforts to achieve victory over their enemies and considered revolution as merely the penalty of defeat in war. Victorious Germany was even well disposed toward the Russian revolution, not only because it removed Russia from the ranks of Germany's enemies, but also because it attracted to itself part of the attention of the Entente. Having seized a large piece of the former Russian Empire, which had not even occurred to them before, the German imperialists had nothing against establishing good-neighbor relations with Russia, playing with her like a well-fed cat with a mouse when it is sure the victim cannot escape.

Now the victor and overlord of the imperialist camp is the Entente, headed by a new country, the United States of America. In recent times this country, together with Germany, has distinguished itself by a rapid and exuberant development of capitalism. While the older capitalist countries, England and France, whose great period of development was the first half of the nineteenth century and who more recently had been living on the fruits of their earlier labor, employed outmoded methods of production and economic organization in which energy, initiative, and continued forward movement gave way to routine, set patterns, and traditional ways of doing things, these countries with a youthful capitalist culture, America and Germany, had to win themselves a "place in the sun." Hence they were compelled to make great efforts, exploiting in the optimum way the resources and human energies of their countries, employing new machinery and better production methods, fostering a spirit of initiative and inventiveness, producing cheap and attractive goods, and ensuring the most flexible and profitable organization of their economies. It took France and England almost a full year of war to come up to Germany's level of technical knowledge.

Germany fell because she could not stand the pace. But the United States did not have to undergo such exertions. On the contrary, she profited from the first three years of the war, completing the organization of her economic and military forces. She could do this slowly since nearly all her competitors were involved in the war. In addition, she was in the position of a *tertius gaudens* (pleased onlooker), warming her hands at others' misfortunes, fishing in muddy waters, and fleecing both hostile camps. As is known, during the early years of the war the United States profiteered from outfitting both the Entente and the Central Powers. This enabled her to complete the organization of her economy and prepare for war, to reinforce her grip on the Americas and put into effect the demand, "America for the Americans" (that is, for American capital), and to grow rich on orders and loans to both the belligerent and nonbelligerent countries. The United States was literally raking the coals with the hands of others. Rivers of European and Asian blood flowed across the Atlantic in the form of a ringing and glittering stream of golden coins.

And the moment both warring camps were half-exhausted the United States stepped forward in arms as the peacemaker, not only through the "epistles" of its holy and apostolic "anointer," President Woodrow Wilson, but also through victory on the field of battle. And the United States chose a very auspicious moment—Germany had reached the zenith of her power, the strength of the Entente and Germany was about equal, and both camps were so exhausted that even a little force could turn the scales one way or the other. Taking Germany's side would have consolidated Germany's hegemony in Europe, and America in this way would have created her own strongest competitor—one with whom she would soon have to enter into an open peaceful and military struggle. France and England, on the other hand, were not so dangerous, and entry of the United States into the war on their side, with their ensuing victory, would actually signify a victory for America.

Indeed, as we have seen, an insignificant military victory by the Entente was enough for Germany to tumble down like an avalanche —demonstrating not the greatness of the victory but the extent of Germany's exhaustion. We have also witnessed the telegraph dialogue between conquered Germany and victorious America. Berlin and New York negotiated the armistice and the peace—nothing was heard about Paris, London, or Vienna.

The United States now finds itself in a position analogous to that of Germany at the beginning of this year, but much better. With the possible exception of Japan, all the great powers are completely exhausted, ruined, and weakened at a time when the United States has succeeded in unleashing its force and its strength. With again the possible exception of Japan, all the world's great powers are frightened by the specter of the revolutionary plague, of communism. The specter of communism has taken on flesh and blood in the Russian, Austrian, and German revolutions. All the powers of the old Europe —the Miliukovs, Rodziankos, Denikins, Charleses, Wilhelms, Hindenburgs, Lloyd Georges, Poincarés, Clemenceaus, and *tutti quanti* are terrified by this specter and ready to throw themselves into the arms of the devil himself, not to speak of the peace-loving Woodrow

Wilson. And Woodrow Wilson manages everything himself, has taken upon himself the role of world gendarme and hangman of the world revolution.

Yesterday's revolutionary and liberator of oppressed peoples entered ruined and plundered Europe to strengthen the grip of American capital and to enable it to continue to impose its will on the peoples of Europe. Around him the revolution has gathered an evil gang of imperialists of various shades—Wilson's erstwhile enemies who are offended by the revolution. All have been unified, all consolidated, into a "small but honest"[1] company of haters of the proletariat. Honor, shame, love of country—everything of which this brotherhood only yesterday was proud and boastful—have been forgotten and sold for the chance to regain its class position, its "nests," its factories, its mills, its shares, its revenues.

The Russian Black-Hundred[2] Cadet (Constitutional-Democratic) brethren initially sided with either the Entente or with Germany. Their heads were humming with ideas about the most suitable orientation. At that time they gained nothing positive for their endeavors—only discredit. Now they have but a single thought, a single desire, a single orientation, a single objective—the great and good American uncle, Woodrow Wilson.

The Austrian and German imperialist bourgeoisie did not suffer as much as the Russian Black-Hundred brotherhood since history did not give them a choice. For them there was only one target, and the German and Austrian imperialist bourgeoisie threw themselves without further thought into the arms of their former enemies. Anything for help against their "rebellious slaves," their own revolution. They had no time to be Hamlets.

And so around Woodrow Wilson, the apostle from the new world, have gathered imperialist brethren of all kinds, united by their terrible hatred of revolution and of the specter of communism. Woodrow Wilson has faithful servants "not because they fear him but for the sake of their conscience," and he has no competitors except, perhaps, Japan. He has all the makings, material and moral, of a world gendarme and a world hangman of the world revolution.

Chapter I V

Russia and the Ukraine
against the Background of World Events

The Anglo-French imperialist bourgeoisie gave the Russian revolution of March, 1917, a very hostile reception. They were afraid, and with good reason, of losing such a rich source of cannon fodder and such a rich market for their capital and goods as tsarist Russia. Before the war a milch cow of the French bankers, during the war weak and entangled in debts, after the war tsarist Russia should have become, for the more advanced imperialist states, a second Turkey, a second "sick man," kept in a chronically weak condition, with accounts eventually being settled at the price of the self-determination of her various lands and concessions. The revolution buried these hopes under the ruins of tsarism. No wonder the "noble allies" met the Russian revolution with venomous hissing!

Imperialist Germany met the revolution differently. For her it meant the withdrawal from war of one of the strongest members of the enemy camp and gave assurance that a German victory on all fronts would soon lead to the complete consolidation of her dominant position in Europe. Revolutionary Russia would be too busy with her internal problems to want war with Germany. Furthermore, the defeated Russia would have to sign a peace treaty dictated by Germany. Finally, Russia would deflect upon herself a part of the forces of her Allies, who would not hesitate to send their punitive detachments to teach her a lesson for her "treachery" and compel her to continue the fight. And German hopes were completely justified. The reality, in fact, even surpassed all expectations of the imperialist dreamers.

In the east Germany gained territories greater than herself. She forced the occupied lands to pay an indemnity. She acquired a position enabling her at any time to attack Russia again and to take from Russia what she needed. She took steps to ensure that her own interests would be unaffected by the social and economic measures of the government of Soviet Russia. It was not in her interest to strangle Soviet Russia. On the contrary, she hoped to be able to do it later, and for the time being Soviet Russia was a convenient buffer against the Entente.

When Kerenski's attempt to compel Russia to continue the war ended in defeat after the June 18, 1917, offensive,[1] the Entente began, after the October revolution, to support all kinds of counterrevolutionary groups in Russia. When the Brest peace negotiations failed, it tried to ascertain if the Bolshevik government would go to war against Germany—to gain a stronghold for the support of the Russian Constitutional-Democratic, Menshevik, and Social-Revolutionary counterrevolution. The attack on Murmansk and Archangel,[2] the idea of a Siberian government,[3] the Czechoslovakian adventure[4]—this long series, one after the other—are the facts of the friendly Allied aid.

As for the Ukraine, her role in the international arena began in December, 1917, and January, 1918, when the Central Rada[5] (Tsentralna Rada) and then the Central Executive Committee of the All-Ukrainian Soviets[6] sent their delegations to the Brest Litovsk peace negotiations.[7] The German government soon realized how easily it could take advantage of the Central Rada's great-power ambitions and how useful could be the struggle between the Central Rada, on one hand, and the Central Executive Committee of the All-Ukrainian Soviets and the Council of People's Commissars, on the other.[8] Indeed, its hopes were not in vain. The delegation of the Central Rada signed the peace treaty at a time when the Germans, after protracted negotiations with the Russian delegation, had reached the peculiar position of neither peace nor war when the negotiations had torn aside the veil of German democratic desires, and when General Hoffman's[9] speech had provoked a labor upsurge in Austria and Germany. This enabled the German government to return home with some sort of "scrap of paper." Soon this same Central Rada requested help against the Bolsheviks, thus giving political sanction to an armed attack on Russia and the occupation of the Ukraine.

The German government made the best possible use of the national hostility between the Ukraine and Russia. Just as it tolerated for a time Soviet Russia as a buffer, so it not only tolerated but even supported the independence of the Ukraine.

The Entente's attitude toward the Ukraine was analogous to its attitude toward Soviet Russia. Until the October revolution in 1917 the Allies were hostile to the Ukrainian National movement because nationalization [Ukrainianization—Ed.] of the army interfered with operations at the front. After the October revolution the Entente attempted to lean upon the Central Rada, hoping it would continue the war. "I am instructed by my government to assure you of its sincerest intentions—it will support to the utmost of its ability the Ukrainian government in the task which it has undertaken, that of introducing good government, maintaining order, *and combating the Central Powers,* who are the enemies of democracy and humanity"*—wrote the British representative, Bagge.[10] But these hopes soon turned out to be unreal, and the Allied attitude became as hostile toward the Ukraine as toward Soviet Russia. It was just that the Ukraine was so far from their lines of communications that they could not get at her.

We should not fail to note the similar attitudes of both imperialist camps toward the Ukraine and Soviet Russia. Neither would have anything against a Soviet or any other kind of Russia, or against an independent Ukraine, if both would stay on the leash of the imperialist bourgeoisie. Objective conditions happened to be such that only Germany could use these territories for her own selfish interests—to supply materials of various kinds and as buffer states against the Entente. The Entente, on the contrary, could not benefit in any way and was actually suffering considerable losses. Hence the hostility to Soviet Russia and to Ukrainian independence.

That is how it was during the first period.

In the second period, October—November, 1918, the Ukraine and Russia found themselves, as we have seen, in an altogether different situation.

And because of this different situation both Soviet Russia and the independent Ukraine evoked different attitudes on the part of Germany and the Entente. But only the attitude of the German imperialists was really changed.

When Germany lost all her conquered territories in the West, she had to agree to all the clauses of the Entente's peace treaty in order to strangle the revolution at home. Then the German imperialists began to reconsider and to assume a different attitude toward Soviet Russia and Ukrainian independence. They had learned by experience that dealing with Soviet Russia was no joke. The "poison" of Bolshevism was threatening to flood all of Europe. It had to be destroyed, but it was already too late. The German imperialists could not wiggle a finger without Woodrow Wilson's consent. So they gra-

---

* O. Shulhyn, *Polityka* (Kiev, 1918), p. 110. [Italics are Shakhrai's— Ed.]

ciously applied to the apostle of the liberation of nations for permission to participate also in the strangling of Soviet Russia. It was absolutely necessary to strangle her, they assured Wilson, but he knew it quite well without their saying so. And the question of Ukrainian independence was entirely superfluous since at the time imperialist Germany was down and out.

In the previous chapter we have seen how the former imperialist leaders united around Wilson, what solidarity existed among them with respect to revolution in general and, in particular, to Soviet Russia and the independent Ukraine. This solidarity emerged at once; all were in agreement.

Since that time there have been only one imperialist center and only one policy of the international imperialist bourgeoisie toward Soviet Russia and an independent Ukraine.

General Denikin, the leader of the so-called Volunteer Army, an army of unemployed officers and spoiled sons, announced at the session of the State Council in Katerynodar the terms of a treaty with the Entente. The Entente would support only the Volunteer Army and those groups of Russian counterrevolutionaries whose aim was the rebirth of a single indivisible Russia. Only defenders of the "one and indivisible" would be admitted to the future peace conference—under no circumstances, Bolsheviks or representatives of any new creations on the former Russian imperial territory which reject the idea of the "one and indivisible." The most prominent of these new creations is the Ukraine.

Denikin's announcement agreed completely with the reply of the United States government to the Ukrainian representative in Bulgaria[11] when the latter asked if a Ukrainian delegate would be admitted to the future peace conference. "President Wilson's government wishes to see at the conference a representative of the one and indivisible Russia" was the curt answer.

In a word, all is clear. Nothing is left unsaid or unexplained. Destroy Soviet Russia and the independent Ukraine, and restore the one and indivisible Russia.

Clear as crystal.

Chapter v

The Strategic Plan for the Rebirth
of the One and Indivisible Russia

Implementation of the wish to destroy Soviet Russia and the independent Ukraine, and to restore the one and indivisible Russia,
requires only the occupation of Russia and the Ukraine.

The one year's experience of the revolution since October, 1917,
has clearly shown that the Black-Hundred, monarchist, Octobrist,[1]
Constitutional-Democratic, Socialist-Revolutionary,[2] Russian counterrevolutionaries cannot restore the one and indivisible Russia by
themselves. Everywhere it exists—in the North, in Murmansk or
Archangel; in the East, in the Urals and Siberia; in the South, on the
Don, in the Kuban and the Ukraine; in the West, in territory occupied
by Germany, Lithuania, and Poland; it is supported by the bayonets
of foreign troops.

But once these troops depart the Russian counterrevolutionaries
will vanish like the dew on a bright summer day.

This means that to attain their goal the Russian counterrevolutionaries and the Entente must introduce a dictatorship, occupying
the whole of Russia, establishing peace and order on the bones of hundreds of thousands of workers and peasants, and rooting out of silly
heads the ideas of Bolshevism and independence.

The events of the past year have shown that the Russian North
and East—Murmansk and Siberia—do not relish the idea of being
the initial strongpoints of this occupation. It would take a long
time, whole years, and it must be done at once so as not to miss the
appropriate moment.

Western Europe and the Baltic Sea would be better. But they
would also require a lot of time. First of all the German revolution
would have to be strangled to secure the rear—and who knows how
long that would take?

A southern strategy would appear to be the best—the Black Sea,
the Ukraine, the Don, the Kuban. From here an offensive could soon

start off northeast to Orenburg, reaching the Urals and Siberia and eventually even Archangel.

From the Ukraine an offensive could be mounted through Belorussia and Lithuania to the Baltic Sea. Thus Moscow could be isolated from Berlin and Vienna, each could be encircled by the occupying army, and the circles could be gradually constricted until the revolution is strangled in one or the other country.

Thus the Ukraine, in the imperialist design, is to be the strongpoint of the counterrevolutionary campaign which will bring ruin to it as well.

Hence the Ukraine and Soviet Russia are bound not only by a common interest in the struggle with a common enemy, the imperialist bourgeoisie, but also by their separate interests in shattering the ingenious and clever plan to strangle both by using one against the other.

For this reason an analysis of the forces presently in conflict in the Ukraine is very significant not only for understanding the Ukraine's own position and her relations with Soviet Russia, but also for indicating what should be Soviet Russia's policies toward the Ukraine.

Chapter VI

Skoropadski and Denikin

Latest news from the Ukraine: His Highness, Hetman Skoropadski,[1] has resigned from the hetmanate and gone into hiding; no one knows where. *Sic transit gloria mundi.*

But in the past seven months we have gotten so used to this comic figure that we cannot pass over him so easily. Also, and what is more, because the forces which raised him up on the historical scene are still with us and because the counterrevolutionary one and indivisible position cannot be understood without Skoropadski.

The same news tells us that on the Russian Black-Hundred horizon has appeared the figure of another tsarist general, Denikin, at the head of the Volunteer Army. One needs not the gift of prophecy to state that in the near future General Denikin will become the focus of as much attention as, in the past, has Skoropadski.

Generals Skoropadski and Denikin are two hieroglyphs which only differ from the Egyptian hieroglyphs in that even the illiterate can read them.

General Skoropadski in the past, and General Denikin in the present, personify the Russian and the world counterrevolution in the Ukraine.

When the Russian Black-Hundred, monarchist, Octobrist, Constitutional-Democratic counterrevolution had broken out in Central Russia and was driven to the periphery of the former Russian Empire (October, 1917—March, 1918); when the hopes for early and adequate Entente aid in restoring the one and indivisible Russia received a shock (because the Entente was at war with Germany and could only send small detachments to save from total extinction the regional counterrevolutionary centers, Murmansk and Archangel in the North, Siberia and the Urals in the East, the Don and the Kuban in the South); when the German troops, invited to the Ukraine by the Central Rada,[2] had established peace and order by fire and sword

16

and, using their bayonets as obstetrical instruments, had helped to give birth to His Highness, Hetman[3] Skoropadski (a former tsarist general and ataman of the Free Cossacks of the Central Rada[4]) ; and when the Miliukovs, Rodziankos, Lyzohubs,[5] Shulhyns[6] saw and heard that a truly Russian heart beats in the blue cossack mantle and in the red baggy pantaloons, wide as the Black Sea, and that the hetman's mace was really an ordinary native, truly Russian bludgeon (*dubinka*), there was a stir in the black sea of Russian patriots. Their souls divided into two groups: one hoping to heaven to be faithful to their first love, the noble Allies, the other attracted by that sinful country of yesterday's enemies of Russia and all humanity, the barbarians of modern civilization, the Central Powers. Then the counterrevolutionary camp split in two—the one half stretching out on the breast of the noble Entente and the other half, at first stealthily through a window and then openly, embracing a new love. But both halves of the camp remained united in their aim to restore the one and indivisible Russia.

Himself, a fierce enemy of the Germans and ardent lover of the Entente, the patriot par excellence, the Constitutional-Democratic Chrysostom and leader, Miliukov, hastened to Skoropadski in the Ukraine and thence directly to Berlin, not in a "sealed wagon" but in a lounge car.

The Constitutional-Democratic Shunammite[7] wanted to embrace the Berlin David, but David said, "I know you not"—not because he was powerless like the biblical David, but because he had better companions and because his blood was racing already.

At that time restoration of the one and indivisible was not in the interests of the Wilhelms, the Hindenburgs, and the Eichhorns, and the Constitutional-Democratic *Mädchen für Alle* was rejected outright.[8]

At this time Hetman Skoropadski, Miliukov's follower and comrade in misfortune, spilled some marvelous information:

> Formerly I was greatly fascinated by the Empire, it is true. It was so beautiful . . . it seemed to be so strong . . . But *now* we must get used to the idea that the Ukraine's only course is independence. (Poor Ukraine!) Believe me, there is no other way.*

So after two and a half months as hetman of the independent Ukraine, His Highness reached the sad conclusion that "The

---

* I cite the hetman's interview after V. Iurchenko, "Na rozdorizhzhi," *Visnyk Ukrains'koho Viddilu Narkomnats,*[9] No. 5, p. 10. [Italics are Shakhrai's—Ed.]

Ukraine's only course is independence. . . . There is now no other way out." This is how the independent hetman became an advocate of independence!

But his followers were not so frivolous and did not abandon hopes of worming themselves into Berlin's good graces.

Backed by German bayonets and the independent advocate of independence, they began preparations. Soon monarchists, Constitutional-Democrats, and Duma members began holding conventions; organizations and bureaus were set up for attracting enlistments into "Astrakhan" regiments and into the Volunteer Army; prayers were made for health and grace and for the dead.[10]

And cooperation between the Allied and the German Shunammites was sincere and complete.

The independent hetman had no army of his own and depended on German bayonets. His whole armed force was a small group of "haidamaks"[11] and a slightly more numerous Volunteer Army. But the Volunteer Army favored the Allied orientation and tended toward the Don and the Kuban.

Thus it happened that when imperialist Germany collapsed and German bayonets became unreliable props, the figure of General Denikin—the true knight *"sans peur et sans reproche"* of the beautiful Dulcinea-Entente—appeared behind the independent Skoropadski and took the place of the Kellers[12] and the Mumms.[13]

His Highness, the Hetman, rushed to the side of the Entente. The "independent"[14] cabinet of ministers was dismissed and a new one formed,[15] the first point of its program being *"Work for the restoration of the one and indivisible Russia* on a federal basis with all rights being reserved to the Ukraine on the basis of her state and national originality."[16]

The independent hetman lost the idea of independence! But now he had to hear what Mumm told the delegation of the Central Rada[17] when it went to find out the German wishes, ready to agree to all terms:

—Too late!

Hetman Skoropadski is no more.[18] He could not be located even at the beginning of the revolution in Germany. Power actually lay in the hands of General Denikin and the Volunteer Army.

To the Black-Hundred Constitutional-Democratic brotherhood General Denikin was the memory of a first love, the rosy dream of its first spring.

Some of the Black-Hundred Constitutional-Democratic counter-revolutionaries passed with Hetman Skoropadski through the full cycle of dialectical development: thesis—fascination by the empire; antithesis—compulsory independence; synthesis—restoration of the one and indivisible Russia.

On revient toujours à ses premiers amours.

The disorder ended among the Black-Hundred brotherhood. But it ended when the new revolutionary surge threatened to wash away the Black-Hundred slime.

All is not yet lost. The Allies are still operating in Odessa and Rumania. The Don and the Kuban are still in the grip of the Volunteer Army. There is still powder in the magazine! The Russian counterrevolutionaries have not lost their power! The struggle continues. The Allies will soon send help![19]

Meanwhile the hetman resigns and flees. Power passes into the hands of the Directory.

Chapter V I I

The Directory[1]

Directory? It sounds completely French! What kind of a hieroglyph is this?

The Directory, they say, consists of five persons. It is headed by V. Vynnychenko,[2] the Ukrainian Social-Democrat and former head of the General Secretariat of the Central Rada, and it includes S. Petliura,[3] commander in chief of the republican forces, former minister of military affairs of the Central Rada, and a Ukrainian Social-Democrat.

"Oh, all familiar faces!"

The Directory is a pseudonym for the Central Rada. The Central Rada died on April 29! *Vive la Centralnaia Rada!* Long live the Directory!

What does it want? We find its program in the first call for insurrection against Skoropadski issued by the Directory's Commander in Chief Petliura.[4]

By order of the Directory of the Ukrainian Republic, I, as Commander in Chief, call on all Ukrainian soldiers and cossacks to fight for the independence of the Ukrainian State against the traitor and former tsarist hireling, General Skoropadski, who arbitrarily appropriated the rights of Hetman of the Ukraine. The Directory's decree outlaws Skoropadski for crimes committed against the independence of the Ukrainian Republic, for destroying her freedoms, for filling prisons with the best sons of the Ukrainian people, for executing peasants, for ruining villages, and for violence against workers and peasants. On pain of court martial, all citizens of the Ukraine are forbidden to help the vampire, General Skoropadski, in his flight, to feed him, or to give him shelter. It is the duty of every citizen of the Ukraine to arrest General Skoropadski and to hand him over to the republican authorities. The Hetman's orders and commands to the army are hereby annulled, and to avoid violence and bloodshed military detachments are to join the forces of the Republic, following those that have already done so. The aim of the Republic's forces is utterly to destroy the order instituted by the Hetman's government, the whip upon which he relied to the last moment. In this great hour when tsarist thrones are falling all over the world, when peoples are being liberated, when throughout the world peasants and workers are becoming the masters, shall we, brother cossacks, permit ourselves to side with the landlords and with the Hetman's government, against our own fathers? Brother cossacks, in this great hour you dared to serve the traitors who were selling themselves, and want to sell the Ukraine, to the former Russian tsarist ministers and to her dominant class, the unemployed Russian officers and plunderers concentrated in the counterrevolutionary lair on the Don.*

This program deserves close scrutiny, and we will examine it. For this purpose we must touch upon recent events. And if this past will not be agreeable to the Directory, nothing can be done about it. *Amicus Plato, sed magis amicus veritas est!*[5] Even more because we only follow the way recommended by the Central Rada in Brest. "History and our descendants will decide who is a revolutionary and who a counterrevolutionary, who defends the rights of his people and who is their enemy," said the delegation. History moves so rapidly that we need not wait for our descendants and their judgment. We can already judge for ourselves.

We shall not dwell at length on Brest or on history generally before April 29, 1918. The reader will find suitable material in V. Skorovstans'kyi's pamphlet, *Revolution in the Ukraine*,[6] and we refer him to it. We will start with the birth of His Highness, Hetman Skoropadski, on April 29, 1918.

This date can evoke nothing but bitter feelings in the Central Rada, that is, the Directory. That is why Petliura's order speaks angrily of Skoropadski having "arbitrarily appropriated the rights of Hetman of the Ukraine." This reproach is not in accord with reality, as Skoropadski became hetman by permission and with the direct assistance of the legal authority in the Ukraine—the German army. And the German troops were invited to the Ukraine by the Central Rada (now the Directory) to establish peace and order. This

* ["Vozzvanie Petliury"—Ed.] *Izvestiia V. Ts. I. K.*, No. 256 (520) (November 23, 1918), p. 2.

task they accomplished by driving out in scorn the Central Rada and installing the hetman. Who can say that the German forces did or did not act arbitrarily? Certainly not one who was harmed! His judgment would not be dispassionate.

It is true that the hetman's edict [hramota—Ed.] stated:[7] "I have decided to assume full authority temporarily. I proclaim myself Hetman of all the Ukraine,"* but this was only verbiage for court use.

To continue. After the overthrow of the hetman, the gentlemen from the Central Rada in general, and the Ukrainian Social-Democrats in particular, recognized the hetman's government as legal and not arbitrary. Isn't this true? Here are the facts!

The Nova Rada, organ of the Ukrainian Cadets, the Socialists-Federalists,[8] who were most active in the Central Rada, stated on June 2: "The whole difficulty and cause of the internal disagreement lies in the fact that the new government does not follow the Hetman's declaration at all and does not manage its affairs in accordance with it." What was this declaration? His Highness, the Hetman, said: "In the new state organization the Ukrainian people will acquire an iron guarantee of their state, national, and cultural sovereignty."† This demonstrates that the Ukrainian state has a good (His Highness, the Hetman) and a bad government, and it is bad because the Ukraine has been invaded by remnants of the Russian bureaucracy.

A second fact. Robitnycha Hazeta—the organ of the Central Committee of the Ukrainian Social-Democratic Party[9]—on August 17, 1918, published an article entitled "Disorders in the Ukraine," which fact is well known to V. Vynnychenko and Petliura, the Ukrainian Social-Democrats. This article classified as follows the driving forces in the present-day disorders:

1. Some social elements primarily dissatisfied with the character of the government's social policy, and especially with its local agents and experts ("the switchman is to blame!") . [Russian saying meaning the blame is usually shifted to those least responsible—Ed.]

2. Others who consider, further, that even the national policies of the government are contrary to the best interests of the Ukrainian national renaissance and Ukrainian state independence.

* V. Skorovstans'kyi [Shakhrai—Ed.]. Revoliutsiia na Vkraini. (Saratov, 1918), p. 86. [Revoliutsiia na Ukraine—Ed.], 2d Russian ed., p. 127.
† I quote after V. Iurchenko, "Na rozdorizhzhi," op. cit., p. 9.

3. Those who have in mind only specifically national moti-
vations. . . .

4. Pillagers unloosed by war and revolution.

5. Bolsheviks in pursuit of that permanent violent "equal-
ization." . . .

6. Bolsheviks supporting the "order" prevailing in Russia
and annexation of the Ukraine to this Bolshevik Russia.

7. Those advocating union with Russia: among them are
found Bolsheviks, left- and right-wing Socialist-Revolutionaries
and even Black Hundreds.

After giving this classification, the *Robitnycha Hazeta* advises
how to deal with these driving forces: "While the struggle with the
two latter groups must be conducted *without mercy*, and while the
struggle with 4 and 5 must be *firm and resolute, an understanding
can be reached* with the first three groups, *and they can even be
turned against the others.*"*

To whom is this advice directed? To the hetman. With whom
can the hetman reach an understanding? With, among others, those
who are dissatisfied with the character of both the social and the national policies of the government, which are contrary to the interests
of the national renaissance and of Ukrainian state independence.
Who are these people? The same Ukrainian Social-Democrats who
were dissatisfied.

*In August the Ukrainian Social-Democrats recognized the het-
man's government as legal, not arbitrary, and offered it their help,
appealing for understanding.*[10]

Furthermore, Petliura accuses Skoropadski of "crimes against
the independent republic and destruction of her freedoms." It must
be assumed that this wickedness began with the organization of the
last cabinet, when Skoropadski announced his aim as restoration of
the one and indivisible Russia, and when it was impossible to hope
that the hetman would reach an agreement with the Ukrainian
Social-Democrats.[11]

Petliura further attacks Skoropadski for "filling prisons with the
best sons of the Ukrainian people, for executing peasants, for ruining
villages, and for violence against workers and peasants." But this
execution, destruction, and violence was started by the Central Rada
(The Directory) and carried out by the German and Austrian forces
called in by the Central Rada. *Robitnycha Hazeta*, the organ of the

---

* V. Iurchenko, "Na rozdorizhzhi," *op. cit.*, No. 4, p. 9. [Italics are
Iurchenko's—Ed.]

Ukrainian Social-Democrats, also urged the hetman's government to
struggle mercilessly with the two latter groups of the above list. To
eliminate all doubt about who was meant in the sixth point above,
we quote the testimony of the *Nova Rada*, a paper which was very
friendly to both V. Vynnychenko and S. Petliura:

"We receive endless complaints about the actions of the new
authorities in the provinces," wrote the *Nova Rada* on June 9, in issue
No. 96. "The day before yesterday there appeared in our office a
group of members of the Peasant Congress who thanked our editorial staff, the committee of the Socialist-Federalist Party, and S.
Petliura for their efforts to free arrested delegates. At the same time,
however, they pointed out that *many arrested persons are still in
Lukianiv prison.* Furthermore, we know that the Kiev provincial
zemstvo is swamped by so many *complaints, applications, and peti-
tions that it has been necessary to institute separate bookkeeping ar-
rangements for their registration and referral to the proper authorities.* S. Petliura, the zemstvo chairman, is virtually buried under these
applications, and we know that he is bringing them to the attention
of both the German and the Ukrainian authorities."

"We consider it our duty to emphasize one detail: in most of
the applications and complaints to come to our attention *there are
almost no grievances* against the German troops. *There are no complaints from places where peasants have clashed with the Germans,
as though they want to fight and thus accept all* the consequences."*
This detail is the gist of the matter. It is known that villages were
destroyed and peasants were shot by just those German troops invited
in by Central Rada. All except the peasants complained to Petliura
because the peasants knew quite well, even without reading *Robitnycha Hazeta,* that for them there was only one way out: a merciless
struggle—fight and accept all the consequences.

Further. "In this great hour . . . throughout the world peasants
and workers are becoming the masters," and because of this, "shall
we permit ourselves to side with the landlords and with the Hetman's
government, against our own fathers?"[12] Well, it means *against* the
landlords—and for . . . whom? Throughout the world peasants and
workers have become the masters, and *this means in the Ukraine
also . . . !*

Oh, no! See what they are after! They should rid themselves of
this silly idea!

* V. Iurchenko, "Na rozdorizhzhi," *op. cit.*, No. 1, p. 19. [Italics are
Iurchenko's—Ed.]

The second Directory commander in chief of the left-bank Ukraine, Bolbochan,[13] states in his order: "I proclaim that *I will not tolerate any kind of soviets of workers' deputies*, monarchist organizations, or, *generally, any organizations striving to gain power*. I emphasize that we are fighting for an independent and democratic Ukrainian republic and not for a united Russia, no matter what kind, whether monarchical or Bolshevik."*

There you have it! Workers and peasants throughout the world have become the masters, and the Directory commander in chief in the Ukraine proscribes worker and peasant organizations, so that they may not gain power and become the masters. *Da liegt der Hund begraben*. The dispersal of the Kharkiv (Kharkov) Soviet has shown that these are not empty words.[14]

Petliura further calls for a fight against the Russian counterrevolutionaries and against the counterrevolutionary lair on the Don. Getting wise at last!

There was a time (October, 1917–April, 1918) when the Directory, or, rather, the Central Rada, had very close relations with this lair; when it allowed armed Cossack troops to pass through and join this lair; when it halted and disarmed Bolshevik troops on their way to fight this lair;[15] when it urged this lair to form a "socialist (with Kaledin!) federative government for the whole of Russia";[16] when this lair was not a lair at all but (as V. Vynnychenko assured the First All-Ukrainian Congress) [17] a self-determined Kaledin[18] Don.

This was the time when the Central Rada was frightened by the October revolution, when it thought to unify the living forces that had been expelled from central Russia.

Then the General Secretaries recited revolutionary phrases and did counterrevolutionary work.

Now things have changed. Now the Directory states obscurely that somewhere in the world the peasants and workers have become masters, and proscribes the Soviets of Workers' and Peasants' Deputies. Now the Directory is afraid to use frightful, revolutionary words, but objectively it plays a revolutionary role. Just as revolutionary phrases (and "honesty to oneself") [19] could not keep the Central Rada from counterrevolutionary activities then, so the fear of revolution and the desire to tame the peasants and workers will not restrain the revolutionary movement now: on the contrary, the Directory itself has in a short time done quite a lot for the development of the revolution and will do more, even against its will.

---

* *Izvestiia V. Ts. I. K.*, No. 265 (520) (December 4, 1918).

The objective situation is such that no other alternative exists. The logic of events outweighs human logic.

But the struggle with this counterrevolutionary Don is rather peculiar—unlike, for instance, that with the Kharkiv (Kharkov) Soviets of Workers' Deputies. The same Bolbochan warns the Cossacks who were pacifying the workers of the Donets Basin with fire and sword, and who routed the Soviets also, that he will use arms against them unless they stop their misdeeds, because their brutalities give birth to Bolshevism. But if they stop, how will the fight be carried on?

By the Allies who support the Don and the Kuban?

By the German troops that once helped the Central Rada?

The Directory is silent. It wants to outwit history.

Silence is golden!

Oh, if we could only avoid outwitting ourselves!

History, the midwife, injured the Directory, so that it does not know which step to take.

The French Directory gave birth to Napoleon . . .

Who is now being born to the Ukrainian Directory?

In the early spring His Highness, Hetman Skoropadski, was born of the Central Rada and of the Directory.

Who will be born this cold winter?

Chapter VIII

The Provisional Worker-Peasant Government of the Ukraine

On December 1 of this year a "Manifesto of the Provisional Worker-Peasant Government of the Ukraine" was published in the *Izvestiia Vserossiiskogo Ts.I.K.S.R.K.K.D.**1

We do not know whether the Skoropadski-Denikin government has completely relinquished its rule in the Ukraine, but, in any case, the Ukraine at that time had three legal governments at once—and they say the Ukraine cannot be independent! Russia has only one government and the Ukraine three, or at least two—who is the more independent?!

Provisional Government! "Once upon a time there was . . . !" And they still say that no miracles happen in our times! There was simply a Provisional Government with one hostage, Kerenski![2] There was a Provisional Coalition Government with six socialist ministers![3] There was a Provisional Coalition Government with ten socialist ministers![4] There was a Provisional Government-Directory with one Kerenski, completely socialist![5] Now we have a Provisional Worker-Peasant Government![6] Collectors will be satisfied: the collection of Provisional governments is complete! The University will have to institute a new professor's chair of Provisional governments! The students' poor heads! five new disciplines, examinations . . . !

"You perished, rascals, perished forever!" [Russian song—Ed.] What does this mean?

"The Provisional Government declares that, when the counter-revolution has been ended and local Soviet rule restored, it will convoke an All-Ukrainian Congress of Soviets of Workers', Peasants', and Cossacks' Deputies to which it will hand over all power in the country."†

* "Manifest Vremennogo Raboche-Krestianskogo Pravitel'stva Ukrainy" [*Izvestiia V. Ts. I. K.* (December 1, 1918)—Ed.]
† [*Ibid.*—Ed.]

27

In other words, the only purpose of the government is to convoke a Constituent Assembly . . . excuse me, Congress of Soviets, after the struggle with the "external" enemy, the Entente, and when the counter-revolution has been "victoriously ended" . . .

Propaganda work again: "Immediate summoning of the Constituent . . . or rather Soviet Assembly!" "Long live . . . etc." Merry life on earth!

"Abraham begat Isaac, Isaac begat Jacob . . ."

Who "begat" this Provisional Government?

"We, the members of the Central Executive Committee of the Soviets of the Ukraine . . . following the decision of the Central Committee of the Communist Party (Bolsheviks) of the Ukraine, have become the leaders of the risen masses and have formed a Provisional Worker-Peasant Government of the Ukraine."

> *Again ye come, ye hovering Forms!*
> *I find ye,*
> *As early to my clouded sight ye shone!*[7]

Thus we must again turn to the recent past to understand this third "Form" of the Ukraine. At this time we will not dwell on the history of the birth of the Central Executive Committee (Ts.V.K.)[8] of the Ukraine and its role from December, 1917, to April, 1918, as we will discuss this later in another connection. Now we will discuss its history after mid-April, 1918, that is, from the moment when, by the decree of history, it was forced to abandon Ukrainian territory. The Communist Party (Bolsheviks) of the Ukraine was born at precisely this time.

We start as follows:

At its last session in Tahanrih (Taganrog)[9] the Central Executive Committee of the Ukraine decided to abolish the People's Secretariat, to send out members of the Central Executive Committee into underground work, and to retain only the organizational insurgent center, the so-called "insurgent nine" (four Communists, four left Socialist-Revolutionaries, one left Ukrainian Social-Democrat).[10]

The position of the nine was not clear: did they stay behind as the government of the Ukraine or as a kind of inter-party organization with the task of coordinating the insurgent activities of the separate parties?

This situation of unstable equilibrium could not last long, and over the radio we soon heard: "To all, to all, to all," an account of the rise of the above secret underground nine to a Worker-Peasant Government of the Ukraine. The People's Secretariat buried in Tahanrih (Taganrog) rose from the dead in Moscow or maybe even on the way from Tahanrih (Taganrog) to Moscow. Future historians may be left the task of ascertaining the exact time.[11]

In any case, paragraph 7 of the "Theses of the Organizational Bureau for convoking a conference of party organizations of Communist-Bolsheviks of the Ukraine" adopted May 18 (that is, one month later) proposes to the Russian Soviet government nothing more nor less than an alliance: "The Soviet government of the Federative Russian Soviet Republic is deeply interested in a closer alliance with the Insurgent Worker-Peasant Government of the Ukraine."*

There is no documentary evidence on how this proposal of legal marriage was received, but the rich parents, in any case, tolerated this government for a while, supplying shelter and a morsel of bread.

And so it is documented that the government, the People's Secretariat of the Ukraine, rose from the dead less than a month after Tahanrih (Taganrog). Or maybe it never died?

The July conference of Bolshevik party organizations in Moscow, which called itself a congress, adopted a resolution, proposed by Comrade Epshtein, "on the People's Secretariat":[12] the First Congress of the Communist Party of the Ukraine[13] decided "To declare the People's Secretariat disbanded."†

This decision brings to mind some ideas about the poor Russian Soviet government's acceptance of the proposed alliance. Comrade Epshtein was the leader of the "Katerynoslav point of view" about which we will speak later. The second leader of this notorious point of view, Comrade Kviring,[15] proposed a "resolution on the current situation" signed by Comrade N. Lenin!

Thus the People's Secretariat was doomed to die a second time. But that same August we read a call to insurrection from . . . the "Soviet Worker-Peasant Government of the Ukraine," signed by the "All-Ukrainian Central Military Revolutionary Committee."[16]

What happened? Nothing at all. The Katerynoslavians who buried the People's Secretariat at the same time resolved: "To instruct the Central Committee of the party to organize a Central Military Revolutionary Committee."

---

* *Izveshchenie o sozyve konferentsii partiinykh organizatsii kommunistov (Bol'shevikov Ukrainy)* (Moscow: Organizatsionnoe Biuro, 1918), p. 16. [Italics are Shakhrai's—Ed.]

† *Kommunist*[14] (Organ of the Central Committee of the Communist Party [Bolsheviks] of the Ukraine), No. 5 (August 15, 1918), p. 14.

The insurgent nine begat the People's Secretariat. The Military Revolutionary Committee begat the Worker-Peasant Government—"the same thing, only in another bowl." [Ukrainian saying—Ed.]

What is so strange about this?

Who needs brains to beget children?[17]

The call to rebellion brought no results, although it seemed impossible to suffer any longer, because insurrection will come by itself, without organization.

It seems that because of this failure the Second Congress in October[18] gave a majority to the Katerynoslavians—the Worker-Peasant Government was buried again. Or maybe it was buried later —we have no documentary evidence. In any case, either before or after the rebellion in the Ukraine led by the Directory (it is a historical fact, no matter how distasteful to us, that the rebellion was headed by the Directory and not the Provisional Government), one had to say: "Good people, bless grandma Palazhka for having died promptly" [Ukrainian saying—Ed.] in order shortly to rise from the dead a third time as a *Provisional* Worker-Peasant Government!

As history teaches, it should have been called *Permanent*, but for our own use we will call it the Permanent Provisional Government, since we could attend neither its birthday party nor its baptism. Take heed, students, or you will be impaled.

At this point we hear the resounding voices of the General Secretaries at the First Kiev Congress of Soviets[19] on the origins of the People's Secretariat.

Shakh-Rai is cheating again.[20] Who, if not he, took part in the birth of the People's Secretariat?[21]

You are right, my dear friends, but at this time there were Soviets in the Ukraine; they could (and did, for a time) do away with the Central Rada and themselves become a government.

But when the Ukraine had been occupied, with the blessing of the Central Rada, and when in May Shakh-Rai made a proposal "for an alliance"[22] in Moscow, he wrote in a booklet,[23] which, it is true, was never published (Do you know what it means to write and then be the sole reader? to write and think "Is this only for my own use?" when you do not know if it will be published or not?) :

They did not even think whether there could be a Soviet government where there are no Soviets. You cannot make a man strong by boasting endlessly about him, if he has no strength to start with ("Untiring and continuous boasting about the existence of a Ukrainian *Soviet* government which did not lay down its arms") .* "The Soviet government of the Ukraine" is now "the irritation of a captive mind!"

The Soviet government of the Ukraine, the People's Secretariat, was born and lived under very difficult circumstances. It made many mistakes, and we could blame it for much, but nonetheless it did some good. Only a blind person could fail to see this. It is so. But, for all that, it could not stay alive.

Nietzsche said: If you don't succeed in life, you will succeed in death.

Unfortunately, this government could not die at the right time.

And it will die without honor.

Great events are happening in the Ukraine. The Ukraine is now passing through one of its greatest tragedies, and in its life it has known many. Throw out your farce, don't spoil the drama completely!†

Unfortunately, as we can say now, nothing need be added or changed in what was written then.

We have investigated the pedigree of our Permanent Provisional Government on the father's side.

Now we pass to the mother's side, to the Communist Party (Bolsheviks) of the Ukraine.[24]

This party's official organ sketches in the following way the party's condition in the Ukraine up until the middle of April:

> From the first days of the February–March revolution the party organizations were confronted with special problems requiring unique, comprehensive, and unambiguous decisions. We had prepared answers to questions of a generally Russian character (the answers given by our common congresses and common central committee) , but we did not have such clear and unambiguous answers to questions exclusively about the Ukraine. The matter of the agreement with the Ukrainian Social Democrats, for example, was decided independently by each local party organization: there was no *single*, collective decision. The problem of the form of the relations between the Ukraine and Russia was resolved on the basis of the abstract formula, "the right

---

* *Izveshchenie, op. cit.,* p. 18.
† [V. Shakhrai, An unidentified pamphlet—Ed.]

of nations to self-determination,"* while we, the vanguard of the Ukrainian proletariat, provided no general answer to the question of the kind of relations demanded by the Ukrainian proletariat. Did it demand regional autonomy, federation, or independence? Or would it perhaps have preferred no political separation at all, but direct ties between every local Soviet and All-Russian center? We did not, and could not, have a generally binding solution to *these* questions because we were not united on an all-Ukrainian scale. Furthermore, did we have a single line on the question of the Rada? No, we did not, and this must be emphasized. When the question arose of opposing our own Soviet center to the Rada, did not the various regions use all their power to impede the strengthening of this center and thereby weaken the struggle with the Central Rada? This was indeed so, and it resulted from the disunity of our party organizations on the all-Ukrainian scale: there were common tasks, but no common action. There were fellow-countrymanship, the cottage-industry mentality, petty reckoning by various Soviets, petty Soviets, secretariats, and sovnarkoms. There was everything imaginable except one thing—strict proletarian centralization and organization. This was lacking, and it was one of the most important causes of our weakness.†

The picture is very vivid and corresponds precisely to the sad reality. *Kommunist* sees the main reason for this disorder in the absence of an all-Ukrainian organization. Indeed, if there were organization, there would be no disorganization—this is the barest tautology, a theoretical marking time.

Nevertheless, during the First Kiev Congress[25] an attempt was made to create such an organization, and a Main Committee of Bolsheviks of the Ukraine[26] was even selected (my proposal to call ourselves Communists was not adopted—V. Sh.-R.), and the C.E.C.[27] [Central Executive Committee—Ed.] itself, composed almost exclusively of Bolsheviks, could have become an organizational center. But this did not happen. Why?

We find the answer in the statement of *Kommunist*: "We had no solution to the problem of the relations between the Ukraine and

* In my preface to the translation of Comrade N. Lenin's essays on the nationality question I show in what way this rebuke in the "abstract" is true and in what way it is not true—V. Sh.-R.

† "Itogi s'ezda," *Kommunist*, No. 5, pp 1–2. Author's emphasis. [See also: V. Skorovstan'skyi, *Revoliutsiia na Ukraine*, 2d Russian ed., p. 147—Ed.]

Russia because we were not united on an all-Ukrainian scale"—con-
versely, *we were not united on an all-Ukrainian scale because we had
no solution at all to the question of the relations between the Ukraine
and Russia.*

We shall prove that this is true.

The same *Kommunist* article indicates that an all-Ukrainian
organization had been formed—the Communist Party (Bolsheviks)
of the Ukraine, as it is officially called—and that the congress,[28] unable to resolve the *national* question, so painful for the Communists
of the Ukraine, gave a *"partial* solution concerning the relations between the Ukraine and Russia."

We shall see that this partial solution is a complete solution.
What else pains them is unknown. In any case, after the partial solution they could only say: "one does not lament the loss of the hair
of a person who has been beheaded" [Russian saying—Ed.]

An examination of the national question at the First Congress
was prevented by the left Socialist-Revolutionaries (the murder of
Mirbach, etc.).

But they [the Bolsheviks—Ed.] managed never to broach it afterwards, neither at the Second Congress[29] nor in the party press. Whoever's in pain, he'll complain [Ukrainian saying—Ed.]—but their
pain is apparently a special, secret one.

As far as we know, only two attempts have been made to
approach this painful and exacerbated issue: (1) the May 18 theses
of the Organizational Bureau[30] on the hetman's coup, and (2) the
essays of a certain Ia. E.,[31] who introduces himself as a representative
of the celebrated Katerynoslav point of view.[32]

According to the Organizational Bureau, the swallowing of the
Ukraine by the finance capital of the Central European center is the
"political expression of the fact that under contemporary world economic conditions an independent Ukraine is an impossibility. The
workers and poorer peasants of the Ukraine are faced with the question of union with the Russian worker-peasant republic just as the
Ukrainian bourgeoisie were confronted with the question of allying
themselves with the finance-capitalist bourgeois German Empire."
For this reason, the theses state, there is an "absolute necessity to
defend the revival of the federal union of the worker-peasant Ukraine
with all Soviet Russia."*

* *Izveshchenie, op. cit.,* pp. 16–17. The former president of the late
People's Secretariat, M. Skrypnyk, proposes "theses" at that time. But he
so hates bourgeois science that he deliberately proposed an unbelievable
complication just to load "bourgeois scholars of state laws" with more work.

That is all. We shall speak of this later and for the time being only underline (thankfully) that the authors at last recognize the existence of the Ukraine. Now we pass on to the Katerynoslav point of view which denies the Ukraine's very existence. Here is the proof, if you don't believe it:

> *Instead of Southern Russia* (as it was known before) *we now have the southern part of the eastern territory (oblast') occupied by Germany.* That the occupation was effected under the label of independence, and even the fact that some fellows whose heads are swelled with a, for them, unexpected surge of Ukrainian national feeling [well, that "for them" is good], regard this occupation as independence, should not prevent us from evaluating it as occupation and nothing but occupation.*

Clear, isn't it?

After this the partial decision on Ukrainian-Russian relations taken by the First Congress, and about which *Kommunist* speaks with such pride, will become perfectly intelligible to the reader. The resolution is as follows: "In view of the fact that:

(1) The Ukraine is inseparably united with Russia;

(2) The economic unification of the Ukraine and Russia in the last decade has laid a firm foundation for the struggle of a united proletariat and of the Ukraine;

(3) For this reason, the separation of the Ukraine from Russia due to the international situation *bears the character of a temporary occupation;*

(4) The idea of 'independence for the Ukraine . . .' is finally discredited among the broad laboring masses of the Ukraine;

(5) The insurrection is unfolding under the slogan of the revolutionary unification of the Ukraine and Russia;

The First Congress is of the opinion that the party should struggle for the revolutionary unification of the Ukraine and Russia on the basis of proletarian centralism within the boundaries of the Russian Soviet Socialist Republic."†[33]

This complication had no practical value, and we leave it to anyone who is interested in it—if they will be.

* "Natsional'nyi vopros v programme kommunisticheskoi partii Ukrainy," *Pravda*, No. 132 (June 30, 1918), p. 5. [Italics are Shakhrai's—Ed.]

† ["Itogi s'ezda"], *Kommunist*, No. 5. [Italics are Shakhrai's—Ed.]

This resolution was proposed by Kviring, the number two leader of the Katerynoslavians. Although it in spirit denies the existence of the Ukraine, it is not opposed to using the word "Ukraine."

This means reunification on the basis of proletarian centralism: that is, to use the words of *Kommunist,* not territorial autonomy, not federation, not independence, but the direct linking of each local Soviet with the All-Russian center.

For heaven's sake, what's new in this? This was really our point of view during the whole revolution; this is what brought us to that unfortunate condition mentioned in *Kommunist!* We have already followed this road! Well, "put your tail between your legs and start running, start again from the beginning" [Russian saying—Ed.].

It looks like it! We see where this point of view *really* leads. This partial solution of the exacerbated Ukrainian question does not really solve it. And just as then it led to rivalry among petty Soviets, Sovnarkoms, and Secretariats, to disorder—so now this partial solution leads to the same result. The same causes give rise to the same effects.

Two facts bear witness to this very clearly. If there is no Ukraine, then (1) why form a party for this nonexistent country, (2) why organize for it a government separate from the Russian one? If the situation is only one of occupation, can these struggles really be characterized as struggles by a Communist party separate from the Russian, in the name of a government separate from the Russian, in the name of a government separate from the Russian Soviet government, for the unification [with Russia—Ed.] of Archangel province, Minsk province, or Siberia?

A pause for consideration of how the leaders of the party of the Communists of the Ukraine look upon this question will be of great interest for understanding the character of this party and of the Provisional Government.

The Tahanrih (Taganrog) conference was faced with two proposals on the "organizational forms of party activity in the Ukraine":

(1) "An autonomous party with its own Central Committee and Congresses, subordinated to the Central Committee and Congresses of the Russian Communist Party." This proposal, made by Kviring, was not accepted.[34]

(2) "An independent Communist party with its own Central Committee and party Congresses, connected with the Russian Communist Party through the international commission (the III International) ." This proposal was adopted by a majority vote.[35]

What motivated this decision? We can only guess on the basis of occasional remarks recorded in the press.

The first and second numbers of *Kommunist* contain a protest by G. Piatakov[36] against M. Skrypnyk's statement that he might oppose the separation of the Ukrainian Communists into an independent party if the convention contained a left-wing majority. "The Tahanrih (Taganrog) Conference," said G. Piatakov, "and the Organizational Bureau never stated that separation into an independent party was absolutely dependent upon this or any other majority at the Congress."*

From this one concludes that there were fundamental considerations. Of what kind?

A Katerynoslav article by Ia. E. in *Pravda*, No. 132, holds that an independent party is not needed. This article, among other things, opposes the Katerynoslav and M. Skrypnyk's view to the view of the Leftists[37] in the following way:

> The tasks of our party in the Ukraine, both in our "Katerynoslav" and in M. Skrypnyk's formulation (we leave aside completely the *insurgent standpoint* of the left Socialist-Revolutionaries and of the *left Communists, whose tactics really call for separation* from the All-Russian center), depend on . . . . [Authors' italics.]

If we are to accept this opposition in views, the conclusion would be that there were fundamental considerations in the view of M. Skrypnyk and the Katerynoslavians and that the leftists were motivated by tactical considerations about whose nature we can only guess from Piatakov's protest (as quoted by us). He considers M. Skrypnyk's proposal (the absolute necessity of a Central Committee representative in the Organizational Bureau) unacceptable in that it introduces a position never before encountered in the party, "the Central Committee sending its representative to the regional [Ukrainian—Ed.] committee as a supervisor or something."† . . . When we recall that the Bolshevik party has always been very centralist, M. Skrypnyk's declaration is seen to contain nothing "hitherto unknown to party history," while Piatakov's protest really does show that the leftists were motivated by "tactical considerations" with respect to separation.

On the other hand, were M. Skrypnyk and the Katerynoslavians motivated by a "fundamental consideration"? Yes, they were, as we see:

---

* *Kommunist*, No. 1–2, p. 25.
† *Kommunist*, No. 1–2, p. 25.

M. Skrypnyk has always regarded the separation of the Communists of the Ukraine into a separate party as dependent upon existing conditions. At the Congress it may become necessary to take a different approach to the formation of a separate party—if there is a change in political conditions. *It may also be absolutely necessary if the convention has a left-Communist majority. . . ."* This he calls a fundamental position—"depending on conditions!" Shchedrin described it differently—"conformably with villainy."[38]

And here is the basic position of the Katerynoslavians. They oppose a separate party but think it "necessary to emphasize that to us [in us? in them, for them!] it is totally immaterial whether the Ukrainian *section* of the Russian Communist Party has a *separate* name, and that we never objected to the name 'Communist Party of the Ukraine."** This is also a fundemental position! The party is unnecessary, and the name—let it go!

The First Congress did not pass any resolutions on the position of the party.[39] But the Katerynoslav point of view was accepted in this, as in other fundamental (not tactical) questions, and we are entitled to state that the Communist Party (Bolshevik) of the Ukraine is not a party but a word. *Im Anfang war das Wort!*

This party is headed by the Katerynoslavians. They make fun of "all the Ukrainian Central Executive's playing at [being a—Ed.] government";† but, at the same time, the party (that is, the Katerynoslavians) forms a government—provisional, but a government just the same. Maybe this government's proclamation lies when it states: ". . . following the decision of the Central Committee of the Communist Party (Bolshevik) of the Ukraine . . . we have formed a Provisional Worker-Peasant Government of the Ukraine"? Maybe the Katerynoslav slave,[40] having served its purpose, has been "sent away"? Or perhaps there is no government of any kind—only a word, a name? Whose health shall we toast, and for whom shall we sing a requiem? [Ukrainian saying—Ed.] Let him decide who has studied in the seminary.

As a result of this investigation of the something that calls itself the Communist Party (Bolshevik) of the Ukraine and bears the name Provisional Worker-Peasant Government, and if we also take into consideration the persons composing this government (with some exceptions) , we reach the following conclusion:

* *Kommunist,* No. 1–2, p. 25. [Italics are Shakhrai's—Ed.]
** [Ia. E., "O sozdanii 'samostoiatel'noi' kommunisticheskoi partii Ukrainy," *Pravda,* No. 132 (June 30, 1918), p. 5—Ed.]
† *Ibid.*

We have a permanent Provisional coalition Worker-Peasant Government which differs from previous provisional coalition governments only in that the latter, as A. Lunacharskii[41] has said, were composed of persons who had their own coalition in their heads, while our provisional coalition government is made up of persons who ("in them, for them"), with some exceptions, have no feeling of personal responsibility for the country which they are trying to rule.[42]

A government which does not respect itself *politically*.

A government which is not respected *politically* by the people who should be supporting it.

And if this is the case, even the exceptionally remarkable reflections on The Government by the head of this government, G. Piatakov, will not help (see the "Funeral Oration Over Skrypnyk's Theses," *Kommunist*, Nos. 3–4) .*

> *. . . for all things, from the void called forth,*
> *Deserve to be destroyed.*[43]

* [G. L. Piatakov, "Nadgrobnoe slovo tezisam Skrypnika," *Kommunist*, Nos. 3–4—Ed.]

Chapter I X

Occupants

Over these three principal governments there hovers, like the Holy
Spirit over the chaos at the beginning of the world, an extraordinary,
super-legal government—the occupation army of the former Hohen-
zollern and Habsburg empires. This army played an important role
in March, 1918, when it was invited to the Ukraine by the Central
Rada; it plays one now that the Directory has organized a rebellion
against Hetman Skoropadski; and it will play one in the future—if
not the German army, then the army of the new victor and "ben-
efactor of mankind," the Entente. [This army—Ed.] has been, and
will be, very influential in the Ukraine. It has had, and will have,
an immense influence on the future status of the Ukraine.

For this reason, it cannot be ignored. On the contrary, this factor
in Ukrainian life should be studied very closely.

The German army came as the defender of Ukrainian freedom
against the Bolshevik anarchy pushing down from the north. The
Central Rada was too weak to hold out alone against the attack of
the Sovnarkom and the Central Executive Committee of the Ukraine;
it had to call on the Germans for help in order to return and stay on
as the Ukrainian government. This "help" arrived, and the German
army began to establish "peace and order" together with the Haidamaks and the Sich Sharpshooters.[1] The Central Rada thought that
this army would not meddle in Ukrainian domestic affairs, and would
be subordinated to the Central Rada in matters unrelated to the administrative and key military objectives of the occupants, but what
happened was altogether different. The "saviors" of the Ukraine soon
disarmed the Ukrainian troops[2] still at the disposal of the Central
Rada and began to issue orders which went far beyond military matters until, at last, the Central Rada was dispersed by a German
lieutenant and its place taken by the Ataman of the Free Cossacks,

General Skoropadski. His Highness, of course, was subject to the will of the lieutenants and carried out all their orders.

For this "help" the Ukraine suffered, as the German occupation led to the burning and destruction of villages, executions of peasants and workers, arrests and full prisons, and the shameless and unscrupulous plunder of the property of the Ukrainian people.

The position of the Ukrainian parties supporting the Central Rada, which was responsible for this terrible pogrom, was bad. As the saying goes: they not only had to take the punishment but were even forbidden to cry out!

When the parties of the Central Rada were punished by the occupants' figurehead, Skoropadski, they had either to stay silent or else whimper impotently that the poor Germans had been fooled by the Black Hundreds, the large landowners, and the capitalists ("survivors" of the Russian counterrevolution); that the Germans were sincere friends of the Ukraine and wanted to help the Ukrainians establish their own state; and that the Germans had just been deceived by the demonic Russian "bureaucrats."[3] The parties of the Central Rada had to turn their backs on the fact that these criminal and ruinous deeds were being committed by the "saviors" whom they themselves had invited, without even hiding behind the facade of the independent hetman. They believed in this facade of independence, they had to believe in it (*der Wunsch ist Vater des Gedankes*), although the occupants themselves pretended they were carrying out the orders of the Ukrainian hetman's government.

This is why the descendant of the Central Rada, the Directory, keeps as quiet about the present, or possibly future, occupants as if it had a mouthful of water.

The discipline of the occupation armies was ruined, or at least perceptibly undermined, by the Austrian and German revolutions. The Austro-German imperialists should have sent their most reliable troops for the Ukrainian occupation, those most immune to the revolutionary plague, those most "worthy of confidence," and actually, according to information we received at the time, they were not very susceptible to infection. They were worthy pillars of German imperalism in the Ukraine. But the occupation army could not be unaffected when the gigantic structure of German world domination, the dream of the German imperialists, collapsed like a sand castle. While one city after the other back in Germany was falling into the hands of the new victors, there was no point at all in hanging on to the Ukraine.

The occupying army is seized by a single thought, a single will:

to get home! *Nach Vaterland!* Its parts break asunder. Where they can, soldiers take the train for home, but this spontaneous movement cannot develop as it should, since the occupiers have penetrated too far into the foreign country. It is difficult, almost impossible, to go alone. For them to reach home, law and order must be maintained on the railroads. They must garrison the railways so that no one will impede their departure. Thus, the occupation has to continue to realize the aims of German imperialism, although now its only aim is to extricate itself from its difficulties.

The German "Soviets"[4] in the Ukraine have charge of everything. The attitude of these Soviets to the three principal centers existing in the Ukraine is determined by their own point of view. To be able to depart for home they need peace and order. That is why they are neutral in the struggle of the Ukrainian parties: to hell with you, cut each other's throats, if only we can leave without hindrance.

But, besides this spontaneous movement, another current may be noted in an altogether different direction. The German imperialists have given up hope of making a stand against their enemies of yesterday, the Entente Allies. On the contrary, they have to ask for help against their own "rebellious slaves." The struggle with their "enemies, their own revolution, will be fruitless as long as revolutionary Soviet Russia, the center of the revolutionary plague, remains in existence." This is why the German imperialists, after being defeated in the West, ceased to battle the Entente and only warned it very respectfully, *for its own good,* not to destroy the German army, and offered their services. "In the struggle with Bolshevism we see the bridge over which the cultural and economic interests of the triple alliance and its enemies will unite. A strong Germany will be able to resist Bolshevism adequately, but if Germany should be defeated in the struggle, the torch of the most brutal revolution the world has ever seen will turn Europe to ashes. The Entente should not overlook this problem."* So stated *Kreuz Zeitung,*[5] a German imperialist newspaper.

We have seen that the Entente, headed by America, undertook the task of restoring the one and indivisible Russia. We have seen that the best strategic point for this campaign is the Black Sea coast, and, in particular, the Ukraine.

We do not know if Woodrow Wilson heeded the entreaties of the

---

* V. Skorovstans'kyi, *Revoliutsiia na Vkraini,* p. 91. [2d Russian ed., p. 133—Ed.]

German imperialists or was himself already aware of the situation. One thing is clear—that the Entente will attempt to make use of the German occupying army to promote its own interests. Of course, just now this army is not too reliable, it is already infected, and is thus not too useful to the Entente. It must be replaced by unexposed troops. It is not safe to rely entirely on the German army at a time when Austria and Germany are slowly being occupied. But what can one do when no other force is yet available?

Both the Austro-German command and the [German army—Ed.] Soviets have surely received suitable orders and will do what they can. Hence the delay in the departure of the occupants from the Ukraine.

But at present the other factors are outweighed by the first mentioned: the spontaneous movement and yearning for home.

The second aspect will become dominant only when the German counterrevolution becomes stronger, but the Ukraine must take it into consideration now. Soon, perhaps in the spring, the Ukraine may be faced with a greater and stronger occupation by the Entente seeking the destruction of the revolutionary specter of communism and restoration of the one and indivisible Russia.

Thus we have been brought to this sad state by the longing of political clowns to remain at the helm at any price. For the sake of independence a stone has been hung around the neck of the Ukraine, and it burdens both the Ukraine and those who asked for help. The Ukraine is suffering because of this help and will suffer more in the future.

The forces now contesting in the Ukraine must take into consideration both aspects of this extraordinary power. On the one hand, they must (and cannot do otherwise) reach agreement with the present infected occupation to benefit from the occupants' desire to get home as soon as possible. This may lead to "understandings," agreements, trades, handing over from one hand to the other, "from the coat-tails to under the coat-tails"[6] (as is done by vendors of salt and dried fish) . For the fact remains that the occupants remain as judges and decide the fate of the Ukraine.

On the other hand, the occupation should be studied to ascertain the right way to liberate the Ukraine from any occupation and the forces appropriate to this end.

This poses the question: how should the Ukraine act to attain full liberty—its social, national, economic, and political liberation?

And where are the forces which can and should lead the Ukraine in this very difficult and complicated struggle?

Chapter x

The Trend of the Ukrainian Movement:
An Independent Ukraine

What path and what direction should the Ukraine pursue to attain its goal of full and complete liberation?

This question leads to another:

To whom shall we look for advice, for an answer to this question? Should it be sought from lesser and greater personages, should it be sought in various general principles, noisy slogans, or legal definitions?[1].

We cannot rely completely on these sources for an answer to our question, no matter how useful they may be, because eminent people, both great and small, either keep silent or evade the question, or at the most give unclear answers. Why they talk this way and not otherwise is another matter—but persons of greater or lesser eminence are subject to the same weaknesses as commoners for whom *der Wunsch ist Vater des Gedankes*. It is impossible to rely on general principles or legal definitions, because these principles and definitions are the work of people and, even against the will of these people, often play the role of juridical law. As the Russian saying goes: the law is like a wagon-tongue; whichever way it's turned, that's the way you go!

And since we consider ourselves influenced by the present time and place, we must find the source which is least influenced by senatorial explanations,[2] which would of itself preclude intentional or unintentional misconstructions.

We want to warn the reader now that we are not free of Ukrainian feelings. We have them "in us," and not only "for us." Of this we can convince the Katerynoslavians who view themselves as vessels of pure internationalism, pure socialism, pure communism. They have, for instance, "in themselves, for themselves" no Great Russian nationalism or chauvinism. God forbid that we should even think such things.

43

To avoid as much as possible the personal feelings of ourselves and others—even those of the "pure internationalists"—we should turn to the real process of the Ukrainian revolutionary movement, lend an ear to the language of facts, feel by intuition the real trend of the Ukrainian movement. Facts are stubborn things, say the English.

To analyze and discover the trend of the Ukrainian movement it will suffice to examine the development of this movement in the years 1917 and 1918. Previous history serves only to prepare and explain, illuminating particular features and details. Revolution, as we know, unveils the real forces and the real tendency of every social movement, tears away the coverings which conceal historical figures and tendencies during the period of peaceful organic evolution. Thus the revolutionary years 1917 and 1918 are incomparably more important for an understanding of the character and tendencies of the Ukrainian revolutionary movement than even the whole previous hundred years of the movement.

One has only to give thought to the history of the Ukraine in the last two and a half centuries to realize how extraordinarily difficult and distressing were the conditions in which the Ukrainian movement existed and developed. All the fearful powers and dreadful weapons made available by feudal serfdom and bourgeois-capitalist society were used to destroy the Ukrainian movement—not only by the bureaucracy but also by the Russian establishment (the large landowners, the bourgeoisie, and the "third element"[3]), and even by the non-Ukrainian proletariat.

We may be reproached for comparing the non-Ukrainian proletariat with the large landowners and the capitalists, or for opposing it to the Ukrainian proletariat. We may be told that we thus disunite the proletariats of different nations and push the proletariat into an alliance with the bourgeoisie. We live in a time of such "pure internationalism" that we must foresee such reproaches, pay heed to them, and answer them seriously. To those who try to catch us we say that we speak not of *how it should have been* but of *how it really was*. And the reality was that the non-Ukrainian proletariat was hostile to the Ukrainian movement, as it was to all national movements generally. It tolerated this movement but warned against nationalism. This movement could be *against* monarchy, large landowners, or capitalists, but it should go no further . . . this was chauvinism! We shall encounter this fact again. This, and only this, is what we have in mind when we say that measures for the destruction of the Ukrainian movement were employed not only by the bureaucracy, but also by the Russian establishment. In different ways, using different methods—but with the same result. Conditions of development were worse than merely difficult or unfavorable. Police proscription, prison, church, press, school—all combined for a single purpose. It was *Vse k tsele odnoi* ("all heading for the same goal") .[4]

All sorts of idealistic, pragmatic, social, and personal considerations were used, different measures adopted, and different methods pursued, and, in short, whether consciously or unconsciously, desired or not desired, the result was the same.

During the war the difficult position of the Ukrainian movement became unbearable. What papers still remained in existence were muzzled; all who seemed infected by "mazepism"[5] came under the suspicious and importunate attention of the tsarist police and were scattered and deposited in various corners of not so distant places. Conquered Galicia,[6] where active Ukrainian patriots found refuge when the Russian Ukraine was no longer bearable, was "blessed" by the benefits of Russian culture in the form of various kinds of police, as well as by governmental, pedagogical, Black-Hundred, and liberal Russifiers up to and including P. Struve, that *enfant terrible* of opposition to his majesty. Whole villages and towns were destroyed by cannon fire, fields crisscrossed by trenches, people driven from their homes. The country was being ruined, and it seemed that the Ukraine could not arise from these devastations. . . .

Thus even greater significance should be accorded to the scale of the revolutionary-national Ukrainian movement which appeared from the very first days of the 1917 revolution. After what happened only those who cannot learn, or who do not want to see what is clear to everyone, who consider themselves (and not only "for themselves") vessels of pure internationalism, can say everything remained as it was, that there is occupation and only occupation. Only a blind man can fail to see the basic trend of this movement—to form an independent sovereign state. Independence may be viewed as a rejection of the occupation in the heads of some fellows with unexpected Ukrainian feelings to precisely the same extent as, for instance, the Katerynoslav point of view may be regarded as "pure, in themselves and for themselves, internationalism." Independence, as the goal of the Ukrainian movement, cannot be viewed as identical with the independence of the hetman's regime. On the contrary, the independence of the independent hetman and the Katerynoslav point of view are two sisters, and both caricatures: one of independence and the other of internationalism. If the hetman's independence reflected the independence which is the aim of the Ukrainian movement, that independence should be buried as deep as possible. And if the

Katerynoslav point of view were a real mirror-image of international-ism, and not its caricature, a cross should have been raised over it [internationalism—Ed.] long ago. But a caricature is a caricature and only a caricature!

Independence is the real content of the Ukrainian movement. That the Ukrainian movement will be satisfied by permission to pub-lish a Ukrainian primer or newspaper, or to allow a Ukrainian play on the stage with music and dancing, or to wear the red trousers and blue cossack mantle, or to cook dumplings and *varenyky*—you your-selves know quite well who could think this way. And what remains of the "inflamed" (as *Kommunist* puts it) Ukrainian national ques-tion after the partial solution offered by the Communists of the Ukraine?

Let us look at the facts. At the outbreak of the 1917 revolution numerous resolutions of many Ukrainian rallies, meetings, and con-gresses of soldiers, peasants, and workers, as well as of party, profes-sional, and educational organizations,[7] were presented to the Provisional Government with two essential demands (1) National-territorial autonomy in a federation with Russia, (2) Ukrainian representation at the future international congress on the [peace treaty—Ed.].

We need not dwell on the legal definitions of autonomy and federation and their differences. We are interested in the meaning which the Ukrainian organizations attached to these demands. Re-gardless of our attitude toward the Central Rada's invitation to the occupiers of the Ukraine, we cannot ignore the fact that the Central Rada was very influential in the Ukraine, and that her demands and Universals reflected the main lines of the Ukrainian movement—in every case embodying either a past or a future standpoint of the move-ment and in every instance marking the beginning of a new chapter in the history of its development. Thus, to understand the essence of the concept of national-territorial autonomy we need only turn our at-tention to the decrees of the Central Rada.

The First Universal,[8] which proclaimed the autonomy of the Ukraine after a three-month quarrel with the Provisional Govern-ment over this inflamed question, directly indicated the will of the Ukrainian people for independence and autonomy in Ukrainian internal affairs. "Henceforth we will manage our own lives," stated the Universal.

How the Central Rada interpreted this formula is seen from the "Constitution of the Ukraine," a statute on the General Secre-tariat adopted at a session of the Little Rada on July 16, 1917, "on the basis of an agreement with the Provisional Government reached on July 3, 1917."[9] That is, after the reaction to the June 18[10] offensive and on the eve of the "July Days"[11] (July 3–5) in Petrograd and Kiev; that is, as a result of concessions and compromises with the Provisional Government due to the dubious state of the revolution; that is, after the decline of revolutionary energy in general, and of the Ukrainian movement in particular, and after the increase in the strength of the counterrevolution. It should not be forgotten that the "agreement of July 3" contributed (together with other events) to the July catastrophe.

How does this statute define the rights of the General Secretariat?*

ARTICLE 1. The supreme State Organ of the Government in the Ukraine is the General Secretariat of the Central Rada, which is formed by the Central Rada, is responsible to it, and is confirmed by the Provisional Government.

ARTICLE 19. All the laws of the Provisional Government are binding in the Ukraine as of the day they are promulgated in the Ukrainian language in the *State Government Herald*.

"Note: In extraordinary cases the General Secretariat will proclaim them in a different way."[12]

Everyone knows that the First Universal was proclaimed at the Second Military Congress when the indignation of the Ukrainian soldiers over the procrastinations of the Provisional Government and Kerenski's prohibition of the [Military—Ed.] Congress had led to extreme tension. The demands of the First Universal may be considered as lacking in energy; it was mild by comparison with the spirited speeches and sharp feelings disclosed by the Congress. It diminished, not enlarged, the demands of the Ukrainian masses. At the time V. Vynnychenko had to argue that it was not necessary to ask for more, nor to proclaim an independent republic, because (1) we did not have enough time to organize properly, (2) we did not have sufficient troops, while our enemies had their own troops in the Ukraine, (3) the large cities would not take our side since their populations were mostly non-Ukrainian. In view of the situation [he continued—Ed.] we had to take what we could get at the time. Eventually we would arrive at the [status of a—Ed.] republic.†

---

* *Robitnycha Hazeta*, No. 87 (July, 1917).

† V. Skorovstans'kyi, *Revoliutsiia na Vkraini*, p. 26. [2d Russian ed., pp. 37–38—Ed.]

V. Vynnychenko expressed the official intentions of the Ukrainian masses. Its gist was autonomy now with status as an independent republic later. In this example we find proof of Lenin's remark:

> . . . autonomy, as a reformist measure, differs in principle from revolutionary freedom to secede. This is unquestionable. But as everyone knows, in practice reform is often merely a step toward revolution. Autonomy is what enables a people forcibly retained within the boundaries of a given state to crystallize into a nation, to gather, assess, and organize all its forces, and to select the most opportune moment for a *declaration* . . . in the "Norwegian" spirit [a reference to the Norwegian Parliament's 1905 resolution to separate from Sweden]: "We, the autonomous diet of such-and-such nation, or of such-and-such territory, declare that the Emperor of all the Russias has ceased to be King of Poland. . . ."*

This was also the true meaning of the First Universal.

We may be told that others thought differently.

We agree and will go even further: When you look more closely at the leaders of the Ukrainian movement, you see that they could not keep up with events, that "The owl of Minerva took to flight only at dusk," that *im Anfang war der Tat* and the "word" appeared later. But this to us is even more significant as an indication of the depth of the national-liberation movement. The masses chose their way instinctively and spontaneously, groping, tearing all kinds of mild forms and harmony from all kinds of sweet and resounding theories. . . .

The second demand—for admission of a Ukrainian delegate to the future peace conference—convinces us of this even more. If we are not mistaken, the Ukrainians were the first of all the peoples of Russia to advance such a demand. The Ukrainian movement supplied an example for others—it was heeded and followed by other national movements in Russia. One does not have to be highly intelligent "in and for oneself" to grasp the idea that the representative of a people living within the boundaries of an alien state can appear at an international forum side by side with the representatives of this state only when this people have actually achieved independence and only lack the pretext for issuing a declaration in the Norwegian Spirit. And only a people which actually has the courage to become

---

* [V. I.] N. Lenin, "Itogi diskussii o samoopredelenii," *Sbornik Sotsial-Demokrata*, p. 22.

independent can issue such a demand, such a declaration in the Norwegian Spirit—although "in and for itself" unable to become conscious of this fact. As an illustration we present the statement of a delegate to the Second Military Congress:

How did we become *samostiinyki?*[13] We learned of the ban on the Congress, and of the Provisional Government's answer, and we realized that *we had pleaded enough; we had to carry on our work independently*—and we called ourselves *samostiinyki.* But now we see that *there are samostiinyki who want to form a separate Ukrainian state. We do not belong to such a party.**

This example may serve to convince the Katerynoslavians that in and for the people the idea of independence is "discredited" (to use the word of the above-quoted resolution on the Ukraine and Russia) , and at the same time the people will declare: we have pleaded enough, we have to carry on our work independently! And what people can carry their work to a conclusion in a state of dependence? Try to place them on the bed of "proletarian centralism,"[14] if the term is taken in its true meaning and you will see before you *samostiinyki.* For example, it may happen in the following way: Soviets, let us say, have again been formed in the Ukraine. To make good on its promises the Katerynoslav government summons a congress, or one may be held spontaneously. And it happens that the *samostiinyki,* those who want to declare the Soviet Ukraine independent, gain the majority at the congress.

What must the Katerynoslav government do? Of course, disperse them because they are chauvinists, against pure internationalism.

What will then be said by the masses who have begun to realize that in and for themselves the best thing is independence? Of course, they will say: "We have had enough of the 'Katerynoslavians.' We have to carry our work to a conclusion independently."

"Henceforth we will manage our own lives."[15]

But what happened was not at all what had been anticipated. The June 18 offensive, the July 3–5 events in Petrograd, the July 5–7 events in Kiev (the disarmament of the Polubotok Regiment) , the execution of the Bohdan Khmelnytskii Regiment,[16] and the institution of the death penalty at the front put the brakes on the cause of Ukrainian autonomy until Kornilov's adventure smashed the evil force of the counterrevolution. The former Russian Empire broke

* V. Skorovstans'kyi, *Revoliutsiia na Vkraini.* [2d Russian ed., pp 36–37—Ed.]

apart, and "authority fell into the hands of the local people." The Central Rada seized power; it was strong enough to do so and was not afraid to proclaim a Ukrainian People's Republic in a federal union with Russia (November 7) .[17] At the time such a republic did not satisfy the people, but . . . no further step could be taken: the Ukraine was full of cossack and Russian troops hostile to separation. "In due course independence will come of itself."* In closing the First Kiev Congress,[18] at which the split occurred, the head of the Central Rada, M. Hrushevsky, noted in his short speech what had been accomplished, adding that such a course would lead to independence and that independence might perhaps be achieved sooner than anticipated. We know that at the Second [Military—Ed.] Congress V. Vynnychenko estimated that we would arrive at the [status of a—Ed.] republic in about two or three years!

That independence was the ultimate aim is also seen from the, at that time ridiculous and wholly counterrevolutionary, theory of the "federative socialist government" proposed by the Central Rada, which did not and could not become a reality. The Rada wanted to form a Russian government by way of agreements among the separate parts of the former Russian Empire: the Ukraine, Great Russia, the Don, the Caucasus, and Siberia. But such agreements could arise only if these lands were politically equal, independent, and sovereign. This theory was not defective in itself, but it was untimely and inconsistent with the Ukraine's actual position. The Central Rada declared that the Central All-Russian government—the Council of People's Commissars—did not exist and wanted to reach agreement with it only as the government of Great Russia. *The Ukraine was a part of Russia* (that is what it was, and that is how the Central Rada viewed it) , *but it acted like an equal and independent body.* This was in contradiction with the state in which the Ukraine found itself at the time.

This contradiction became apparent in another case as well. The Central Rada sent a separate delegation to the Brest Litovsk peace negotiations. Like a mentor "wise after the fact" (so to speak) , the Katerynoslavians talk contemptuously about the error of the All-Russian delegation's "recognizing" the delegation of the Central Rada at Brest Litovsk.† The Katerynoslavians should give a little thought to the matter and recall the objective position not only of the

* V. Skorovstan'kyi, *Revoliutsiia na Vkraini*, p. 26. [2d Russian ed., p. 38—Ed.]

† [Ia. E., "O sozdanii 'samostoiatel'noi' kommunisticheskoi partii Ukrainy"—Ed.], *Pravda*, No. 132 [June 30, 1918, p. 5—Ed.]

Ukraine and its delegation but also of Russia and its delegation. What would the Katerynoslavians have had the All-Russian delegation do? Not recognize? But then all the negotiations would have come to nothing, since they were based on the "right of nations to self-determination"—the ninth paragraph of the Bolshevik Program,[19] the principle which the Katerynoslavians *recognize even today.* The Russian delegation had to recognize the delegation of the Central Rada because "facts cannot be ignored," as was clear to Count Lvov, the head of the Provisional (not the present) Government. Facts are stubborn things, and one has to have a Katerynoslav head not to understand it.

Not to recognize was impossible, even though the recognition was incomplete, insincere, improperly explained. On the other hand, the declaration of the Central Rada's delegation was also incomplete and insincere in talking about the unity of the revolutionary front and claiming to stand on the same side of the barrier as the Russian delegation while actually ruining the revolutionary front in the presence of the Austro-German imperialists and polemicizing, thus discrediting the authority of the Russian government.

The contradiction in the Ukrainian position became even more apparent when another Ukrainian delegation arrived—from the Central Executive Committee of the Ukraine.[20]

Regardless of who stood in the position of the Central Rada, what could it or the Ukraine have done? The only solution was a declaration of independence.

The Central Rada reached this logical conclusion at the session of January 11 (24), 1918. The Fourth Universal proclaimed the independence and sovereignty of the Ukrainian People's Republic.[21]

The "i's" were dotted and the contradictions resolved. The delegation of the Central Rada concluded a separate peace, and the Russian delegation broke off the negotiations with the well-known declaration: "No peace, no war." *No peace,* because that would mean agreeing to the ultimate demands of Germany and thus recognizing the treaty signed by the Central Rada; that is, recognizing the Central Rada as the legal government of the Ukraine and itself as the aggressor—admitting the Central Rada's assertion that the war between itself and the Bolsheviks was a war between the Ukraine and Russia. *No war,* because the war could not continue for lack of troops.

Thus the Central Rada arrived at independence, not through conscious leadership but because it was impelled by the facts. It cherished ("in and for itself") mild sweet thoughts about a mild organizational effort in order, slowly and with brief rests, to attain full independence. But behind it was something stronger than itself: facts, the real and objective processes of life which impelled it, stimulated its thoughts, *forced* it to reach suitable logical conclusions.

Let us now examine the position and role of the other factor in the Ukrainian revolutionary process—the Soviets and, in particular, the Bolshevik Party.

The following quotation from *Kommunist*, No. 5, states: "We . . . provided no general answer to the question of the kind of relations demanded by the Ukrainian proletariat. Did it demand regional autonomy, federation, or independence; or would it perhaps have preferred no political separation at all, but direct ties between every local Soviet and the All-Russian center."*

There is much truth in this assertion. We gave no answer to the Ukrainian question, indeed, because we were not aware of it and considered it only a petty-bourgeois whim (we speak only about the factual relations of the Bolsheviks in the Ukraine, not about personalities). But this means that at the time we were unaware of any Ukraine; there was only "Southern Russia," and we did define an attitude to that: "no political separation, direct ties between every local Soviet and the All-Russian center."** This, it is true, was connected with "the right of nations to self-determination," but "this was to come later"—"maybe, most likely, somehow!" Just now there could be no "political separation, only direct ties between every local Soviet and the All-Russian center."

This view, it would appear, guards against any kind of chauvinism, against any kind of independence, even "in and for ourselves."

But where did we actually end up? At independence! This is a fact.

We are attacked at this point by the Katerynoslavians, screaming with contempt and indignation about the "rash recognition, after federation, of the independence of the Central Executive Committee of the Ukraine and of the Ukrainian Central Executive Committee's playing at government."† But there was really no other way! If the Katerynoslavians knew how to reckon with facts, they would understand this. Then they would understand the fact that, while denying the very existence of the Ukraine, they themselves form a separate party and a separate government for this nonexistent country; they

---

* ["Itogi s'ezda," *Kommunist*, No. 5; V. Skorovstans'kyi, 2d Russian ed., p. 147 n.—Ed.]

** [Ia. E., "O sozdanii 'samostoiatel'noi' kommunisticheskoi partii Ukrainy," *Pravda*, No. 132 (June 30, 1918), p. 5—Ed.]

† [*Ibid.*—Ed.]

would understand that "in and for themselves" they confirm the existence, as a state-political unit, of the country whose existence they deny, but that they do it blindly, damaging their own cause. Facts are stubborn things, and even a copper forehead cannot cope with them! [Ukrainian saying—Ed.]

We demanded "direct ties between every local Soviet and the All-Russian center"—and under the *pressure* of events the Katerynoslavians should have formed a Central Executive Committee of the Ukraine, that is, a center which would rally the disunited Ukrainian Soviets and become a connecting link between every local Soviet and the All-Russian center. . . .

We did not want any kind of political separation and rashly had to recognize independence after federation because, asleep, we missed the Ukrainian movement and did not arrive at a positive answer: yes or no on the Ukraine (indeed, this could not have been done at the time). We had to act rashly because facts are stubborn things— just as the Katerynoslavians had to hurry after the Directory, although they clamored and made a lot of fuss about an insurrection.[22]

In order to oppose the Central Rada we had to form the Central Executive Committee of the Soviets of the Ukraine, thus to complete the Ukraine's organization into a state-political unit and to confirm it in fact. Let the Katerynoslavians try to delete this point from the history of the Ukraine!

To oppose the Rada in the international arena we had to send a delegation to Brest; although it was not our intent, we thereby confirmed in the international arena the Ukraine's status as a state-political unit. Let the Katerynoslavians strike this point from the history of the Ukrainian nation!

One is driven to both laughter and tears in reading how the present Central Committee of the Katerynoslav party attempted from Poltava to outwit[23] the German socialist government at a time when the Central Committee was still very far from Poltava, which was the seat of either Skoropadski or Petliura.[24] No matter how curious this act may appear to us, even in caricature, it still serves to confirm that facts are stubborn things!

To fight the Germans called in by the Central Rada, we had to proclaim the independence of the Ukraine. We had to, we had to, we had to. . . .

While we can discuss the Central Rada only *cum grano salis*, with many reservations, about us one can sing without any reservations:

> *They married me without me—*
> *I was in the mill.* [Russian saying—Ed.]

In the same mill where the Katerynoslavians have lived to this day. They have good reason to write with this song as a pattern: "in them, for them" and "me without me!"*

Compelled by facts, events, and the logic of the real revolutionary national liberation movement in the Ukraine, the country's two most authoritative organizations, the Central Rada and the Central Executive Committee of the Soviets, came to the idea of independence.

The outcome of all of the various designs, viewpoints, desires, and philosophical, socio-political, and ideological considerations—the ultimate point at which all arrived—was independence!

Certainly there were mistakes, vacillation, and inconsistencies. But to explain the outcome only by "mistakes," "vacillation," "inconsistencies"—would be . . .

"Always 'good luck'—grant me at least a little bit of brain!" said Suvorov[25] to those who explained all his victories and conquests by good luck and accidents.

We maintain: "Always 'mistakes' and 'inconsistencies'—give us at least a bit of historical content in this process." And we add: "because nothing in history can be understood by following the method of the Katerynoslavians."

* ["Natsional'nyi vopros v programme kommunisticheskoi partii Ukrainy," *Pravda*, No. 132 (June 30, 1918), p. 5—Ed.]

Chapter XI

Revolution in Austria. Galicia

Our analysis of the trend of the Ukrainian movement would be incomplete without an analysis of still another inseparable feature of this movement.

The revolutionary Ukrainian movement was concentrated chiefly in the Russian Ukraine. But its events had their counterparts also in Galicia, the Austrian part of the Ukraine.

These two parts, forcibly torn asunder, had never lost contact even in the past. From the natural, ethnographic, social, and economic points of view the Ukraine and Galicia, separated by an artificial boundary, form a single whole with its own historical traditions. Hence the Ukrainian movement on one side of the border had a great influence on the fate of the other side. In territory and population the Russian Ukraine is almost ten times as great as Galicia, but the political conditions in which it lived were far more difficult. The chains of tsarist despotism were far heavier than those of the Habsburg fragmentary dual or triple monarchy.

For this reason Galicia played a major role in the development of the Ukraine. As a center of the Ukrainian movement it was known as the Ukrainian Piedmont. Its beacon, never extinguished, threw sparks across the border.

The Russian revolution made a profound impression on the Galician citizens and the Galician political parties. All who were politically independent and nationally conscious were hostile to "Muscovy" [Moskovshchina—Ed.]. Muscovy has destroyed the political freedoms of the Ukraine; Muscovy throttles the Ukrainian movement; our chief enemy is Muscovy—such was the general feeling. Everything is permitted, everything is right, which leads to the liberation of the Ukraine from Muscovite enslavement. From this it was only a step to the "Union for the Liberation of the Ukraine,"[1] which did not shun direct assistance from the Austro-German government.

"In the current war the general staffs are making the utmost use of any national or revolutionary movement in the enemy camp: the Germans utilize the Irish rebellion, the French—the Czech movement, etc."* Nor were the Austro-German imperialists reluctant to exploit the Ukrainian movement, to give it money or to permit it to spread propaganda among prisoners. There is no doubt that some parties and groups accepted this assistance, but for this reason to consider the Ukrainian movement an Austro-German invention suits only the Russian bourgeoisie which was always frightening the masses with German money—one judges others by one's own standards.

With the Russian revolution came a change in the attitude of the Ukrainian parties, even that of the Union for the Liberation of the Ukraine. The dazzling slogans of this revolution awakened hopes for immediate "peace and good will among men." The old tsarist chains dropped to the ground, and with great enthusiasm the peoples of Russia strove for "peace based on national self-determination."

Is it possible that one's own country will be denied self-determination?

Many Galician political and social leaders were scattered in various corners of Russia. Now they gathered in Kiev, and thus direct contact was made with Galicia.

The Galician parties[2] openly and directly advocated two complementary objectives: (1) unification of the two parts of the Ukrainian people, Russian and Austrian, into (2) a single, independent, sovereign state.

In the Russian Ukraine only the second objective played an active role—the demand that the Ukrainian people organize a free, independent, sovereign state. The first objective had no operative meaning, not because it was redundant or unimportant for the national liberation movement but because at the time the Russian revolution was limited to the remaining territory of the former Russian Empire. It seemed that the revolution would find no response on the other side of the front but that the war in any case would soon be over, and the national question would be decided at the imminent peace conference. Therefore, even greater importance was attached to the demand that representatives of the Ukrainian people be admitted to this conference without distinguishing between the Russian and Austrian parts.

* [V. I.] N. Lenin, "Itogi diskussii o samoopredelenii," *Sbornik Sotsial-Demokrata*, p. 27.

People only talked about the peace conference, no one did anything—no one even asked when and where it would take place. But there was much talk about the socialist conference in Stockholm.[3] The Ukrainian socialist parties were briskly discussing the questions of the future conference and preparing to send a delegation. The Galician Social Democrats even sent delegates to Stockholm with a memorandum advancing, among other things, both of the above demands.

Thus, although it did not play an active propaganda role in the Ukrainian national revolutionary movement, the demand for union with Galicia was not forgotten. The feeling was that "It will come of itself in due course."[4]

Here the occupation of the Ukraine was of primordial importance. Although the influence of this factor cannot even be fully measured, one thing should not be forgotten. Regardless of how we view the invitation to the German troops, regardless of how we censure and condemn this act of the Central Rada, regardless of how pejorative a light it cast, among the Ukrainian masses, on the very act of national liberation, it accomplished one thing without any doubt: in severing the connection with Russia the occupation drew the Russian Ukraine closer to Galicia. But this had another aspect: in drawing closer to Galicia, the Ukraine was at the same time drawing Galicia closer to itself. The Austrian delegation headed by Czernin,[5] and the Austrian government in Vienna, understood this quite well, and that is why they were so cool to the idea of peace with the Ukraine. That is why the Reichsrat was slow to ratify the Ukrainian treaty.

The Ukrainian parties appear not to have placed much hope in the Austrian (and German) revolution. They intended and desired to follow a policy of peace and diplomacy.

The Austrian revolution set the Ukrainian question on a new course of revolutionary struggle and added the creative power of the broad national masses.

We have only fragmentary reports about the events in Austria, but the basic features of this movement are known to us. The former Habsburg Empire has been replaced by separate national independent republics. Although this process may lead to a new unification, to us it seems pointless to hope that the old boundaries will be preserved.

An interesting aspect of the Austrian revolutionary movement reported in the press is the existence of an "Eastern People's Republic," a republic in Ukrainian eastern Galicia headed by a National

Rada [Council—Ed.].[6] We hear further of preparations for a constituent assembly. We have news reports about battles between Ukrainians and Poles for possession of Galicia (the Poles consider Eastern Galicia a Polish land). Although incomplete, these news items make one thing clear—with the outbreak of the Austrian revolution a new chapter opened in the history of the Ukrainian movement. The course of events has placed on the agenda the slogan, "Union of Galicia and the Ukraine"—and you have to reckon with it willy-nilly.

Thus the principal trend in the Ukrainian national-revolutionary liberation movement is that the Ukrainian people should constitute themselves a nation—an independent, self-governing, and sovereign political organism—irrespective of the former boundaries.

Chapter XII

Is a Ukraine Possible, Independent of Russia?

What conclusion do we draw? We do not deny that the tendency of the Ukrainian movement is to form a sovereign independent state, to unite, to draw its lands together, and to constitute itself a nation. But the aspiration to create an independent sovereign state is not peculiar to the Ukrainian movement; it is found in every national movement. Paragraph nine of our Marxist program contains the slogan: the right of nations to self-determination. Its meaning can only be that every nation has the right to form an independent sovereign state because, as historical experience demonstrates, through self-determination a nation tends to form an independent sovereign state. But this does not mean that every nation can organize itself into an independent sovereign state. The same historical experience convinces us that many nations have disappeared completely, others have been scattered, others partly assimilated, still others incorporated within the boundaries of an alien state. The history of the Ukrainian national movement and its outcome (the hetman's regime) prove to us, as we are told, that "under contemporary world economic conditions an independent Ukraine is impossible."*

Thank you, we answer, for reminding us of the content of this abstract formula—the right of nations to self-determination. Better late than never.

But to what extent are the theses of the Organizational Bureau correct in asserting that the historical national-revolutionary movement in the Ukraine is a "political expression of the fact that under contemporary world economic conditions an independent Ukraine is impossible"? If this were really so, it would be stupid for us to struggle for an independent Ukraine. So, to what extent is this statement correct?

* *Izveshchenie, op. cit.*, p. 16.

59

To our regret the theses of the Organizational Bureau postulate and present these absolute truths but do not prove them. They disclose the true meaning of the help which the Central Rada received from German imperialism and tell us how Austro-German imperialism exploited the Ukrainian national movement, how it replaced the Central Rada by an independent hetman, and, generally, how the Ukraine fell into the claws of Austro-German imperialism. All this is true, but is it enough to state that, *ergo*, an independent Ukraine is impossible under present world economic conditions? No, it is not enough. It only shows what unexpected obstacles and difficulties arise in the path of liberation from capitalism in general, and in the path of the national liberation movement in particular. No one denies that the path is difficult nor that the liberation movement may be exploited by this or that imperialist beast of prey. Did not France, Germany, and others take advantage of the Russian 1905 revolution? Was not the present revolution exploited in the same way by the Central Powers?[1] But what is one to say about people who, on this basis, conclude that a republican Russia is impossible under contemporary world economic conditions and that only a monarchist Russia can exist? *Ça dépend.* We have no guarantee, to be sure, that no tsar will be appointed for us if the counterrevolution is victorious. But maybe not—maybe such an appointment will never be possible. The same goes for Ukrainian independence. We have already pointed to a great many unifiers. If they are successful, it will not be unexpected. But maybe they will not be successful. No matter how terrible are the Wilsons, Lloyd Georges, Clemenceaus, and *tutti quanti*, the facts may prevail and convince the world imperialists. History has its own course which is not marked out only by presidents, bankers, and finance capital.

No, such arguments are not enough. The conclusions of the theses are based on too little evidence.

But let us accept them for the time being, accept them on trust, accept the authoritative declaration of the Organizational Bureau.

Thus we admit that an independent Ukraine is impossible under the conditions of the present world economy. Does this prove that it would be impossible under the conditions of a future socialist economy? The theses do not discuss the contemporary bourgeois, but the future Soviet, Ukraine. Is an independent Soviet Ukraine possible? To be sure, under present world economic conditions a Soviet Ukraine is just as impossible as a Soviet Russia. But can we conclude from this that "under present world economic conditions an independent Russia is impossible?" Then we should leave to the Miliukovs, the Rodziankos, and the world imperialists behind them, the task of uniting a bourgeois Ukraine and a bourgeois Russia. When the Organizational Bureau issued its call for unity (on a federal basis) we think it had in mind the Soviet Ukraine. Well, is an independent Soviet Ukraine possible or not?

We will give the relevant arguments.

"7. At the present moment the Ukraine appears, with respect to Soviet Russia, to be an outpost of the counterrevolution, and the Soviet authorities of the Russian Federative Soviet Republic are consequently very interested in a closer alliance with the insurgent Worker-Peasant Government of the Ukraine. The establishment of closer relations between Russia and the Ukraine is also a definite necessity because, if cut off from the Ukraine, the Worker-Peasant North will be in an almost critical situation. Therefore, since the workers and peasants of the Ukraine are interested in having a Soviet government in the North, it is absolutely necessary to promote the establishment of a federative union of worker-peasant Ukraine with Russia."* That is all.

"If cut off from the Ukraine, the Worker-Peasant North will be in an almost critical situation."** So be it. To what conclusion does that lead us? You say—"unite the Ukraine to Russia." And we say, on the contrary, "in present or future world economic conditions an independent Russia is impossible, because if cut off . . . etc., and therefore we will unite Russia to the Ukraine." Help, police, chauvinism, nationalism!

What a clamor you would raise, my friends,
If I said a thing like that![2]

Well, we think that with an independent Soviet Ukraine—really independent, not on paper, not in words, but in reality—the Worker-Peasant North would not find itself in an almost critical situation, no worse, at any rate, than in a union. You think that an independent Soviet Ukraine would not supply grain, sugar, or coal? But we will supply them, and more readily and generously than when forced to unite because of sugar, coal, or grain.

"The workers and peasants of the Ukraine are interested in having a Soviet government in the North."† Yes, indeed, interested. But does this interest not depend precisely on the idea that Soviet rule in the North is the greatest and best guarantee "under present world economic conditions" that the enslavement of the Ukrainian

---

* *Izveshchenie, op. cit.,* pp. 16–17.
** [*Ibid.*—Ed.]
† [*Ibid.*—Ed.]

people, a nation of workers and peasants, will soon end in complete liberation? And complete liberation is independence! Is it possible that we are mistaken?

No, these arguments of the Organizational Bureau are not sufficient to support the conclusion that "an independent Ukraine is impossible under present world economic conditions."* The thesis remains unproven.

We pass now to the Katerynoslav point of view. We already know that this is the official view of both the Communists of the Ukraine and of the Provisional Government. Hence the reader should not complain if we entertain him for some time with this dish.

After stating that there is no Ukraine, that formerly it was only "Southern Russia" which has now become "the southern part of the eastern region occupied by Germany," and that it is "occupation and only occupation," the Katerynoslavians ask the question: "Does Ukrainian 'independence' correspond to or contradict the region's economic nature and the tendencies of its economic development?"**

From the Katerynoslavian point of view this question is the equivalent of another:

"Did the economic development of the Ukraine in recent decades create the sort of close mutual economic ties between the Ukraine and Russia which could serve as the material base for the union of these two countries and would oppose their separation, or was the inclusion of the Ukraine in the Russian Empire only the result of political oppression and compulsion?"†

To these questions they give the following answers:

"It is generally accepted that the present economy is based on three things—coal, ore, and cast iron.

"Where is the foundation of the domestic economy of Russia located?

"The basis and foundation of the Russian economy is the heavy industry of the Donets Basin.

"The vital impulses of the whole Russian economy come from the Donets Basin. This can be proven by a few figures.

"In 1913 the Donets Basin gave industry 1,561 million puds[3] of coal out of a total Russian production of 2,223 million puds—that is, more than 70 percent of the total Russian production.

---

* [*Ibid.*—Ed.]
** ["Natsional'nyi vopros v programme kommunisticheskoi partii Ukrainy," *Pravda*, No. 132 (June 30, 1918), p. 5—Ed.].
† [*Ibid.*—Ed.]

"In addition to the southern industry with which it was very tightly linked, the Donets Basin also served the railways, steel industry, and processing industry of Petersburg, the Moscow textile industry, the steamships, etc.

"The Donets Basin was the principal source of this black food for Russia.

"And through its metallurgical giants which, fed on coal and ore, have grown into powerful combined enterprises, it also supplies Russian industry with a second (after coal) absolutely essential component: cast iron, iron, and steel.

"In 1915 the South supplied the Russian market with 99 percent of all double T-beams and channels, 79 percent of the large rails, 68 percent of the shaped iron, and 96.7 percent of all wire products. An average of three-fourths of the cast iron, shaped iron, and steel products arriving on the Russian market in recent years has come from the South.

"The Donets Basin is the most essential link in the contemporary chain of industry.

"Any attempt at removing this link from the chain of Russian industry (Manilov-like attempts[4] in the light of future prospects) represents either self-delusion or a reactionary utopia.

"The Ural, Moscow, and Kuznetsk regions have hitherto served local needs and have been, more or less, of only local importance.

"Decades of stubborn revolutionary work will be needed to alter the importance of these regions in the general Russian industrial system.

"But this connection is not unilateral: it is not being transformed into a dependence favorable to one side alone.

"Even the large Russian landowners and capitalists who have preempted power in the Ukraine, in order to extend it over all of Russia, do not dare, despite their hatred for Soviet Russia, to break economic ties with Russia—and not for nothing: over them is hanging the specter of manufactured goods, kerosene, petroleum, and timber.

"The Ukrainian textile industry is in its earliest stages, and Germany can give it nothing . . . only Russia can supply the Ukraine with oil and timber, and stoppage of the Russian machine-building industry because of a lack of Ukrainian coal would hurt southern industry by depriving it of the necessary instruments of production.

"We have been considering fundamentals without entering into details. But precise figures and details are not needed for recognition of the basic fact that the recent decades of the Ukraine's economic development have so tightly unified the Ukraine and Russia that we are justified in pointing to a contradiction between the economic development of the Ukraine and the desire for its separation. This also implies that the productive forces of the Ukraine would indignantly reject any such separation."*

That is all.

"That the productive forces of the Ukraine would indignantly reject any such separation"** sounds altogether "à la Marx!" How little is needed to draw such a frightening conclusion!

Just imagine: the productive forces would themselves revolt against the separation of the Ukraine. But it is clear to anyone, even to a Marxist who never studied in a seminary, that productive forces ultimately comprise the whole social, economic, political, and ideological development of a society, its whole life. This is the base—and this base will revolt against separation. It is not strange that Ukrainian independence will come crashing down if this base revolts. See what this learned fellow can do—he makes the thing clear as mud!

"He tries to frighten me, but I am not afraid," said L. Tolstoi about the intimidating L. Andreev.

The Katerynoslavians frighten us with the base, but we are not afraid of it. They want to beat us with the base, but instead we strike into their base.

It is a well-known fact that the mining and heavy industry of the Donets Basin played a primordial role in the Russian economy.

It is also well known that the Ukraine has no textile industry and that she has received oil, kerosene, and manufactures mainly from Russia.

That the economic ties were reciprocal is also an undeniable fact.

But what is new in this? What has this to do with the "revolt of the productive forces against separation?"†

All sorts of economic relations among countries (and among independent states or between colony and metropolitan area) bear a more or less reciprocal character, but this does not mean that the parties have the same status, the same interests, or economic equality.

No country can forego economic ties with other countries, satisfying all its own economic needs in a state of "autarky"—but this does not preclude the existence of independent autonomous states under contemporary world economic conditions.

* [*Ibid.*—Ed.]
** [*Ibid.*—Ed.]
† [*Ibid.*—Ed.]

The Katerynoslavians don't know "what's what," as Comrade Lenin has said. To prove that the productive forces revolt against the political separation of the Ukraine they talk about the well-known economic ties between Russia and the Ukraine, which differ in no particular way from other general economic ties in modern economic life.

They needed to show how these *economic* ties influenced *political* relations, and they were satisfied by this one frightfully scientific thesis: "the productive forces revolt against separation!"* To prove this thesis they had to pass from economics to politics, from productive forces to separation, and this is much harder than to postulate absolute truths. The jump from productive forces to separation is not as simple as the Katerynoslavians like to think. If they could make this jump, we would have grave doubts about the totality and the stability of the thesis: productive forces revolt against separation.

The Katerynoslavians raised the question: "Was the inclusion of the Ukraine in Russia the result only of political oppression and compulsion?"

They appear to think that the two countries were united by productive forces, but unfortunately this question did not receive a direct answer. If the Katerynoslavians were capable of knowing and understanding "what's what," they would have noticed that the economic relations and ties between Russia and the Ukraine are essentially those between contemporary great powers and their colonies. Great powers are also bound economically to their colonies, and productive forces revolt against separation. But do the productive forces of great powers revolt? No. On the contrary, the productive forces of the colonies revolt against union.

The Katerynoslavians point with contempt to the Russian counterrevolutionaries, the large landowners, and capitalists who are striving to regenerate the one and indivisible Russia. We are sure that they too want to do this because the productive forces of the Ukraine revolt against separation. And we are also sure that the Russian large landowners and capitalists know far better what sort of productive forces were uniting Russia and the Ukraine. By comparison the Katerynoslavians are puppies and guttersnipes.

And when it comes to the economic justification for their endeavors to regenerate the one and indivisible Russia they will use such Marxist philosophy as will make the Katerynoslavians appear to be nothing more than great Russian petty bourgeois shopkeepers who

* [*Ibid.*—Ed.]

can barely manage their own little shops but try to pass judgment on heavy industry, metallurgical colossi, and combined enterprises. They should be discussing a combination of three fingers,[5] not combined enterprises! Their Gothamite fathers got lost among three pines, and the sons are still wandering.

These are exactly the matters which have been discussed by numerous committees made up of representatives of the first Provisional Government and delegations from the various Ukrainian organizations and parties.

Even with regard to internationalism the Cadet-Octobrist land-owners and capitalists can spot you a hundred points. The Katerynoslavians argue very sloppily about economic ties—it would appear that Russia needs the Ukraine very much, but, as for the Ukraine, well—there . . . is a "mutual advantage." The result is that the Ukraine is blamed because "someone is hungry." The Cadets see this differently. The Cadet paper, *Poltavskii Den'*, published in Poltava, published an article opposing Ukrainian autonomy, asserting, as it were, that the productive forces of the Ukraine are against it; this well-written article maintained in a very internationalist manner that autonomy would harm the Ukraine, not Russia, that Russia would lose nothing.

Who is gifted with more internationalism? The Cadets, by God!

No, the Katerynoslavian productive forces have not yet spent themselves but they have failed to intimidate us, regardless of how indignant they may be.

The Katerynoslav point of view is only another variety of what comrade Lenin calls "imperialist imperialism." Economics—base, politics—superstructure; there is an economic tie, *ergo* "productive forces revolt against separation!"

It is true that politics is dependent on economics, but the tie between them does not follow the Katerynoslav pattern. It is much more difficult and complicated, not so simple and direct.

Economic ties and productive forces sometimes lead not to political union but to political separation. The process is two sided, dialectical. The productive forces and economic ties of a colony are aggravated in a different way from the productive forces and economic ties of the metropolitan area.

In 1905 the economic ties and productive forces of Norway and Sweden led to separation, not to union (of course, they were not bound together as closely as the Ukraine and Russia). One knows and understands without studying in a Katerynoslav seminary that these ties and relations were analogous to those between colony and metropolitan area.

The literature on the national question was quite correct to speak of Russia's annexation of other countries, including the Ukraine.

Can the Katerynoslavians possibly think that it was only a "word?"

Chapter XIII

How Is History Written?

We have just seen that the thesis of the Katerynoslav point of view—that the productive forces of the Ukraine reject separation—has no firm foundation. This foundation is nothing but a sand pile of commonplace truths which the Katerynoslavians have not managed to bind together with a strong cement despite their use of such frightening words as "metallurgical colossi," "combined enterprises," and "productive forces."

But this does not mean that any reference to base, to productive forces, to economics is superfluous and unnecessary in a discussion of political questions (and the question of the Ukraine's independence is political). On the contrary, in any political issue an investigation of the base, economics, and productive forces is extremely useful and merits the closest scrutiny. Every political question has an economic basis and economic consequences and in one way or another affects the development of productive forces, evoking either aggravation or satisfaction. But these ties, influences, and consequences do not follow the Katerynoslav pattern.

We will also try to examine the base of the Ukrainian national liberation movement. No matter how diligently we have followed the literature on the Ukraine coming out of Russia last year we have not been able to perceive the slightest desire to approach it from that point of view. While propaganda has its place, to be sure, even that would benefit from such an examination. We agree completely with V. Skorovstans'kyi's view as expressed in the introduction to his pamphlet, *Revolution in the Ukraine*. He writes: "It is true that in the past year and a half all sorts of writers have been paying considerable attention to the Ukraine. One could be grateful for this attention if . . . it had been directed at the Ukraine and not just aroused by the Ukraine. Mountains of paper and streams of ink have been spent on the Ukraine, but, how odd, not a word has actually been written about it. Everything written on the Ukraine can be summarized in a verse of M. Lermontov's "Prophet":

> Look at him, children,
> How gloomy and lean and pale he is,
> Look, how naked and poor,
> How everyone despises him.

"Moralizing and sermonizing about the Ukraine and because of the Ukraine, but not a word about why and how everyone 'despises' it."*

We know of only one attempt to understand the "how" and "why" of the Ukraine—Comrade I. Kulyk's *History of the Revolution in the Ukraine*[1] which is being printed in the *Visnyk Ukrains'koho Viddilu Narodnoho Komisariatu Sprav Natsional'nykh.*** Issue number 8 of the *Visnyk* contains a chapter, "Autonomy—Federation—Independence," on which we will dwell a while.

We do not know the official attitude of the party to the theory of Comrade Kulyk. We do not know how it is officially regarded by the Katerynoslav point of view. But we still think that Comrade Kulyk's views are not peculiar to him alone.

> The kulyk[2] is a little bird,
> But it is a bird just the same.†

For this reason, therefore, we will consider his thoughts. We will quote an appropriate portion, although the reader may not like it, since, after all, someone once said: "Give me a phrase, and I will lead any author to the gallows."[3] To avoid the role of such a judge we will try to quote not only isolated phrases but the context also, showing in what connection a given phrase has been used.

The quotation is as follows:

> The elements at the head of the national movement in the Ukraine may be divided into the following groups:
> a) The well-to-do peasants who wanted to organize a special

---

* V. Skorovstans'kyi, *Revoliutsiia na Vkraini*, pp. I–II. [See also Predislovie k ukrainskomu izdaniiu. 2d Russian ed.—Ed.]

** [I. Kulyk, "Istoriia revoliutsii na Ukraini," *Visnyk Ukrains'koho Viddilu Narkomnats*, No. 8, 1918—Ed.].

† We humbly ask the honorable Comrade Kulyk to forgive us this liberty. This verse was given to us by Comrade Kulyk himself. We quote it here not to offend Comrade Kulyk, whom we respect sincerely, but because "you cannot throw the words out of a song."

Ukrainian land fund so as not to have to give up the land which was to be divided among peasants from Great Russia.

b) The Ukrainian artisans—potters, weavers—who wanted to escape competition with Russian manufactures, mainly textile products.

These two groups were close to separatism, but a complete separation leading to customs barriers was not in their interest since nearly all the grain and most artisanal products were sold in Great Russia. They would have been satisfied with autonomy, especially in a federal system with the Russian Republic.

As for the other groups:

c) The bourgeois intelligentsia dreamed of becoming the Ukrainian bureaucracy in the event the country became independent, and

d) The rich bourgeoisie of manufacturers and landowners (a minority) felt that the complete separation of the Ukraine from Russia was unqualifiedly in their interest.

Although the two latter groups formed a small minority, they were stubbornly agitating and drawing some of the others over to their side. In addition to the material advantages of separation there was also the hatred of Russia, the result of long years of slavery, and (most important) fear of the Russian revolution, which was steadily assuming a more distinctly proletarian character.

This fear forced them to carry on their harmful work more actively, disguised by ambiguous slogans such as: Through autonomy and federation to independence, etc., or else concealing their secret intentions completely.

The same kinds of policies—the secret but certain movement toward independence—were pursued by the petty-bourgeois government of the Ukraine—the Central Rada.*

We have quoted this passage literally, without any changes except of typographical errors.

We would first like to ask Comrade Kulyk the following question: we regard his classification as complete, but under which rubric would he put the Ukrainian proletariat? What position did the proletarian parties defend? How did they regard "autonomy—federation—independence"?

In this argumentation one is first of all struck by its strange reasoning.

* [I. Kulyk, "Istoriia . . ." *Ibid.*—Ed.].

The National movement is a bourgeois movement. *Ergo,* national demands for federation and independence were made only by the bourgeoisie.

The petty bourgeoisie lacks consistency and is afraid to advance resolute demands—*ergo,* for it "autonomy was enough." The rich bourgeoisie, landowners, capitalists, and intelligentsia dream of becoming the bureaucracy and are more resolute—*ergo,* they demand independence.

And so forth and so on.

We will examine his arguments more closely.

Let us leave the peasants with their land fund for the time being. We will return to them later.

Comrade Kulyk states that the peasants and "artisans—potters and weavers"—had to escape competition with Russian manufactured goods. But how could they do this through autonomy? Could they be helped by an autonomous Ukraine? Could an autonomous Ukraine raise customs barriers and impose duties on Russian goods or even forbid their sale in the Ukraine? No, because this would be the very raising of customs barriers which Comrade Kulyk himself states was not in their interest. How then would the weavers and potters be helped by autonomy? That is Comrade Kulyk's secret.

To continue, "most artisanal products were sold in Great Russia." This means that the weavers and potters had no reason to fear competition with Russian goods, since they themselves were already competing with Great Russian factories.

What, for heaven's sake, have customs barriers, artisanal products, and "mazepism" to do with this?

Consider the following formula: the Ukrainian movement is petty bourgeois; the petty bourgeoisie are peasants and artisans; artisans have their own economics and production methods; yes, their pots crack and that's that: the pots say "we will cook only in autonomy!"

That the Ukrainian movement bears an almost exclusively petty-bourgeois character, and that the artisans and, especially, the peasants, are greatly involved in it, is true, but not in the way Comrade Kulyk imagines. Pots do have a connection with the Ukrainian movement, but it is completely different from the one Comrade Kulyk thinks they have. The pots don't say they will cook only in autonomy, but the Ukrainian movement says: call me even a pot, but don't shove me into the oven of autonomy!

Consider further "the bourgeois intelligentsia which dreamed of becoming the Ukrainian bureaucracy." The intelligentsia participated directly and actively in the Ukrainian movement (as in other movements) and in the workers' movement also. The bourgeois intelligentsia dreamed of becoming a bureaucracy, but the proletarian intelligentsia is not reluctant to become, let us say, the bureaucracy of the Soviet Republic. Will Comrade Kulyk contradict this? But why does this bourgeois, or, rather, petty-bourgeois intelligentsia (and not it alone) particularly desire independence? Would it not be satisfied with autonomy?

Doesn't the autonomy which Comrade Kulyk is talking about require a bureaucracy? Or maybe the bureaucracy in his autonomy would be sent out from the center?

In the beginning the Ukrainian intelligentsia was satisfied with autonomy, and it was led to independence by the force of events.

The intelligentsia played an important role in the Ukrainian movement and dreamed of becoming a bureaucracy (is there anyone who has not and does not dream?), but not according to the above "formula."

Consider further: the capitalist and landowning minority were undeniably interested in the complete separation of the Ukraine from Russia!

Comrade Kulyk! Who do you think your readers are? Why do you abuse them? Why make fun of them?

The landowners and capitalists wanted separation?! When? Where? How? Your readers would have to be insane to believe you! Don't say it, Comrade Kulyk, be ashamed to look people in the face!

This revolution took place before our very eyes and is still going on. Do you think we have forgotten it?

Show us just one group of capitalists and landowners that had any influence at all on the Ukrainian movement.

Quite to the contrary, our daily experience convinced, and convinces, us that the capitalists and landowners stand for a one and indivisible Russia.

Take Skoropadski, the most exemplary representative of the Ukrainian nobility, landowners, and capitalists. In him we find everything: tsarist general and bureaucrat, landowner and capitalist, descendant of an old Ukrainian family, the first ataman of the Free Cossacks, the first (and we think the last) hetman of an "independent" Ukraine—in a word, the most prominent figure in the Ukraine, and it took him a whole two and a half months as head of the state, holding the hetman's mace, to reach the sad conclusion:

"The Ukraine's only course is independence. Believe me, there is no other way."

As soon as the situation changed Skoropadski opposed independence, announcing his desire to "regenerate the one and indivisible Russia." He won't play first fiddle in that Russia. He will have to take a back seat. But, all the same, give him the one and indivisible—he will not agree to less!

In the demand for separating the Ukraine from Russia "in addition to material advantages" (separation also afforded advantages to the very capitalists and landowners who stubbornly and resolutely stood for the one and indivisible!) "there was also the hatred of Russia" (on the part of those who dream about the one and indivisible Russia!), "the result of long years of slavery" (it was the landowners and capitalists who were enslaved! poor capitalists and landowners! and we didn't know), "and (most important) fear of the Russian revolution" (see, the capitalists and landowners were hiding from the revolution in a separated Ukraine; thus, those who sought shelter from the revolution see and will see this shelter in a regeneration of the one and indivisible Russia!) !

Whose portraits do they paint?
Where do they get that kind of talk?
And if it happens to them,—

it is certainly to be found in the Katerynoslav point of view. But

We don't want to hear them—[4]

a few sweets are enough, otherwise you get a stomach ache. Enough of this fare.

Chapter X I V

The Ukrainian National Movement Against the Background of the Modern Capitalist-Imperialist Economy

One need not have studied in a seminary to know that we live in the epoch of the higher stage of capitalist development, the epoch of the domination of finance capital, the epoch of capitalist imperialism.

In this epoch the tendency of the capitalist economy to involve all parts of the globe in world trade, all-encompassing economic ties, and economic interdependence is becoming extremely powerful, and finance capital has all the necessary means for implementing and putting into effect this tendency.

The network of railroads covers almost the whole globe; every day gigantic steamships ply the seas and oceans in all directions; subways, submarines, and airplanes, telegraph and telephone wires enfold the earth like a spider's web, under water and in the air. Thousands and millions of people communicate over them every day and every minute; goods are moved; every news event is broadcast over the whole world within a few minutes; every inquiry or disturbance is at once echoed in the most distant lands. The thousands of economic ties stretching out in every direction are supplemented by those of a cultural character. Financial ties among banks, enterprises, and states; commercial deals; international syndicates and trusts; trade agreements, colonial policies—all establish the closest ties among the countries of the world, strengthen them, and make them more all-encompassing. The bears' dens whose inhabitants never leave and never hear any news, whose interests do not extend beyond their village, district, or region, are steadily vanishing.

The multilateral international interdependence of individual institutions and of the whole economies of various countries; the international organization of banks, enterprises, and trade relations; the internationalization of learning, literature, languages, technology, arts, fashions, manners, and customs; the many-sided continuing, lively, political relations; the continual intermingling of people of different nations—in a word, the internationalization of all spheres of life by the gigantic productive forces of contemporary capitalist society, are indisputable facts.

But there is another side to this increasing interdependence of modern society and the increasing involvement of outlying areas in its economic life. Side by side with this internationalization of economic, social, political, and spiritual culture goes a nationalization, an intensification of national feeling in the masses, an awakening of their national consciousness. This leads to the consolidation of nations, revives backward and seemingly lost nations, leads them from a state of helplessness and ignorance to one of national consciousness, and impels them to create their own literatures.

And this is entirely understandable. The development and spread of capitalist production among backward peoples draws them out of their patriarchal and feudal conditions of life, by destroying their old methods of production and introducing them to new goods, new ideas, new customs and needs promotes their advance, and by compelling them to seek work in factories and in cities, on railways, leads them into the new culture. Regardless of how simple it is, factory or railroad work demands greater intelligence than work in a village. All this impels them to study, faces them with the necessity of learning how to read and write in order not to get lost, so as to better their position. Before them are spread the wonders and riches of modern capitalist culture. If they are not adopted by the people, they will crush them. But this culture can be adopted only when presented in a suitable form, in a language the people understand. Although some are able to learn one or more foreign languages, and thus acquire an alien culture, the whole nation cannot do this. The people cannot spend so much time in study: one must work, keep house, earn a crust of bread. Someone, therefore, must undertake to acquaint them with the results of scientific investigations and artistic achievements in a suitable form—that is, in their native language. Their children must be schooled in their native language, and this means a need for teachers. They need officials (whether elected or not is unimportant here) who know and use the native language.

In thus awakening the national masses of the most oppressed, crushed, and undeveloped nations, capitalism creates the need for conscious and educated men—the intelligentsia.

The intelligentsia is generated out of the people, although the birth process differs from one nation to the other. Different classes have participated in different ways in contributing to the intelligentsia: bureaucrats, teachers, parliamentarians, party leaders, lawyers, engineers, writers, technicians, speakers, and scholars. We know that every social class has its own intelligentsia. But irrespective of these different class origins and views, the intelligentsia of all classes have common features which justify our viewing them as a separate social group. The principal feature or characteristic of the intelligentsia as a social group is its role in satisfying the spiritual needs of society or of some special social group or class. To perform this task properly the intellectual needs an appropriate means of production. The intellectual's means of production is the word—his language. In addition, every group of the intelligentsia needs its own special means of production: the physician, medicine and medical instruments; the writer, paper and pen; the scholar, office or laboratory. But the primary and essential means of production of each of them is language—the printed or spoken word, literature, knowledge.

These productive forces affect the intellectual in many ways. On this base is erected the superstructure of the intelligentsia with all of its features good and bad: altruism and the sincere love of one's own people and of all humanity, disdain for the material side of life, a broad outlook: but also the desire to become a bureaucracy, to live more gaily and spaciously, narrowmindedness, petty-bourgeois attitudes, and timidity.

The intelligentsia is an indispensable product and agent of bourgeois society. In a communist society it may be possible to abolish the intelligentsia as a separate group by transforming all classes into intelligentsia. But until this happens, no class or group can dispense with the intelligentsia. Nor can any nation do without its national intelligentsia.

A nation is interested in having its own intelligentsia to care for its spiritual needs, but on the other hand, the intelligentsia is concerned that the nation be great, strong, and educated because these factors determine the demands for the books of its teachers, officials, authors, and doctors. The capitalist mode of production enforces an increasingly extensive division of labor, the improvement and perfecting of instruments, machinery, and so on. It also leads to an improvement in the means of production of the intelligentsia—his language—because on this depends his ability to express the subtlest variations of thought, feelings, impressions, and so on, and even the further development of the nation. Furthermore, pedagogy holds that the education of the child and his further development as a human being are promoted more effectively by teaching in the native language. This is true generally for all members of a given nation, but it has additional importance for the child who will become an intellectual, for in this way he will learn the language better and use it in all its strength, beauty, and richness—thus with more success. With the exception of a few particularly talented persons, only one who has used a language from early childhood will gain a deep knowledge of it. In modern education it appears that, as a rule, only the native language can be used accurately.

"To master the accomplishments of international culture the intellectual should learn foreign languages, but if he is to make a contribution to culture, this must be done primarily in his native tongue. His initial audience are the members of his own nation. That intellectual is fortunate who is a member of a great nation, and especially of a nation whose language has become a world language. In such a case he speaks to the whole world. On the other hand, the intellectual from a minor nation which is, furthermore, poor and backward, can of course acquire a profound knowledge of international culture by learning foreign languages, but his own contribution to this culture will often fail to reach a public even though his works show extraordinary genius. He is forced to use a foreign language in which his thoughts are less well expressed.

"For this reason no one so ardently desires to see his nation achieve greatness as an intellectual from a minor nation.

"It is precisely those well-educated people who have mastered foreign languages, are most influenced by international culture, and are most concerned with the purity of their own language, who worry about expanding the area in which it is used and about reducing the number of people who read only foreign authors. In short, *the most internationalized elements of the nation at the same time appear to be the most nationalistic.*"*

But we should warn the reader against an error which is often set forth as absolute truth. This is the view that the nation is the invention of the intelligentsia. We must warn the more strongly against this error in view of the currently widespread fashion of scolding the intelligentsia. The intelligentsia indeed deserve this rebuke, but it is not necessary to throw out the baby with the bath water. The intelligentsia may be punished, may be brought to its knees, but the nation cannot dispense with it without doing harm to itself. This is the more true in view of the fact that the sharpest rebukes also come from the intelligentsia.

The intelligentsia's role in modern society in general, and in national movements in particular, can be explained by analogy with

* K. Kautsky, *Natsional'nye problemy* (Petrograd, 1918), pp. 50–51.

the role of machinery in contemporary capitalist production. The analogy extends to cover the mode of coping with the shortcomings of both intelligentsia and machines.

There can be no doubt that the existence of machines has placed another weapon in the hands of the capitalists for use against the proletariat and against the broad masses of toilers; that machines have given rise to an unprecedented exploitation of the workers; and that they have, by accelerating production, helped the capitalists to gain domination over millions of toilers, thus leading to expropriation, proletarization, and hardship. But there can also be no doubt that the movement against the use of machinery in production which arose in England in the late eighteenth and early nineteenth centuries, at the dawn of the modern capitalist era, hurt the workers and not the capitalists. Not only did it fail to help in the struggle with hardship and misery, it even worsened the position of the workers. One should not oppose the machines, but rather their capitalist exploitation at the expense of the toiling masses. One should not abolish the intelligentsia but rather use it in one's own interests, thus to free all from slavery, transform everyone into intelligentsia, and abolish the abyss between mental and physical labor.

The intelligentsia's role in a national movement is analogous to the role of the machine in capitalist production. It is not because of the machinery that capitalism exists, develops, and expands; on the contrary, machinery exists because of the existence, development, and expansion of capitalism. National movements do not come into existence and wax strong and active because of the national intelligentsia; on the contrary, the national intelligentsia comes into being because national movements exist and become strong and active.

Capitalism uproots millions of people of different nations, moves them from place to place, mixes them all together, pounds them in the mortar of capitalist production, cooks them in the boiler of the factory, grinds them in the mill of combined enterprises, melts them down in the ovens of "metallurgical colossi," and shapes them into a new type of iron, cast iron, and steel. Thus nations are born and develop, and national movements appear over and over again, grow stronger, and demand autonomy and independence. This is not reasonable; the productive forces of certain shopkeepers, philistines, and financial titans grow angry at it—but what can you do, history is so foolish, it did not study at the Katerynoslav seminary.

The observation and study of national movements, of the awakening and development of nations, show that the existence of a peasantry is of prime importance for the preservation and formation of a nation. Capitalism, with its capacity for cracking the concrete and iron Chinese walls of particularism and provincialism, even affects the peasant masses when conditions are suitable: a territory, large or small, inhabited by more or less the same nationality. Capitalism wakens these masses, forces them to leave their villages and districts, makes them aware of problems beyond what can be seen from the village belfry. The peasants who migrate to the cities become workers or intellectuals. Although at the beginning of the process isolated workers and intellectuals are quickly assimilated, acquire the veneer of the new culture, and are ashamed of their peasant language and peasant origin—as the process continues, and as they learn more about the new and higher culture, they come to understand the deep abyss which exists between the more cultured and educated and their own browbeaten and illiterate village people. Then they return to their own villages and begin to work with enthusiasm at awakening the peasants' consciousness, at raising them to the higher cultural level.

"The prestige of the nation to which they belong is not a matter of indifference to the elements in the framework of capitalist production—and least of all to the existing classes and to the wage-worker"* The history of the past century presents much glaring evidence that workers do borrow these and other national slogans.

But, although the wage worker can learn a foreign language quickly and become assimilated (this applies likewise to the capitalist, the landowner, and the intellectual), the peasant has no such opportunity. He lives in a village where foreigners do not penetrate, or at the most pass through for brief visits. He himself rarely visits a foreign city, and, if he does, for such a short period that it is pointless to talk of his acquiring a foreign language.

Thus the peasantry, as the base, and the intelligentsia as the ideologues, the superstructure, have (in recent decades, at least) been the principal agents of any national movement. This contrasts with the beginning of the capitalist era, the period of its struggle with feudalism, when the national liberation movement was headed by the urban bourgeoisie and intelligentsia. To be sure, even today, the bourgeoisie takes quite an active part in the national struggle, as does the proletariat. None of the attempts yet made to remove the proletariat from the national movement, to place them outside or above it, has yielded definite results. Each class or group of course interprets the movement in its own way, but all participate in it.

* K. Kautsky, *Natsional'nye problemy*, p. 49.

National movements, in the modern acceptance of the term, appeared at the same time as capitalism itself. And they have appeared not because they were invented by one or another exploiting class of capitalist society for the interest or profit of that class (this feature is very important for national and other movements), but because capitalism has involved the most closely knit and diverse groups of people in world trade and in a common economic—meaning a common spiritual—life. National movements are more closely associated with the progressive aspect of world capitalism than with its destructive tendencies, its exploitation and degradation of the national masses. This latter fact has a considerable impact on the development of national movements, but the movements, and their depth and pervasiveness among all classes of contemporary society, cannot be explained by this fact alone. No class, including the proletariat, fails to participate in national movements or to advance nationalist demands. Of course, this does not mean that all classes advance the same demands with the same force and enthusiasm. At different times and in different places various classes have espoused various national demands with varying force and obstinacy.

The two eras of national movements must be distinguished from the general historical point of view. The dividing line between these eras was the Franco-Prussian War of 1870–71 which brought about the national unification of Germany.

"There is, on the one hand, the period of the collapse of feudalism and absolutism, of the formation of the bourgeois-democratic society and state, when the national movements first became mass movements and through the press and through participation in representative institutions involved all classes of the population in political life. On the other is the period of fully formed capitalist states with long-established constitutional regimes and a highly developed antagonism between the proletariat and the bourgeoisie—a period which may be called the eve of capitalism's downfall.

"The typical features of the first period are: the awakening of national movements and the involvement in them of the peasants, the most numerous and most sluggish sector of the population, through the struggle for political liberty generally, and for the rights of the nation in particular. The typical features of the second period are: the absence of bourgeois-democratic mass movements and the prominent position of the antagonism between the internationally united capital and the international working-class movement, this being due to the fact that developed capitalism brings closer together the nations that have already been involved in commercial intercourse and causes them to intermingle in an increasing degree."*

Lenin continues in the same vein:

"Of course the two periods are not partitioned off from one another; there are numerous transitional links, as countries differ from one another in the rapidity of development of their national movement, in the national composition and distribution of their populations, and so on."**

In another place he gives the following classification of countries "with respect to the degree of their self-determination":

1. The advanced capitalist countries of Western Europe and the United States. Here the progressive bourgeois national movements have long since come to an end. Each of these "great" nations oppresses others in the colonies and at home.
2. Eastern Europe: Austria, the Balkans, and especially Russia. Here bourgeois-democratic national movements have developed, and the struggle has intensified, particularly in the twentieth century.
3. The semi-colonial countries, such as China, Persia, Turkey, and the colonies, with a combined population of one billion (1000 million). Here the bourgeois-democratic movements have either hardly begun or else have a long way to go.†

The above description of the two periods in the history of national movements is evidently applicable only to countries of the first type, but even with respect to them, some limitations must be introduced. England falls in the second group of states with respect to the Irish question. And Norway's separation from Sweden occurred in 1905, that is, only in the second period.

Again, the description of the second period as characterized by the "absence of mass democratic movements" can be regarded as accurate only within distinct limits. Of course there are no democratic mass movements where bourgeois-democratic movements have ended, where nationally homogeneous capitalist states have been formed, and where a constitutional order has been established—this is only

* [V. I.] N. Lenin, "O prave natsii na samoopredelenie," *Prosveshchenie,* Nos. 4–6 (1914).

** *Ibid.*

† [V. I. Lenin, "Sotsialisticheskaia revoliutsiia i pravo natsii na samoopredelenie,"—Ed.] *Sbornik Sotsial-Demokrata,* No. 1 (October, 1916), pp. 3–4.

a tautology. But where this has not occurred we see an altogether different phenomenon. We can call it an exception, if that is convenient, but an exception that violates the very rule.

The most characteristic point of difference between the two periods relates to the question: "Who heads the mass democratic movements?"

Formerly it was the bourgeoisie; now it is the proletariat. This is agreed in any discussion of democratic movements generally. But when it comes to that sub-variety of democratic movements which is the national-democratic or national-liberation movement, the objection is at once raised in international phrases that the working class, the proletariat, is an international class concerned with international problems, that it is indifferent to the national question, that the proletariat should pay no attention to national matters, and that nationalism is an invention of the bourgeoisie to deceive the proletariat. These accusations are all absolutely correct when used properly, but harmful if used to attack the essence of the national liberation question. For the gist of every national liberation question lies precisely in the fact that each nationality strives for the formation of its own independent sovereign state. Now what is, and should be, the attitude of the proletariat toward this aspiration to form a national state?

Historical experience shows that the proletariat participates directly in the national liberation movement and cannot stay away from it. It cannot be set aside, placed above the national movement, or in any other neutral position. And regardless of how many international phrases are used, the national question cannot be ignored. The task of the proletariat is not to ignore it, but to solve it.

International social democracy has also proclaimed the "right of nations to self-determination," that is, to the formation of sovereign, independent national states, as a way of solving the national question. International social democracy set itself the task formerly performed by the bourgeoisie—when it was revolutionary, when it was destroying absolutism and feudalism.

"Social democracy inherited from bourgeois democracy the striving for a national state. Of course we are not bourgeois democrats, but we resemble them in viewing democracy as more than a trifle, as something superfluous and unnecessary. As the lowest class in the state, the proletariat can only assert its rights through democracy. But we do not share the illusion of bourgeois democracy that the proletariat will gain full rights when it does achieve democracy. Democracy is only the basis for the acquisition of its rights. The liberation struggle of the proletariat does not end with democracy but merely takes on a different form.

"Democracy is a vital necessity, not for the bourgeoisie, but precisely for the proletariat. The bourgeoisie has now renounced its former democratic ideals and, at the same time, the idea of a national state. Its present concept of the ideal state goes beyond the boundaries of the national state. It throws these survivals of liberalism into the warehouse of historical curiosities. But we have no reason to do this. We should not take the materialist interpretation of history to mean that the proletariat had to adopt the general tendencies of bourgeois development just because they are determined by economic relations. The proletariat has its own tendencies of development, which are no less economically determined, and it should follow them without worrying about whether or not they contradict bourgeois tendencies."*

Thus we see that national movements admit of only one solution —full democracy. And full democracy means the organization of sovereign and independent national states. This was true for the era of the destruction of feudalism and absolutism and the birth of bourgeois-democratic states. And it is also true for our own era, the era of imperialist capitalism, the eve of the birth of socialism. The same will be true for socialism. We see the past and the present, and we see what will be in the future. And in saying what things will be like under socialism we base ourselves not on what has already been accomplished but on that "tendency in the development of the proletariat" mentioned by Kautsky.

This is what Comrade N. Lenin states:

"Victorious socialism must necessarily establish full democracy and, consequently, not only introduce the complete equality of nations but also *implement* the right of oppressed nations to self-determination, i.e., their right to free political separation. Any socialist party whose activity *now, during the revolution, and after victory* does not make clear that it will liberate the enslaved nations and establish relations with them on the basis of a free union —and free union is a false phrase if it does not include the right to secession—would be betraying socialism."†

"Marx wrote in his *Critique of the Gotha Programme:* 'Between

---

* K. Kautsky, *Nationalstaat, Imperialistischer Staat und Staatenbund* (Nurnberg, 1915), pp. 11–12.

† [V. I.] N. Lenin, "Sotsialisticheskaia revoliutsiia i pravo natsii na samoopredelenie," *Sbornik Sotsial-Demokrata*, No. 1 (October, 1916), p. 1. [Italics are Shakhrai's—Ed.]

capitalist and communist society lies the period of the revolutionary transformation of one into the other. In this period of political transition the state can be nothing but the revolutionary dictatorship of the proletariat.'

"Hitherto this truth has been indisputable for socialists, and it includes recognition of the fact that the *state* will exist until victorious socialism develops into full communism. Engels' dictum about the *withering away* of the state is well known.

"And since we are discussing the state, this *means* that we are also discussing its *boundaries*. In his article, 'The Po and the Rhine,' Engels writes, among other things, that during the course of historical development, which swallowed up a number of small and non-viable nations, the 'boundaries of the great and viable European nations' were increasingly determined by the 'language and sympathies' of the population. Engels calls these boundaries 'natural.'

"Today, these democratically determined boundaries are being increasingly broken down by reactionary, imperialist capitalism. There is every indication that imperialism will bequeath its successor, socialism, a heritage of *less* democratic boundaries, a number of annexations in Europe and other parts of the world. It is to be supposed that victorious socialism, which will restore and implement full democracy all along the line, will refrain from demarcating state boundaries democratically and ignore the 'sympathies' of the population?"*

In this we see how deeply and strongly the national liberation movements are linked to the progressive side of the world development of capitalism. Of course, the national liberation movement is not an exception among democratic movements and has other aspects which should not be forgotten. Of course it can be exploited by the bourgeoisie. It should be clear enough that we are speaking here of a "tendency which is to be followed, not blindly, but in full awareness."†

The Ukrainian movement does not appear to be a unique phenomenon in history, but it has assumed such vivid forms and developed in such a distinct and classical manner that it is very important for understanding the character, essence, and laws of development of national liberation movements in general. This study is, and will be, of not only theoretical interest. "Today, these democratically determined boundaries are being increasingly *broken down* by reac-

---

* [V. I.] N. Lenin, "Itogi diskussii o samoopredelenii," *Sbornik Sotsial-Demokrata*, pp. 12–13.

† K. Kautsky, *Nationalstaat, op. cit.*, p. 12.

tionary, imperialist capitalism [of the great and viable European nations whose boundaries were earlier being increasingly determined by the language and sympathies of the population—V. Sh.-R.]. There is every indication that imperialism will bequeath its successor, socialism, a heritage of *less* democratic boundaries, a number of annexations in Europe and other parts of the world."*

The Ukrainian movement, along with others, will supply much material for working out the principles and tactics of the proletariat. While the proletariat's attitude toward national movements has been, up until recently, more negative, when it has to act as the "dominant class of the nation" it will be forced to adopt a positive policy.

The Ukrainian nation inhabits an uninterrupted area from the Carpathians in the west almost to the river Don in the east, and from the Black Sea in the south to the line of the Prypiat in the north. The area of this territory is nearly 850,000 square kilometers.† Even if this figure is considered exaggerated, it will be clear that territorially the Ukraine does not fall among the smaller countries.

Here are the areas of some of the larger states of the world without their colonies:

State	Year	Territory (thousands of Sq. K)	Population (millions)
United States of America	1897	7,872	63
Turkey	1897	1,631	22.8
Austria-Hungary	1890	602	42.9
Germany	1895	476	52.3
France	1896	465	38.5
Spain	1887	450	17.6
England (including Ireland)	1891	275	38.1

And there are other states with territories of less than 400,000 square kilometers. So even if the Ukraine's area were reduced by half, that is, if we took only the eight provinces (gubernias) of the former Russian Ukraine (Poltava, Kyiv [Kiev], Kharkiv [Kharkov], Katerynoslav [Ekaterinoslav], Chernyhiv [Chernigov], Volyn, Podillia [Podolia], Kherson) in which the Ukrainians comprise an absolute majority of the population, it would still be territorially comparable

* [V. I.] N. Lenin, "Itogi diskussii o samoopredelenii," *Sbornik Sotsial-Demokrata,* pp. 12–13.

† S. Rudnitskii, "Ocherk geografii Ukrainy," *Ukrainskii narod v ego proshlom i nastoiashchem* [Ed. F. K. Volkov (Petrograd, 1916), Vol. II, p. 361—Ed.].

to France, Germany, Austria-Hungary, and Spain, and greater than any other European state except Russia.

We cannot say precisely how many people inhabit this territory, but an estimate of 35 million cannot be an exaggeration. Thus even with respect to population the Ukraine occupies approximately the same place among European states. The number is equally valid as an expression of the population of the territory where Ukrainians form an absolute or a preponderant majority or as an expression of the total Ukrainian population, including those living outside this territory.

For a better understanding of the character of the Ukrainian national movement, its class essence and its various forms, it will suffice to give information on the above eight provinces alone. They differ in no way from the rest of the territory, and their characteristics may thus be considered typical.

Of the 22 million persons inhabiting these provinces in 1897, 16.4 millions or 74.6 percent were Ukrainians, 2.4 millions or 10.7 percent were Russians, 1.9 millions or 8.5 percent were Jews, 0.4 million or 1.9 percent were Germans, and 0.4 million or 1.9 percent were Poles.

Of the Ukrainians 90 percent are peasants, and the cities are inhabited predominantly by non-Ukrainians. The following are a few characteristic figures:*

	Percent of Ukrainians in the Population	
District	Including the cities	Without the cities
Poltava	88.7	98.7
Kremenchuh (Kremenchug)	80.8	98.2
Chernyhiv (Chernigov)	86.1	97.4
Kamianets Podilskyi (Kamenets Podolskii)	78.9	87.0
Kharkiv (Kharkov)	54.9	88.8
Kyiv (Kiev)	56.2	84.0
Katerynoslav (Ekaterinoslav)	55.7	74.1

For this reason one significant characteristic of the Ukrainian movement has been the opposition between the Ukrainian village and the non-Ukrainian city.

* [A. Rusov, "Statistika ukrainskogo naseleniia evropeiskoi Rossii"— Ed.], *Ukrainski narod v ego proshlom i nastoiaschchem,* [Vol. II], pp. 386–88.

Furthermore, social contradictions have been clothed in national colors. Manufacturers, merchants, and landowners were usually either Russians, Poles, Jews, Germans, or Ukrainians of the Skoropadski type. The Ukrainian noble strata had been russified or polonized during the preceding two and one-half centuries. Only during the revolution, when the strength of the national movement became clear to everyone, did some landowners begin to recall their Ukrainian ancestry. All of the grand bourgeoisie—landowners, merchants, entrepreneurs, and bankers—had close ties with Russia because of profitable business interests. Separation of the Ukraine brought them only clear loss. And when the landowners and capitalists now do everything possible to regenerate the one and indivisible Russia, they show a much better understanding of their own interests than Comrade Kulyk imagines.

It could, of course, be maintained that the aristocratic intelligentsia has played a prominent role, especially in the early stages of the new Ukrainian movement in the first decades of the nineteenth century. Thus one could "write history" as follows: I. Kotliarevskii's[1] *Aeneid* "gave birth" to the Ukrainian national movement. And Kotliarevskii was (1) of the intelligentsia, (2) a bureaucrat and high official of the Poltava governor-general, and (3) concerned with the problems of landowners (he was an official for *special assignments* of the governor-general who was himself a *landowner*). *Ergo*, as early as the end of the eighteenth and beginning of the nineteenth century the landowners and intelligentsia foresaw the 1917 revolution, and the fear of this proletarian revolution forced them to seek shelter. Their prognostications came true, and we see them first seeking refuge with the Central Rada and then dispersing it and setting up Skoropadski! But this made the productive forces angry, and Shevchenko[2] was made a soldier while Minister Valuev[3] (who was clever, even though a landowner!) said: There were no Ukrainians, there are none now and there will be none in the future!

No, the Ukrainian movement depended mainly on the village and was led by an intelligentsia in constant communication with the village. The Ukrainian workers also played an important role in awakening and activating the national consciousness of the peasants and maintained contact with the village. The Ukrainian worker felt the national oppression on his own neck.

The central figure of Ukrainian literature and of the intelligentsia is Taras Shevchenko, son of a peasant serf. Throughout the century Ukrainian literature and art bore a primarily rustic character. It depicted peasant life, took its heroes from the village, and was imbued with a deep and sincere love of the illiterate, browbeaten, and helpless village population. Not from the national character but through a consideration of the Ukrainian people's exceedingly difficult and abnormal living conditions can one understand the idealistic enthusiasm which runs like a red thread through the history of Ukrainian literature and social thought and of the Ukrainian intelligentsia. The role and character of the intelligentsia in the Ukrainian national liberation movement is better understood if compared with that of the Russian intelligentsia in the general history of the revolutionary destruction of serfdom and despotism. Not in vain did they live together under the roof of the tsarist autocracy!

It was hard work! The enslaved village was silent, only occasionally sending out its sons to anounce that

> *The species has not perished,*
> *The country is still alive.*[4]

But conditions changed at the beginning of this century. The capitalism which invaded the Ukraine with a clattering and whistling of locomotives and a wailing of factory sirens also aroused the village. The Ukraine was lighted up by the glowing coal of the blast furnaces; the straw-thatched villages were set afire by the sparks from locomotives and factory chimneys. It is no accident that the rise of capitalist production in the Ukraine, the peasant insurrections in Poltava and Kharkiv (Kharkov) provinces, the divisions among Ukrainian groups along party lines, and the advent of an urban type of literature (particularly in the writings of the talented V. Vynnychenko) all occurred at the same time. "The stone which the builders rejected has become the cornerstone." That very same 70 percent of coal, 99 percent of beams and channels, 79 percent of rails, and 68 percent of shaped iron with which the Katerynoslavians attempt to strangle and bury the Ukrainian movement were the base of this movement. Ukrainian independence rests precisely on this industry, and not on any higher feelings ("in them, for them") of these or other "benefactors." The same combined enterprises which the Katerynoslavians use to offer the Ukrainian people a combined unity will see to it that the Katerynoslavians are left with combined enterprises made up of their own fingers.

We know that revolution rejects all that is superficial and conventional and reveals the sources of deep springs and forces. A revolution is an examination. What do we learn from the revolutionary national liberation movement?

As early as May, 1918, we wrote (in a book which was never published) :

The national movement for the first time gives evidence of its own vigor and strength. Before the revolution the general attitude was that the Ukrainian movement was the invention of an eccentric "Little Russian" intelligentsia, was incompatible with the interests of a majority of the population, had no mass following, and was not supported by any wide circles of "Little Russian" citizens.[5] The movement was considered as limited to so-called cultural demands: schools in Ukrainian, free use of both spoken and printed Ukrainian, etc. The desire for autonomy, for the organization of Ukrainians into a political unit, was viewed as "separatism," "an Austrian orientation," "supported by German marks" in order to arrive at the police deduction: "grab 'em and hold 'em."[6] Although formerly one might have thought that the Ukrainian movement could not pass beyond literary, cultural, and educational matters, since the revolution only those who are hopelessly ignorant of its real relation to political life can call the Ukrainian movement a "bourgeois invention" or can advance such petty arguments as that the peasants understand Russian better than "Galician" and so on. These views would not be so annoying if held only by the common people, but it is regrettable that even those in high positions in our party[7] advocate them even after the proclamation of the Ukrainian Republic.

Only the blind can fail to see that the movement has embraced the broadest and deepest circles of Ukrainian citizens and has revealed their general desire to become not only a cultural, linguistic, and ethnographic group, but also a sovereign political nation. The initial demands for national territorial autonomy and then for republican status in a Federated Russia evoked a broad and immediate response.

All congresses—peasant, worker, military, party, professional, or educational, whether All-Ukrainian, regional, or district—have unanimously adopted this objective.

The power of this movement for rebirth of the nation in statehood has been so unexpected that even the leaders of the movement can hardly give it suitable political expression. The movement has also been very influential in Galicia and has awakened the desire to do away with the border dividing the two parts of the Ukrainian nation.

It can be stated with certainty that the Ukraine will not agree to die, or to accept national captivity, regardless of what misfortunes may befall it. This should be kept in mind by every party working in the Ukraine.

The will to organize the Ukraine as a state-political unit within ethnographic boundaries is an incontrovertible fact.

What "ideological" elements enter into the Ukrainian movement?

First, the language. One's native language, one's own word,[8] evoke the deepest national feelings. Every Ukrainian has loved his native tongue. In it are historical memories, songs, literature, and also the social-national protest of a people using a "peasant" language against those speaking "noble" languages (Russian or Polish). It contains a vision of equality with the "noble" nations. It contains the recognition of national unity: we are Ukrainians above everything else.

There were recollections of the historic past—the Cossack campaigns, the struggles with Poland and Muscovy—whose strength was a source of delight. Others—the Petrograd erected on Cossack bones[9]—awoke bitter feelings about a greater culture and enlightenment in the past.[10]

There was protest against socioeconomic and national-political oppression by the Russians, Poles, Rumanians, and Hungarians who were the large landowners, merchants, manufacturers, and officials.

There was protest against the city which leads a luxurious life on the power and money it derives from the village and gives hardly anything in return.

Among Ukrainians there was a desire to organize their own land fund, to increase production, to raise their culture to a higher level.

There was protest against the centralism and imperialism which returned to the Ukraine only half of the taxes which it paid.

There was the desire to exercise one's own will and power in one's own house.[11]

Ukrainians felt that they represented the only democracy in the Ukraine—in contrast to the other nationalities which they viewed as autocratic.

"We have no bourgeoisie, only democracy."

"We have only socialist parties!"

In the detailed memorandum sent to the Provisional Government and the Petrograd Council of Workers' and Soldiers' Deputies we read:[12]

"The ruling circles of the Ukraine are not Ukrainian. Industry is in the hands of the Russian, Jewish, and French bourgeoisie, and the capitalist traders, together with a large proportion of the agrarian bourgeoisie are Poles and *Ukrainians who have long since called themselves 'Russians'* [italics ours]. Similarly, administrative posts are all in the hands of non-Ukrainians.

"But the exploited strata—the peasantry, a majority of the urban proletariat, the artisans, and petty officials—are Ukrainians. Hence, at the present time there is no *Ukrainian* bourgeoisie [italics in the memorandum] which considers itself Ukrainian. Although the class interests of some individuals and small groups are identical with those of the economically dominant classes, no bourgeois class, we repeat, exists.

"This is why no Ukrainian party has yet failed to include the idea of socialism in its platform."

What forms did this movement take? How did it make itself noticed?

Through gigantic rallies, mainly of soldiers, in places such as Kiev and Petrograd where there were many Ukrainians; through thousands of peasant congresses, military congresses, and workers' educational, cultural, and party congresses; through meetings in villages, cities, railroad yards, and factories.

And at times of particular tension it took the form of near-insurrections. There were three such occasions: in the early days of June when Defense Minister Kerenski forbade the convocation of the Second Military Congress, and it assembled in spite of him (the upshot of this "peaceful" insurrection was the proclamation of the First Universal and the declaration of autonomy)—then during the October revolution when the Third Military Congress carried with it the vacillating Central Rada (resulting in the Third Universal and the proclamation of the Republic)—and finally there was the insurrection against the "Bolshevik Russian" government and the Fourth Universal proclaiming independence and appealing to the "German people" (in reality, to Kaiser Wilhelm, Hindenburg, and Hertling) for help against the "Russians" and "Bolsheviks" . . .

We have not even mentioned the newspapers, proclamations, announcements, and so forth.

But after all this has happened some people still call it an "invention"—a "bourgeois invention" perhaps, but an "invention" nonetheless!

In the same way the Cadet *Rech*, and even the left-wing Zimmerwaldists in *Berner Tagwacht*, called the Irish insurrection a "Putsch."[13]

Here is what N. Lenin wrote about this "Putsch," this "invention":

"The term 'putsch' [and 'invention'], in its scientific sense, may be employed only when the attempted insurrection is exposed as nothing but a circle of conspirators or stupid maniacs who have aroused no sympathy among the masses. The centuries-old Irish movement, after passing through various stages and combinations of class interest, manifested itself, in particular, in a massive Irish National Congress in America (*Vorwaerts*, March 20, 1916) which called for Irish independence; it also took the form of street fighting by a section of the urban petty bourgeoisie *and a section of the workers* after a long period of mass agitation, demonstrations, suppression of newspapers, etc. Whoever calls *such* a rebellion a 'putsch' [or an 'invention'] is either a hardened reactionary or a doctrinaire, hopelessly incapable of envisaging a social revolution as a living phenomenon."*

The Ukrainian people as a nation, regardless of class, have expressed their will with respect to self-determination and their political status.

In tens and hundreds of resolutions at meetings, at congresses of various kinds, large and small, in the party and the public press, in demonstrations on an imposing scale, in armed clashes—the desire has everywhere been expressed to:

1. Organize themselves as a state-political nation.

2. Unite the various Ukrainian lands and regions in which there is a Ukrainian majority, regardless of existing political boundaries, into a united Ukrainian Republic.

3. Declare themselves for an independent republic not in theory but through personal experience and through the course of events.†

This we wrote eight months ago.

---

* [V. I.] N. Lenin, "Itogi diskussii o samoopredelenii," *Sbornik Sotsial-Demokrata*, p. 26. [Italics are Lenin's—Ed.]

† V. Shakhrai, an unidentified pamphlet—Ed.]

Chapter x v

Unity or Independence? Two Policies

We have already noted that *Kommunist* views the nation's right to self-determination as "an abstract formula," and, therefore, "we . . . provided no general answer to the question of the kind of relations demanded by the Ukrainian proletariat. Did it demand regional autonomy, federation, or independence; or would it perhaps have preferred no political separation at all, but direct ties between every local Soviet and the All-Russian center."*

The Katerynoslavians adopt a different approach to this formula.

"In response to the categorical demand of the Ukrainian social-democratic parties for an indication of the attitude of the Communist Party organizations toward the Ukrainian question, we have busied ourselves with what, for the Party, was an empty and objectively stupid matter pertaining to an *oppressed* nation. [Here, here! What kind of nation? non-existent? And if it exists, then where?—"in us and for us" or "in you and for you"? Because there is no Ukraine. There was Southern Russia, which became the southern part of the eastern territory under German occupation—S. M. and V. Sh.-R.] . . . repetition of 'words' about our recognition of the Ukraine's right to separation at a time when the All-Russian Council of People's Commissars [Sovnarkom—Ed.] demands from us a different attitude toward this right—*clear and categorical statements and strong agitation in favor of a possibly closer connection between the Ukraine and Russia, against separation and for proletarian-revolutionary unity.*"†

The Katerynoslavians, therefore, view the right of a nation to self-determination as "an abstract formula" and, furthermore, just

---

* ["Itogi s'ezda," *Kommunist,* No. 5; V. Skorovstans'kyi, 2d Russian ed., p. 147n—Ed.]

† ["Natsional'nyi vopros v programme kommunisticheskoi partii Ukrainy"—Ed.], *Pravda,* No. 132 (June 30, 1918) [p. 5.] [Author's italics—Ed.]

a "word" to which they have no objection. But a little earlier in the very same article the Katerynoslavians talk enthusiastically about the way in which this formula was justified (for itself?) by the test of the Russian revolution. It was only in practice that it limped a little, that is, it "did not at all suit our program on the national question."*

This means, according to the Katerynoslavians, that all is quiet on the theoretical Shipka![1] Theory was no good at all! say the leftists. Practice was so bad that we could not bear to look! shout in unison the right-leftists, the Katerynoslavo-Kievans.

We will not dwell here on the relations between theory and practice in the matter of the right of a nation to self-determination. A special pamphlet on this will, we hope, be published soon. We will only quote a few passages from V. Zatonskii's[2] article, "Iz nedavnogo proshlogo" ("From the Recent Past") ,† in which "practice" is painted in very bright colors.

"The fundamental question—the attitude toward the national movement, which to a great extent determined the policies of the Ukrainian proletariat—was given an extremely vague answer by the party: 'the right of nations to self-determination . . .' But concrete decisions were taken in a purely *ad hoc* manner.

"March–April, 1917. The Ukrainian national position is formulated in the jungle of cooperatives and associations, and the Rada [Central Rada—Ed.] creeps out into the sunshine—the party gently affirms self-determination.

"May. The Rada raises its head.

"June–July. The Rada endeavors to stand on its feet—the party patronizes self-determination.

"September. The Rada is nearly forgotten.

"October. The Rada runs wild—sympathy for self-determination. ('We do not understand the question.')

"November–December. The Rada issues a threatening ultimatum and . . . the right of nations to self-determination.

"January. The Rada is anathematized.

"May. The Rada is overthrown in a complete bankruptcy of Ukrainian nationalism . . . still the right of nations to self-determination, as immovable as a rock and as uncommunicative as a rock.

"That vacillating tactics were adopted with respect to the Ukrainian national movement, and that the Rada was not under-

---

* *Ibid.*

† [V. Zatonskii, "Iz nedavnogo proshlogo"—Ed.], *Kommunist*, Nos. 3–4 [July 1, 1918]. [See also V. Skorovstans'kyi. 2d Russian ed., p. 147n.—Ed.]

stood earlier, were not so bad; what was serious was that these dizzying changes of course followed no internal logic. (Is there such a logic now?)

"Sometimes contradictory directives were given at the same time (aren't they still?) as, for instance, when the Soviet Ukraine was being blessed with the right hand and the Donetsk Republic[3] with the left, orders were issued to combat Ukrainian chauvinism and also the advancing petit-bourgeois reactionaries in the South. It reminds us of the Ukrainian anecdote about the old woman who placed candles before the picture of Satan and the icon of Saint Nicholas at the same time, thinking,

Who knows where I will have to spend eternity,
It's a good thing to have a friend in both places.[4]

"The party as a whole had no platform. Its policies vacillated unpredictably, and the results were, naturally, nothing to brag about. At the local level the mess was unimaginable.

"Every organization, and almost every member, resolved all questions of tactics on the Ukrainian national movement at his own peril. The movement grew and was becoming an increasingly important factor in the Ukrainian political struggle—and it soon became clear that the serious principle of the self-determination of nations (not of the proletariat) which should have been followed, if one was to believe the writings and oral traditions of the Church fathers, was all very well with respect to India or Egypt—as long as we (sic!) do not have to work there (the Tatars and Bashkirs are already giving us enough trouble with it) .[5]

"It is fine to make noble gestures, like a repentant lord to a Muscovite on Tverskaia street (in "Lux"?)[6] or to a German on the Friedrichstrasse (are there still repentant lords there today?) , but it is not clear at all how those damned problems in various regions, such as the Ukraine, are going to be decided.

"Not for nothing did the national (ah me!) communist parties, such as the Polish and Latvian, within the Russian party, dispatch the principle of national self-determination to the place where the Constituent Assembly[7] already rests in peace.

"But their position is simpler than that of the Ukraine.

"The Latvian and Polish parties are actually made up of Latvians and Poles (no one yet has doubted that Latvians and Poles actually exist) .

"It is not the same with the Ukraine. Here the Bolshevik party, and the greater part of the industrial proletariat as well, is made up of persons who are Russians—culturally, even if not by nationality. It is awkward to oppose national self-determination because, even without this, sincere Ukrainians call these people 'russifiers.' But to acknowledge the Ukraine as the Ukraine is unpleasant (*and even more so because, to this day, many comrades are still profoundly convinced that Hrushevsky invented the Ukraine deliberately*).*

"So the search begins. Self-determine yourselves up to the point of separation (and perish in the process!), but must it be precisely here in my party's private domain. If we can't avoid an independent Ukraine, let it be somewhere in Australia or, at the worst, in semi-savage Volyn [Volhynia] or Podillia [Podolia]—but why right here in Katerynoslav or Kherson (not to speak of Kharkiv [Kharkov])?[8] For one thing, the peasantry in these particular areas (for the information of comrades: they are nationally all Ukrainian), when left to an arbitrary fate and abandoned to the monopolistic exploitation of the Ukrainian social-chauvinists, were self-determining themselves, both poor peasants and kulaks, in the way the Rada wanted.

"What shall we do? Scandal. Self-determine yourselves, those who can. Such was the beginning of all those deliberately invented (only not by Hrushevsky) diplomats' republics. They handed over the Western Ukraine to a group of Petliuras in order to save their Palestines from the horrid name of Ukraine (they are not afraid any longer!)"**

Comrade Zatonskii states further: "Ukrainian chauvinism suffered the fate of the Rada—it was wiped out of the consciousness of the peasant masses (not to mention the proletariat) (for the comrade's information, this does not prevent the masses from remaining nationally Ukrainian)."†

One is amused that it would be necessary to prove to the comrades of the Communist Party of the Ukraine that Ukrainian workers and peasants are nationally Ukrainians. But why does Comrade Zatonskii recommend that they "take this truth into consideration"? That it should remain "in them, for them"? Is this truth needed for a solution or not? And if it is necessary, then how?

We do not think that the theory of the nation's right to self-determination—as expounded by Comrade N. Lenin—follows precisely the outlines ascribed to it by the Katerynoslavians. We think that theory and practice cannot be differentiated and that the giving

---

* Sic! [Italics are Shakhrai's—Ed.]
** [V. Zatonskii, "Iz nedavnogo proshlogo"—Ed.] *Kommunist*, Nos. 3–4 (July 1, 1918), pp. 9–20.
† [*Ibid.*—Ed.]

of advice includes a proposal to carry it out. The theory of the nation's right to self-determination contributed to the practice of the party in the Ukraine. But we cannot agree with the leftist view that theory and practice are simply bad. The rightist Katerynoslavians and the leftist Kievans are united by their unanimous view that practice is empty, abstract, and stupid. One has the impression that these people delight in sullying themselves, although, it is true, they do it with holy intentions. Hohol's [Gogol's—Ed.] smith, Vakula, deliberately painted a loathsome and ugly devil so that every old woman could point her finger at it and say, "Look what a monstrosity," then turn reverently to the luminous paradise. For the Communists of the Ukraine, whether right or left, everything in the past was a monstrosity. Now, however, it is a real paradise. We have seen this paradise before, and will soon see it again. To the extent that it is not just empty space (they have not yet completely solved the "in them and for them" morbid Ukrainian question!) they just chew over the old practice. And as for invective, it is just "words and voice, nothing more," although, after you have berated someone you feel much better and look more independent than before.

Whether we were right or wrong we at least gave answers to the question of the relations between the Ukraine and Russia. Whether right or wrong, we applied these theories in practice. We stated (and put this into practice) that it was necessary to promote a "possibly closer connection between the Ukraine and Russia," that we were "against separation and in favor of proletarian revolutionary unity." We supported the idea of a "direct tie between every local Soviet and the All-Russian center." And we did this on the basis of a verbal, abstract formula. At the same time, to be sure, we used words about the right to self-determination. But only a Katerynoslavian could fail to see the absolute necessity of these words. They call these words "empty and objectively stupid for the party of an *oppressed* nation." But, objectively, we were not the party of an oppressed nation. Objectively, we were a non-Ukrainian party even though living and working in the Ukraine, and even though the birth certificates of some of us showed that we were barely Ukrainian. We were a Russian, or, more properly, a Great Russian, party. It is not so much that we defended unity and were unenthusiastic about slogans of autonomy, federation, and independence. The point is that we completely avoided the national liberation movement, that even today Comrade Zatonskii has to persuade his comrades that the Ukrainian workers and peasants are indeed Ukrainian workers and peasants, that there is such a nation, that it was not invented by Hrushevsky. The point is precisely that Comrade Zatonskii himself reached this conclusion only after long meditation on what constitutes a nation.

The point is:

> For several decades a well-defined process of accelerated economic development has been going on in the South, i.e., the Ukraine, attracting hundreds of thousands of peasants and workers from Great Russia to the capitalist farms, mines, and cities.
>
> Within these limits, the "assimilation" of the Great Russian and Ukrainian proletariat is an indisputable fact. And *this* fact is *undoubtedly* progressive. Capitalism replaces the ignorant, conservative, settled *muzhik* of the Great Russian or Ukrainian backwoods with a mobile proletarian whose conditions of life break down the specifically Great Russian or Ukrainian narrow-mindedness. Even on the assumption of an eventual state boundary between Great Russia and the Ukraine, the historically progressive nature of the "assimilation" of Great Russian and Ukrainian workers is as certain as is the progressive nature of the grinding down of nationalities in America. As the Ukraine and Great Russia become increasingly free, the development of capitalism will be *increasingly rapid and extensive*, and this will attract even larger numbers of workers of *all* nationalities from all regions of the state and from all neighboring states (should Russia become a neighboring state of the Ukraine) to the cities, mines, and factories.
>
> Mr. Lev Iurkevych[9] (a Ukrainian national-socialist from *Dzvin*[10]) acts like a real bourgeois, and a short-sighted, narrow-minded, obtuse bourgeois, i.e., a philistine, at that, in dismissing the benefits to be gained from the intercourse, amalgamation, and assimilation of the *proletariat* [of the two nations—Ed.]— for the sake of a momentary success of the Ukrainian national cause [*sprava*—Ed.]. The national cause comes first, and the proletarian cause second, say the bourgeois nationalists, and the Iurkevyches, Dontsovs,[11] and other would-be Marxists repeat it after them. We say the proletarian cause comes first because it protects not only the permanent and fundamental interests of labor and of humanity, but also those of democracy, and without democracy neither an autonomous nor an independent Ukraine is conceivable.*

We agree completely that *such* "assimilation" is progressive. But

---

* V. Il'in [Lenin], "Kriticheskie zametki [po natsional'nomu voprosu,"
—Ed.] *Prosveshchenie*, Nos. 10–12 (1913). [Italics are Lenin's—Ed.]

it should not be forgotten that the Russian assimilation of the (comparatively) less developed Ukrainian masses has not reached the point where we are justified in talking about the "grinding down of nations." This "assimilation" led to denationalization only in the beginning; afterwards it actually led to an awakening of national feeling and national consciousness. For that reason we can discuss "assimilation" here only in quotation marks. This is the second aspect of "assimilation" and it should be borne in mind when we consider the development of the Ukrainian national movement and the labor movement. In place of the "ignorant, conservative, settled" peasant appears an active proletarian who demands schools, newspapers, and books in his own language. The intellectual acquires a co-worker with a will of his own, who makes demands, expresses his needs, and himself urges on the intellectual.

The revolution has revealed both of these aspects of "assimilation": the division of workers into Ukrainian and "non-Ukrainian," supplemented by the division between the "alien," "non-Ukrainian" city and "our" Ukrainian village.

Our party was Russian, that is, Great Russian, both in name and in reality. And such a party is obliged to use words about separation while at the same time conducting propaganda for unity. The unfortunate thing is not that we used words about separation, but that for a majority of our party members they were only words—just as the Social-Democratic Mensheviks and Russian Socialist-Revolutionaries treated words as just words in some other matters. And the following was particularly unfortunate:

> An internationalist Social-Democrat does *not* think only of his own nation but sets *above* it the common interests of all nations, their common liberty and equality. [Author's italics— S. M. and V. Sh.-R.] *Everyone accepts this 'in theory' but in practice manifests an annexationist indifference. There is the root of the evil.* [Italics ours—S. M. and V. Sh.-R.]*

It was unfortunate that, as Zatonskii writes, the words about separation were understood to mean: "Self-determine yourselves up to the point of separation (and perish in the process!), but must it be precisely here in my party's private domain. If we can't avoid an independent Ukraine, let it be somewhere in Australia . . . etc."† This

* [V. I.] N. Lenin, "Itogi diskussii o samoopredelenii," *Sbornik Sotsial-Demokrata,* p. 23.

† [V. Zatonskii, "Iz nedavnogo proshlogo," *Kommunist,* Nos. 3–4 (July 1, 1918—Ed.]

was bad because it had a bad effect on that unity about which so much fuss had been made, and because the masses thus rightly learned not to believe words but only actions. An empty space cannot be covered with words; lack of content cannot be hidden with a signboard.

The party used words about separation in order to champion unity. As long as the words were believed, we were able to achieve this unity, but when it became clear that they were only words, the unity began to be replaced by a terrible enmity and discord. On the occasion of the First Universal *Pravda* wrote as follows about the absolute need for these words, for the sake of unity:

"If the Russian revolutionary democracy is to be a real democracy, it must break away from the past (the oppression of stateless nations by tsardom) and attract to itself—to the workers and peasants of Russia—the fraternal trust of the workers and peasants of the Ukraine. This can only be done through complete recognition of Ukrainian rights, including the right to separation. We do not favor small states. We stand for the closest union of the workers of 'our own' and all other countries against the capitalists. But precisely to ensure that this union be voluntary, the Russian worker, without trusting for a moment the Russian or Ukrainian bourgeoisie, now defends the right of the Ukrainians to separation—not *thrusting* his friendship upon them but *winning* it by treating them as brothers and allies in the struggle for socialism."*

We believed these fine words, because we hoped they would be followed by appropriate actions, even though at almost every step we encountered the "Katerynoslav supporter of independence in Australia." But now, after all these experiences, the bitter thought arises: what if these were only words? Fine words, but . . . "I believe, O Lord, help thou my unbelief!"

At that time we were in such a state, objective conditions were such, that we had no other choice but to defend the unity of the workers' movement with words about self-determination. We followed this course, whether badly or not, because we had to (and we agree that it was done more badly than well).

Now, after what has happened, we vie with each other in seeking for past errors and revile the past in very strong terms. Now . . . we have gotten "smarter!" So let us now look at this past, at the objective state of the Ukraine, not only with respect to internal affairs and

---

* We cite this article after *Robitnycha Hazeta*, No. 65 (June 20, 1917). [Italics by *Robitnycha Hazeta*.] ["Ukraina," *Pravda*, June 28 (June 15, O.S.), 1917, p. 1—Ed.]

the relations among the different classes, but also with respect to the
All-Russian revolution and international relations, to the development of international events. We formulate the question as follows:
if 1917 and early 1918 should return, and with them the objective
relations and conditions in which the Ukrainian revolutionary movement developed, and if the wise Katerynoslavians and Kievans from
Kommunist were placed in our midst, how would they act?

The very same way, although perhaps better or worse in some
details.

The reader will have no difficulty persuading himself of this.
Now we pass to another question. We have seen that our "right leftists," or Katerynoslavo-Kievans, after abusing one another over the
past, now boast of their "new" positions as something never seen before. Actually, all that is new is that, instead of the "abstract formula"
(leftists!) or "wonderful theory" (not for application—Katerynoslavians!), they have a concrete empty space—the left Socialist-Revolutionaries prevented them from taking their malady to a physician to
cure their secret morbid national question.[12] By this abuse we simply
make clear how the most common

> *Russian brain and Russian spirit,*
> *Speaks of things past and lies for two!*[13]

We will examine the Katerynoslavian partial solution for
Russian-Ukrainian unity. Nothing has occurred to lead us to revise
our solution, they say. The only thing is that formerly we Katerynoslavians had unity with an abstract formula or a wonderful theory,
while now we have unity with an empty space to boot.

"In them and for them" almost nothing has changed, but this
is not so in life. Let's take a look at it.

We already know that "[the Social-Democrat from a small nation
—Ed.] may, without failing in his duties as an internationalist, favor
both the political independence of his nation and its integration into
the neighboring states of X, Y, Z. But he must in all cases fight *against*
small-nation narrow-mindedness, seclusion, and isolation, consider
the whole and the general, subordinate the particular to the general
interest."*

During these two years has anything happened to require from
us a different solution of that same Ukrainian question?

Two things have happened: one of a Russian-Ukrainian character, the other of a world or international character.

---

* [V. I.] N. Lenin, "Itogi diskussii o samoopredelenii," *Sbornik Sotsial-
Demokrata,* p. 23. [Italics are Lenin's—Ed.]

The first is the separation of the Ukraine from Russia, the second is the revolution in Austria and Germany. Of course, the first also had international significance, especially when placed side by side with the events occurring in Austria and Germany.

From the Katerynoslav point of view the whole Ukrainian movement is a kind of nonsense, a chain of errors. And the Central Rada's invitation to the German troops is occupation and only occupation. But from the point of view of the real historical process the invitation to the Germans is more than occupation and only occupation. Of course, to the German imperialists this act of the Central Rada from the very beginning meant occupation and only occupation, and it was an episode of extraordinary advantage to Germany. To be sure, they sent troops not to defend the freedom of the Ukrainian people, its independence and sovereignty, from the attack of the Russian Bolsheviks. To be sure, they did not think at all about "building a home for the Ukrainian people," as was imagined by the fools from the *Nova Rada*. To be sure, they came for the grain, sugar, coal, and other valuables. To be sure, their management of the Ukraine took the form of robbing, looting, and exporting as many goods of all kinds as possible. In short, it was plunder and extortion, occupation and only occupation.

Of course, to the Russian merchant who knows about the Ukraine only as much as he needs to know (that the iron for the roof of his shop comes from the Donets Basin and the sugar he sells in his shop also comes from the same "khokhols"[14]) the separation of the Ukraine is occupation and only occupation.

But the content of historical events is not exhausted by the point of view of a German or Russian annexationist or shopkeeper. From the point of view of contemporary world events the act of occupation and only occupation has a much deeper content and much greater significance. It represents one more link in the long chain of the Ukrainian people's struggle for national liberation, for their complete freedom and independence. It serves to make one of its most characteristic and classic episodes and indicates the depth of national liberation movements in our time.

This was only one manifestation of the indignation of the productive forces of the Ukraine against the slavery of centuries. But productive forces do not always "become indignant" in the same way. They may send a delegation [to Petrograd—Ed.] to beg gently for mercy and for gratification of their demands;[15] they may confront the Provisional Government with the *fait accompli* of a proclamation of autonomy; they may entertain the dear guests who have come on their own [to Kiev—Ed.] to reach a peaceful agreement; they may scratch the nape of their neck when it itches as a result of the "agreement"; they may proclaim a republic in order to live as a free member of the family of free nations; they may turn the Katerynoslavians around—often so suddenly that the head still faces north when the body is turned completely south[16] (such things do not happen only in Dante's *Inferno!*) ; and sometimes it happens that a Samson shakes the walls of the building and perishes together with the Philistines.

What is one to do? History is so unreasonable. To observe that railway ties, rails, beams, coal, and sugar are fine, warm, sweet things (for instance, when traveling over these rails in a first-class compartment which is well heated by coal, drinking sweet tea with all the trimmings and wondering at the marvels which the eye encounters) —is fine for the soul and not bad for the body. But when the rails, ties, and beams begin to rebel, it is better to walk! Or when the shop is on fire and the iron roof drops with a clang on the shopkeeper's head—that is also bad for the soul: to hell with the sugar, let it burn up! If only those heavy, warm, and sweet things would rebel "nicely," that is, in the Katerynoslav manner. But no, they insist on getting some idea about independence in their foolish heads . . . Say what you will, that is a bad thing.

All the great events of history have been the outcome of struggle and hostility. Such things as the liberation of enslaved nations can very seldom end nicely. The accommodation of the superstructure to the economic base does not happen directly, not nicely. The eyes give out sparks when the productive forces are indignant. It's a good thing if the eyes themselves don't pop out. F. Engels said that revolution cannot be distinguished from any other kind of destruction.

And this basic historic meaning of the Central Rada's shameful act is not weakened by the fact that it led to the "independence" of Skoropadski. Even the "independence" of the present Directory (which should not be compared to Skoropadski!) is thus far only a fine wish "in them and for them." Today the Ukraine is further from independence than it was in November–December, 1917. The act[17] of the Central Rada may even have cut the Ukrainian Samson's hair so short that years of work will be needed for it to grow out again. This is so. But the real historic meaning can be nullified neither by this independence "in them and for them" nor by occupation and only occupation "in them and for them."

The Ukraine has not yet gained independence, but separation from Russia is a real fact. And the Ukraine has been steadily crystallizing into a state-political unit regardless of the occupation, of the Katerynoslavians, or of Skoropadski's independence.

The occupation and only occupation in its rude way put into effect the Central Rada's decisions of January 11 (24) (the Fourth Universal) as well as the resolution of the Second (Katerynoslav) Congress of the Soviets of the Ukraine on the independence and sovereignty of the Ukrainian Republic.[18] Of course, these economic, socio-political, and cultural ties, which came into existence when the Ukraine was a Russian colony, could not be severed at once as though with a knife. Of course, some threads still run through the torn places. It is like breaking a stick—the stick cracks, but the two pieces do not fall apart. They are still held together by the splinters. But the stick cannot be made whole again regardless of how you press the pieces together. It is better to even off the two broken ends and join them with a piece of tube. Or the comparison may be made with a living organism: when it is deeply wounded, the torn pieces must be cleaned off because they do not help the wound to heal but only irritate it, festering and poisoning the whole body.

Of course, those who consider the catastrophe of February–March, 1918, as an occupation and only an occupation may say that the stick is not broken but only a little bent, that there is no wound but only a little bruise. Then, of course, it would be unnecessary to trim the ends, to clean out the bruise. Of course, it is better for those with a secret disease to pretend that everything is fine. But we cannot accept such reasoning.

We are actually confronted with a crisis, a deep wound; the history of the Ukrainian movement during the revolution (and not only during the revolution) convinces us of this. And we become even more convinced when we consider the Ukrainian movement in the light of certain events which we have witnessed during the present war and, especially, during the revolutions in Austria and Germany.

The crisis of capitalist society—the war and revolution—brought to light the deep springs and forces of the gigantic historical struggle of the present era. It has clearly revealed the two tendencies of capitalist society: the internationalization and nationalization of the struggle. Moreover, the difference is not only of form but of content. It is said that this struggle is national in form and international in content, and while there is a little truth in this, it is not the whole truth, and hence the statement is incorrect. It is a relic of the dualistic religious view which opposes the lifegiving spirit—God, energy, force, international content—to lifeless matter—the clay, the national form. This is a variant of the Katerynoslavian view of a wonderful theory opposed by bad practice, of pure internationalism opposed by pure nationalism. In reality the theory is, and must be, the reflection in people's minds of their own practice, just as, on the contrary, a wonderful theory yields bad practice.

In this case, therefore, internationalism and nationalism differ from one another not as content and form, but as two points of view in one and the same process. It can be explained by the following analogy: an ordinary circle looks different from a point outside it than when observed from its center.

The war and revolution revealed the contradictions between the gigantic productive forces and the property relations of modern capitalist society; between the social character of production and the private character of appropriation (i.e., private ownership of the means of production). The war and revolution revealed capitalist society's inability to resolve this contradiction by its own efforts. They laid bare the real content of the life of capitalist society—class struggle and civil war, not peace. They revealed the aspiration and the trend toward replacing the contemporary capitalist economy and society by a socialist economy and society. At the same time, they revealed a tendency toward an alteration not only of the base—the economy, but also of the superstructure—political, spiritual, and other aspects of social life.

Furthermore, the war and revolution tore the healthiest and most active members of the broadest and deepest strata of the population away from their traditional living conditions, threw them together in barracks, gave them arms, taught them how to use these arms individually and as members of armies numbering millions, stirred their consciousness, compelled them to think, faced them with the absolute necessity of the masses deciding the cursed questions of war and peace, led them to the brink of hunger and hardship.

We have seen how the imperialist war changed before our very eyes into a civil war, and the civil war into a revolution. The leaders of the first were the imperialists, of the second, the proletariat. Imperialist hostility has been replaced by class hostility. Class against class!

Here the clever Katerynoslavians interrupt us and say: "Ah, yes, class against class—why do you keep talking about nationality?"

The Katerynoslavians imagine the social revolution as follows: on one side is an army saying "we are for socialism," and on the other side another army saying "we are for capitalism." But in reality the social struggle cannot be so pure, not only because the masses are (naturally) cautious but also because the social revolution is made by masses of various nationalities, entangled with themselves and with imperialism. For these masses (including the proletariat) the social struggle means fighting not only to abolish social oppression (i.e. for common ownership of the means of production) but to abolish political and other kinds of oppression as well.

This is why the armed and trained masses in the barracks fight so eagerly—not only for socialism but also for the concomitant demands for national freedom, sovereignty, and independence. From their very outset the war and revolution made use of the wonderful theory, the words about the right of nations to self-determination.

Regardless of the hypocrisy on the part of imperialists of various kinds (including the Katerynoslav real shopkeepers) which these words concealed, they played a very great role in arousing the consciousness of the national masses. The imperialists and Katerynoslavians called forth spirits which they cannot now exorcise.

Now the masses have arms and are fighting for their own interests. On one hand they display the ability and inclination for an organized, conscious struggle, on the other, terrible hostility and savagery. War and revolution not only organize and arouse consciousness, they also scatter and corrupt, lead people to savagery.

One would have to be a Katerynoslav historian to write, like Comrade Kulyk, that the Ukrainian military movement was one of egotists and savages, the result of fatigue and villainy. Needless to say, this also occurred. But is there any place now where this does not occur? Is all well in the Red Army? But this does not exhaust the content of either the Red Army or the Ukrainian military movement. We notice plenty of consciousness and idealistic enthusiasm.

The revolutions in Russia, Austria, and Germany have shown what deep roots a national movement puts down and what power and strength it displays. While the Austrian, German, and Russian revolutions generally, and the Ukrainian revolution in particular, formerly maneuvered between the two hostile imperialist camps, now they are opposed by a single imperialist front and, in Austria and Germany, possess an ally. The revolution has clearly revealed an aspiration to reorganize the map of Europe (and not only of Europe) on foundations other than violence, dejection, and the sword. This aspiration has the sympathies of the population. It will lead to a partnership, a federation of free, independent, sovereign states. Although the road to this "idyllic state" leads through an armed struggle of the masses, as historical experience teaches us, can a goal be reached in any other way on this sinful earth?

The war and revolution have completely laid bare the fallacy of the self-determination and liberation of nations propounded by Miliukov, Rodzianko, Wilson, Lloyd George, Clemenceau, Kühl-mann, Czernin, and *tutti quanti.*

The war and revolution have also brought into question another policy—that of the proletariat, especially its most revolutionary part.

Of course we know that the proletariat will not become holy and immune to error and weakness "just because it will carry out a social revolution."

Of course we know that "possible errors (and selfish interests—the attempt to saddle others) will inevitably lead it to realize this truth."*

But will not these errors have the same significance for, let us say, the Third International, as the error of August 4, 1915, for the Second International?[19]

Again we rely on history. It will inform us.

Now we return to our theme, to the Ukraine.

We are of the opinion that the two eras in the history of the revolution in the Ukraine are divided by the "occupation and only occupation" and the revolution in Germany. The Ukraine's different objective status in these two eras, different with respect to both international and domestic relations, required two different solutions of the Ukrainian national question, two different policies of the proletariat.

The difference can be expressed in the form of two slogans: in the first era—union of the Ukraine with Russia and simultaneous acknowledgment of the right of nations (including the Ukraine) to self-determination; in the second era—Ukrainian independence.

"The significance of the 'national culture' slogan is not determined by the promise or intention of some petty intellectual to 'interpret' it as meaning 'development through it of an international culture.' The significance of this slogan is determined by the objective alignment of all classes in the country and in all countries of the world."†

This applies not only to the national culture slogan, but to the international culture one as well, and also to unity and even independence. It applies not only to the petty intellectual, but to the intellectual, even to the Intellectual, even to the INTELLECTUAL. "The sons of princes and of beggars are all Adam's children!"[20]

* [V. I.] N. Lenin, "Itogi diskussii o samoopredelenii," *Sbornik Sotsial-Demokrata,* p. 25.

† V. Il'in [Lenin], "Kriticheskie zametki po natsional'nomu voprosu," *Prosveshchenie,* Nos. 10–12 (1913).

The best way to test the accuracy of this solution, therefore, is to "study the attitude toward this question of the *various classes* of society. This test is obligatory for the Marxist. We must proceed from an objective basis; we must examine the relations among classes on this point."*

Let us examine the relations among classes with respect to the Ukrainian question before and after the catastrophe of February–March, 1918.

The objective position of Russia, which influenced either directly or indirectly all classes and parties, their interrelations, and their solutions to various questions arising from the catastrophe of February–March, 1918, was determined by the fact that it participated in a war within one of the imperialist camps, that of the Entente.

This made the Russian revolution directly and immediately dependent on international relations and, on the other hand, afforded it the possibility of exerting a direct influence on the course of international events.

And this objective state of being was also reflected in the consciousness of the Russian revolution, which recognized itself as the product and agent of the development of international events.

Every political grouping and party started with a slogan on war and peace and returned to it again and again. Every current event began and ended with war and peace. "Peace without annexations and indemnities on the basis of national self-determination" was the principal theme of speeches, reports, conventions, meetings, and conferences.

Between the 1905 revolution and the war of 1914 the Russian imperialist bourgeoisie divided into political parties which sometimes quarreled quite sharply. The war of 1914–17 did away with this hostility, since one could forget political enmity and establish civil peace for the sake of Constantinople, the Straits, the "indigenous Russian lands of Red Rus'," and Galicia.[21] Their mutual hatred for the "enemies of humanistic culture," the "barbarians of modern times," the Germans, impelled the Cadet, Miliukov, to exchange kisses with the Black-Hundred Purishkevich.[22] The revolution of 1917 completed this merger. During the revolution all the bourgeois-capitalist press—from the *Novoe Vremia* to *Rech* and *Russkiia Vedomosti*—played the same fiddle. The Cadet Party, being the most

---

* [V. I.] N. Lenin, "O prave natsii na samoopredelenie," *Prosveshchenie*, Nos. 4–6 (1914).

"opportunist" of the bourgeois parties and the one least discredited by tsarist policy, drew to it Black-Hundred and the landowner-capitalist brethren of all sorts and became their only representative.

The whole policy of this landowner-capitalist Cadet Party was determined by its imperialist aims—Constantinople, the Dardanelles, Galicia—and its crudely imperialist dependence on its noble Allies. In its own interest and on orders from Paris and London it tried in every way to suppress the revolution, so that Russia would not have to leave the war and could be forced to toil in it to a "victorious conclusion."[23]

The Russian bourgeoisie could not treat one of the revolutionary currents—the national movements which sprang up suddenly "from the cold Finnish cliffs to the flaming Colchis"—otherwise than as separatism or German espionage. "Grab 'em and hold 'em!" was the only response. We need only recall its procrastination with the Ukrainian delegation seeking autonomy.

"We reckon only with facts!" said Count Lvov, the head of the Provisional Government, to the Ukrainian delegates. In other words, we will not give up anything if you don't take it yourselves.

The bourgeois position on the matter of concern to us was: the full and unconditional totality, unity, and indivisibility of Russia. The Cadet Party[24] in the Ukraine was supported by the Union of "Agrarians"—the grand bourgeoisie, the landowners, and the urban bureaucrats. Let Comrade Kulyk try to point out one other political party of landowners and capitalists in the Ukraine! And let him tell us how that party used cunning arguments to fool the Ukrainian masses about the independence of the Ukraine.

"One and indivisible Russia" was its slogan.

The second group was composed of the Russian socialist parties, the Social-Democrats, Mensheviks,[25] and Socialist-Revolutionaries.[26] Attracting the Russian intelligentsia and a part of the Russian workers, these parties had little influence in the Ukraine. As they were part of the Russian socialist parties which ruled the Soviets, they were represented in the ministry and, in the Ukraine, supported the same policy of marking time until the Constituent Assembly or until the (they were ashamed to say "victorious") end of the war. And, just as in Russian questions generally they employed revolutionary terminology while acting in reality as lackeys of the imperialist bourgeoisie, so in their Ukrainian policy they uttered words about the nation's right to self-determination, pointing to appropriate paragraphs in their programs (the Socialist-Revolutionaries even used the word "federation"!) , while in practice they resorted to bayonets, to "grab 'em and hold 'em!"

Although not unanimous in words, the Cadets, Socialist-Revolutionaries, and Mensheviks behaved identically in all matters relating to the Ukrainian movement. It was a Great Russian, Non-Ukrainian, Anti-Ukrainian bloc—not a formal one but nonetheless real, and this is the salient fact of the Ukrainian revolution. Although they used different words, the touchstone was identical: the one and indivisible Russia. As for autonomy . . . we will take that up at the Constituent Assembly, if it can't be avoided, but why right now?

The Ukrainian parties opposed, with even greater unanimity, this one and indivisible front of the Russian non-Ukrainian parties. Here there was not only a de facto bloc but a formal alliance—the Central Rada, which incorporated all the Ukrainian parties. This greater unanimity was not the outcome of the greater chauvinism of the Ukrainian movement (on the contrary, the cultivated Cadets and internationalist Mensheviks and Social-Revolutionaries were more chauvinist) but was due to the more homogeneous social basis of the Ukrainian movement.

We have already seen that nearly 90 percent of Ukrainians are peasant-farmers (not of the Cadet type like Skoropadski) while the other 10 percent are workers, artisans, and intellectuals. Furthermore, because of their origin and social position the workers and intellectuals were in close contact with the villages. "We have only democracy. All our parties are socialist!" This was due to the uniform social base. As a counterweight to the categorical call for a one and indivisible Russia Ukrainian parties initially made an equally categorical demand for Ukrainian autonomy. As each side pressed its demands stubbornly the initially amicable relations grew more antagonistic. National hostility grew apace.

The Bolshevik Party occupied a completely different position,[27] as it could not do otherwise. This party also stood for and advocated a one and indivisible Russia—but one erected, not on historical traditions, but on the solidarity of the working masses, on a living union of workers. The party also used words about the right of nations to self-determination up to and including separation in order to demonstrate to the oppressed nations (including the Ukrainians) that the Bolshevik Party had no intention at all of forcing them to remain within the boundaries of Russia. Under the circumstances this was the only way to "neutralize" itself from national antagonisms. And since the Mensheviks also employed words about self-determination, our party seized every opportunity (e.g., articles in *Pravda** on the occasion of the First Universal and of the resolution of the Poltava committee[28]) to point up our differences with the Mensheviks. Despite the fact that we never lacked Katerynoslavians who also used words in the Menshevik manner, we succeeded in at least suggesting, if not in demonstrating and proving, the difference in the Menshevik and Bolshevik use of these words. The Bolsheviks were for self-determination, and not only in the sense of a Ukraine in Australia.

The Ukrainian masses at once became terribly hostile, surprised, and indignant at the October revolution and the ensuing war between the Bolsheviks and the Central Rada.[29] This meant that the Bolsheviks were lying, that they were just as much enemies as the Cadets and the Mensheviks. In the popular consciousness we appeared to continue the Menshevik policy and to rely upon the very same national elements. Only by setting up the Soviet government of the Ukraine, only through the error of recognizing the Ukrainian Republic at first as part of the federal union and then as independent,[30] were we able to regain some of the sympathy of the Ukrainian masses. The rest was done by the Central Rada and the occupying army.

Thus, when we used words about self-determination (and not in the sense of the Mensheviks and the Katerynoslavians), we were gaining the sympathies of the Ukrainian masses against the one and indivisible front of the Cadets-Socialist-Revolutionaries-Mensheviks; by our opposition to the one and indivisible Russia, and not in the Menshevik or Katerynoslav manner, we directed the attention of the Ukrainian masses to the main task of the times: preserving the unity of the revolutionary front against Allied, Russian, and German imperialism.

Let us now take a look at the second era—after the catastrophe of February–March, 1918, and the Austro-German revolution.

The Ukraine is cut off from Russia. Many regions of the former Russian Empire are occupied by counterrevolutionaries with the help of the only remaining imperialist armies. All the governments of these regions,[31] whether Cadet-Monarchist or Socialist-Revolutionary-Menshevik–Constituent-Assembly, defended the one and indivisible. And only in the Ukraine (Finland is a special case) did the Ukrainian parties favoring Ukrainian independence unanimously oppose

* ["Ukraina," *Pravda*, June 28 (15 O.S.), 1917, p. 1—Ed.]

the one and indivisible front of the Cadet-Monarchist and Socialist-Revolutionary-Menshevik reactionaries. And these were not land-owners. Under the Central Rada one could point to the figure of the ataman of the Free Cossacks, the future Hetman Skoropadski, but now all these elements returned to their first love.

If we compare the two camps in the Ukraine: (1) the one and indivisible Russia represented by the Monarchists, Cadets, Mensheviks, Socialist-Revolutionaries and Communists of the Ukraine, and (2) the independent and sovereign Ukraine side by side with Russia, represented by the Ukrainian parties, this piquant situation becomes quite odious for a proletarian party. This is the language of facts, of class alignment.

We know that the petty intellectuals, Intellectuals, and INTEL-LECTUALS will revile us for this classification. How can one compare Cadets, Mensheviks, and Communists?! It is completely un-Marxist! Where is the class content of this classification?

We know that Communists are not the same thing as Cadets and Mensheviks. But are Mensheviks and Cadets the same thing? No, but this does not prevent the Communists from placing them in the same classification.

Class content? Here we wish to point out the very interesting and unfortunate fact of class division by nationality: non-Ukrainian landowners and capitalists (i.e., all the grand bourgeoisie with a few exceptions), petty bourgeoisie, workers, and intelligentsia on one side and Ukrainian petty bourgeoisie, workers, and intelligentsia on the other.

At the beginning of this chapter we quoted the Katerynoslavians as saying that it was an empty and objectively stupid matter for the party to use words about self-determination. The Katerynoslavians don't know what they are talking about [Literally, a Ukrainian saying: "hear a bell but don't know where the noise is coming from"— Ed.]. *Right now* objective conditions in the Ukraine are such that to use the word self-determination is empty and objectively stupid, not only for the parties of the oppressed nation but also for those of the ruling nation. But the Katerynoslavians interpreted this to mean that it was empty and objectively stupid *then*. Existence determines consciousness, and Katerynoslav existence determines the consciousness of the Katerynoslav head, and in the Katerynoslav manner.

The Ukrainian people, the Ukrainian nation, has *already* determined itself, and expressed its will. Now we must talk, *not casually or in general terms* about the right of all nations to self-determination, but about our attitude toward *this* act of self-determination, *this* desire to form an independent nation. Not only the Ukrainian social-patriots, but the facts themselves, ask "Is it so or not?" No!, shout the Russian, or russified, or polonized, "non-Ukrainian" landowners and capitalists. No!, clamor the Russian, non-Ukrainian Mensheviks and Socialist-Revolutionaries. No!, scream the Russian Communists, including the Communists of the Ukraine. No!, is the cry in London, Paris, New York, and other cities.

Now is the time to give proof of one's internationalism in action. It is time for the proletariat, the leading and revolutionary part of the Russian and world proletariat, to show *in action* how its self-determination differs from that of the imperialists, what the difference is between the self-determination of Woodrow Wilson and the self-determination of Comrade N. Lenin.

Up until now nothing has indicated the absence of a difference between the two positions on this question. And if we still refrain from putting the final dot on the final "i," it is only because we still nurse a little hope, we still want to believe that other events will occur. We still believe that Comrade Lenin wrote his articles on the national question not just as a reprimand to the Mensheviks or to poke fun at the leftists.

Because we want a "yes or no" answer on the separation of the Ukraine. No one can tell us that we cannot understand the meaning of these articles.

"The demand for a 'yes' or 'no' answer to the question of secession in the case of any nation may seem very 'practical.' In reality, however, it is absurd; it is metaphysical in theory, and it leads in practice to subordinating the proletariat to the policy of the bourgeoisie. The bourgeoisie always places its national demands in the forefront, and does so in a categorical fashion. With the proletariat, however, these demands are subordinated to the interests of the class struggle. Theoretically, one cannot say in advance whether the bourgeois-democratic revolution will end in a given nation seceding from another nation, or in its equality with the latter; *in either case* the important thing is for the proletariat to ensure its own class development. The bourgeoisie has to hamper this development by placing its 'own' nation's aims before those of the proletariat. That is why the proletariat, so to speak, confines itself to the negative demand for recognition of the *right* to self-determination, without giving guarantees to any nation."*

---

* [V. I.] N. Lenin, "O prave natsii na samoopredelenie," *Prosveshchenie,* Nos. 4–6 (1914). [Lenin's italics—Ed.]

We will not give a theoretical analysis of this argument, as the reader can see for himself what's "what" and what's "not what." We hope to do this in a separate pamphlet on the theory and practice of self-determination.

Now we will only direct our attention to some facts. If the reader will open *Izvestiia V. Ts. I. K. Sovetov*, No. 282 (546), of December 24, 1918, and will look at page three, under the heading: "Acts and Orders of the Government," there he will find: (1) the decree on recognition of the Soviet Republic of Latvia; (2) the decree on recognition of the independence of the Lithuanian Soviet Republic; (3) the resolution of the People's Commissariat of Foreign Affairs stating that "because of the annulment of the Brest Litovsk peace treaty, the Ukraine is no longer recognized as an independent state by the Soviet Government of the Russian Republic"; (4) the same resolution on Georgia.

We now ask the reader to answer these questions. If it is impossible to give a "yes or no" answer, because this would be "absurd . . . metaphysical in theory, and [would lead—Ed.] in practice to subordinating the proletariat to the policy of the bourgeoisie," then why is the answer yes given for Latvia, Estonia, Lithuania, and Byelorussia, and the answer no for the Ukraine and Georgia? Why does the Russian proletariat not limit itself to the, so to speak, "negative . . . recognition of the *right* to self-determination"? That is one question.

Here is the second. Does the yes answer in the cases of Latvia, Lithuania, Estonia, and Byelorussia, and no in the cases of the Ukraine and Georgia, mean that the "bourgeois-democratic revolution" will inevitably lead to the separation of Estonia, Lithuania, Latvia, and Byelorussia and to equal rights for the Ukraine and Georgia?

The third: In recognizing the independence of Lithuania, Latvia, Estonia, and Byelorussia, does the proletariat "not oblige itself to give away *something at the expense*" of, for example, the Russian or Jewish nations to the Lithuanians, Latvians, Byelorussians, and Estonians? And by not recognizing the independence of the Ukraine and Georgia, does the proletariat not oblige itself to give something to the Russian nation *at the expense* of the Ukrainian and Georgian nations?

The fourth: Why do the yes answer for Latvia, Lithuania, Estonia, and Byelorussia, and the no answer for the Ukraine and Georgia not result in subordination of the proletariat to the bourgeoisie?

The fifth: If the independence of the Ukraine was not recognized, what was the sense of "playing a comedy" with the Provisional Worker-Peasant Government of the Ukraine? We do not know how the government will react to this act. Perhaps it will say "God's dew," rub the spit out of its eyes [Ukrainian saying meaning that weaklings usually pretend that they are blessed with God's dew when actually they are being spat upon by someone stronger than they—Ed.] and go "back to work!"?

Is the Ukrainian national movement less strong, less widespread, or less deep than the national movements in other countries?

Comrade Kulyk tries to frighten the Ukraine with separation, stating that "given the presence of finance capital and the active colonial policies of the great powers, there is no room for small independent states." Let him then explain what kind of policy is pursued by Soviet Russia.

Now let us listen to the former chairman of the Russian delegation to the peace negotiations with the Ukraine. Kh. Rakovski lived about three months in the Hotel Marseille in Kiev, received a few letters from the peasants of the Kiev and Poltava regions, and considers himself a Ukrainian expert entitled to give authoritative advice to the Russian proletariat. In his article, "Beznadezhnoe delo" [A Hopeless Affair—Ed.], published in *Izvestiia V.Ts.I.K.S.*, No. 2 (554), January 3, 1919,* Kh. Rakovski sets himself up as an expert on the Ukraine and argues, from the ethnographic and socioeconomic points of view, against the existence of the Ukrainian people.

> First of all, the ethnographic differences between Ukrainians and Russians are in themselves insignificant . . . More important is the fact that the Ukrainian peasantry lack what is generally called "national consciousness" . . . The Ukrainian proletariat is completely Russian in origin . . . It is also a well-known fact that three-fourths of the population of Kiev is non-Ukrainian, while only 10 percent of the population of Odessa is Ukrainian. It is also well known that within the borders of the Ukraine as it was imagined by the authors of the Third Universal, i.e., including the eight provinces and the Tauride but leaving out the Crimea, there lived 2,100,000 Great Russians, according to the 1897 statistics. . . . Finally, even those who are only superficially acquainted with the Ukraine [Kh. Rakovski considers himself a real expert] know that the industrial *bour-*

* [Kh. Rakovski, "Beznadezhnoe delo; o Petliurovskoi avantiure," *Izvestiia*, No. 2 (554) (January 3, 1919), p. 1—Ed.]

geoisie and the greater part of the landowning class is of Russian, Polish, or Jewish origin. . . .

His conclusion?—that the Ukraine was invented by persons in the cooperative movement, teachers, and court officials like Shelukhyn.[32] For an unfortunate mouse there is no stronger beast than a cat. For Kh. Rakovski there is no stronger beast than Shelukhyn, and he became convinced of this during negotiations about which the Soviet Union will never boast.

Well, let it be. The peasants lack "national consciousness," and the workers, landowners, capitalists, and officials are of Russian origin. That leaves only the intelligentsia. But there is one curious thing. In the end Kh. Rakovski appeases someone in the following way:

> The danger of Russification under the Ukrainian Soviet government appears groundless. The Ukrainian peasants and Ukrainian (?) workers who will need schools and administration in the Ukrainian language will secure them much better under the Soviet government than under a Ukrainian intelligentsia made up of new officials, turned out by short courses, who see in Ukrainian independence not so much the conditions for the cultural development of the Ukrainian people as the conditions for their own bureaucratic rule.*

What's this? How's this? Why does Kh. Rakovski have to persuade anyone that there is no "danger of Russification"? Whom does he want to appease? The peasants? But Kh. Rakovski, who "knows" the Ukraine more than superficially, has assured us that the peasants do not even want to read the Ukrainian proclamations, saying "Not again? In Ukrainian?" Perhaps Kh. Rakovski wants to appease the Russian workers, the Russian landowners, capitalists, and so forth? Or perhaps the "intelligentsia" which is "inventing" the Ukraine? Kh. Rakovski started by talking about the Ukrainian workers who will want an education in the Ukrainian language. But then, as an expert, he was assuring us that the "Ukrainian proletariat is of purely Russian origin." When does Kh. Rakovski talk as an expert and when superficially?

Kh. Rakovski further assures us that there will be no danger of Russification under the *Ukrainian* Soviet government. Does this require proof? Well, we didn't realize it before. But we don't believe the expert Kh. Rakovski, even after his analyses and proofs. There must be something wrong here.

* [*Ibid.*—Ed.]

Why and for whom is it the *Ukrainian* Soviet government? Does this word have to be introduced for the sake of Shelukhyn? And what is the meaning of the phrase appearing before the end of the one quoted above: "The Russian Soviet Government will not sell its birthright (in the Ukraine) for a mess of pottage, even if this mess of pottage takes the form of sugar and grain"?*

The bureaucrats don't let Kh. Rakovski sleep. What does it all mean? Does he see a competitor among them? Ah me, that Shelukhyn.

Not at all. One can "bless him and christen him," but the Rumanian background still sticks out. The truly Russian tsarist Russia had a sincere friend in Purishkevich, and Soviet Russia has a new prophet in the Bolshevik Rakovski. The Russian proletariat should take care in accepting the advice and services of its sincere friends. Because an obliging—how does Krylov[33] put it—"an obliging friend is more dangerous than an enemy!" In its own interests the Russian proletariat should be careful not to follow the advice of its "friend," Kh. Rakovski. Because if the Ukraine hears that the Russian Soviet government and the Ukrainian proletariat (purely Russian in origin) will not sell their birthright in the Ukraine because of 2,100,000 Russians, workers, landowners, and capitalists, then no one will believe our internationalism at any price.

We warn the Russian proletariat against any kind of comforting self-deception with respect to Ukrainian independence. It must say to itself once and for all: "The Ukrainian national liberation movement is a serious matter. The Ukraine wants to become independent. Let it be independent! We will help it out of the difficult situation into which the Central Rada (now the Directory) has got it. But we will not help because we want to regain our birthright, not for a 'mess of pottage,' but because we want to help it. We are neither Katerynoslav shopkeepers[34] nor Rumanian internationalists,[35] and we are not afraid of alien bureaucracy. Among proletarians, between really free nations, there can be no talk about birthrights nor about any 'mess of pottage.' If the Ukraine has difficulty getting to its feet because of its history as a stepchild, its past status of colony—we will help it. We recall Engels' advice to the West European proletariat to seize colonies for a short while in order to make them independent as soon as possible. We prove this by the examples of Estonia, Lithuania, Latvia, and Byelorussia.

"Is it possible for us to be enemies of Georgia's independence and, even more, that of the Ukraine whose territory is as great as that

* [*Ibid.*—Ed.]

of any European state and which has a population of 35 million, whose people have shown such power and strength during the revolution and have created their own literature and science in their own language despite the most difficult historical conditions? Is it possible that we will give up an international solidarity, not of words but in deed, for the 'mess of pottage' of our Russian 'birthright' in the Ukraine? The Ukrainian people have declared for independence, the international unity of the working masses of all nations is dearer to us than anything else, and for its sake we are ready to help the Ukrainian people to 'build their own home,' although not in the manner of the German occupying armies."

Or, perhaps Engels' colonies are one thing and Europe another?

Chapter XVI

The Proletariat Allied with the Petty
Bourgeoisie Against World Imperialism

The Ukrainian revolution revealed another glaring fact.

While in Russia the petty bourgeoisie (meaning the peasants who made up its great bulk) went along with the workers from the very beginning and during the whole course of the revolution, the Ukrainian peasantry from the very beginning followed a course different from that of the workers.

The unity of the Russian proletariat and petty bourgeoisie was reflected in the joint Soviets of Workers' and Peasants' Deputies, in the alliance between the Mensheviks and Socialist-Revolutionaries until October, and in the alliance between the Bolsheviks and left Socialist-Revolutionaries after October until, in July, 1918, the left Socialist-Revolutionary adventure discredited the advocates of rebellion and pushed the poor peasant toward the Communist Party.

In the Ukraine the worker and peasant movements went separate ways from the very outset, and there was no lasting or stable alliance between the Peasants' and Workers' Soviets. On the contrary, from the very outset of the revolution we find two centers—the Central Rada and the Soviets—sharply and tensely opposed to one another.

If we characterize the events in the Ukraine, which were largely the outcome of the relations between the Central Rada and the Soviets, as a division into separate peasant and worker movements, this must be taken with some reservations, *cum grano salis*. We mean only the prevailing trend, the dominant coloration of what we perceived in the relations between the Central Rada and the Soviets.

In the first place, the Central Rada included, besides a Council of Peasants' Deputies and a Council of Soldiers' Deputies (whose class content was the same since the Council of Soldiers' Deputies represented the same villagers, only the most competent and energetic ones, dressed in uniform), a Council of Workers' Deputies whose one hundred members were elected at the All-Ukrainian Workers' Congress on July 11–15.[1] But even before this Congress the Ukrainian workers had taken part in the national liberation struggle, the most striking evidence being the existence of the Ukrainian Social-Democratic Workers Party, which was born in 1904–5 and appeared on the historical scene not as an invention of the intelligentsia but as a result of the 1902 wave of peasant uprisings in the Poltava and Kharkiv (Kharkov) regions. One needs a really thorough knowledge of the Ukraine, as derived from the windows of the Hotel Marseille in Kiev, to state as absolute truth, with the supreme arrogance of a man "who has seen everything by just peeking out," that "the Ukrainian proletariat is purely Russian in origin." As usual, the "thorough" Kh. Rakovski "missed the elephant." If the chairman of the peace delegation in Kiev had been a little more interested in the Ukraine than he was in last year's snow, even without leaving his room in the Marseille he could have read M. Porsh's little pamphlet about the Ukrainian worker, based on the same 1897 census quoted by Kh. Rakovski. To our regret we have no copy of this pamphlet handy and thus cannot give its title or the relevant figures. But, as far as we can remember, M. Porsh, on the basis of a thorough (not Rakovski's type of thoroughness) analysis and investigation of the 1897 census (and the defects of this census are well known),[2] concluded that at that time there were about 500,000 (we think the exact figure is 416,000) non-Ukrainian workers in the Ukraine—thus, unless we are mistaken, only one-third of all the workers in the Ukraine. Even on the assumption of an increase in the number of workers of purely Russian origin, they would still be no more than half of the Ukrainian proletariat. Thus at least one half is of purely Ukrainian origin.

If not, perhaps the Marxist intellectual, Kh. Rakovski, can explain how the Ukrainian Social-Democratic Party could exist and become so influential.

Thus the workers also participated, and are still participating, in the Ukrainian national liberation movement. But because of the generally lower educational level of the Ukrainian masses (the result of the tsarist educational policy and national slavery) the Ukrainians were found mainly in the lower strata of workers, maintained ties with the village, and played a secondary role in the workers' movement. The leading role in the workers' movement was played by the more developed non-Ukrainian workers (not only those of purely Russian origin), while the peasantry was the backbone of the national liberation movement. What is characteristic, however, is that the principal leaders of this national liberation movement were not the

Ukrainian Socialist-Revolutionaries, but the Ukrainian Social Democrats.

On the other hand, the Soviets were not pure class organizations any more than the Central Rada was a purely national organ. Only a lax Russian or "internationalist" intellectual, like the eternal student and drunkard Onufrii from L. Andreev's *Days of Our Life* who looked for a "quiet family" in which to cause a scandal with much face-slapping, would look everywhere for "pure internationalism" in order the better to set off his "pure" Russian or Rumanian origin! For two and a half centuries the Ukraine was a Russian colony. For two and a half centuries the truly Russian Rumanians, Purishkeviches, "cosmopolitans" of the Russian breed (Valuevs, "Ukrainians," " 'Me-too' Little Russian"[3] Rodziankos and Skoropadski's) tried to drive out of the foolish "khokhol" heads various peculiar separatist thoughts. For whole centuries national and international science tried to prove that the "ethnographic differences between Ukrainians and Russians are in themselves insignificant" because both walk on two legs, because Ukrainians also speak a human language (although to the educated international intellectual the Ukrainian version seems very simple and naive), and even because Ukrainians have the same kind of noses as Russians. The intellectual, V. Vynnychenko, lied when he stated at the Second Military Congress that the Ukrainians do not yet have noses of their own![4] For centuries science has been trying to prove that Ukrainian peasants have no national consciousness, that they are jostling and clamoring to get into Russia. We don't want the Ukraine! they shout in unison when "court officials of the Shelukhyn variety" (where does this cursed weed come from?) try to draw them in by force. Kornfeld[5] [editor of—Ed.] *Satirikon*, had to be assigned to duty in the Main Guardhouse in 1912 to learn from an old newspaper pasted over a hole in the window that the first State Duma had been dissolved; he then took this "discovery" to the captain in command. Kh. Rakovski had to stay in the Marseille three months to be able to report to the Russian proletariat the "discovery" that neither in Bucharest, nor in Moscow, nor even in the Marseille in Kiev was there any national consciousness. Can you imagine: twenty-five thousand peasants writing every day and clamoring: "Police! Help! 'Ukrainian again!' " And the peasants wrote below the Russian language proclamations: "Read with pleasure!"

The Ukraine, like the rest of Russia, was militarized. The result of the tsarist system of troop distribution, taken over by the Provisional Government, was that the Ukraine was covered with garrisons of Russian and Polish troops while the Ukrainians themselves were scattered on the northern front, in Petrograd, and along the Volga.

Thus the Soviets of Workers' and Soldiers' Deputies in the Ukraine had a more non-Ukrainian look because they were composed mostly of workers, soldiers, and intellectuals of purely Russian origin. Here again, of course, we are talking only about the dominant coloration.

This should be borne in mind in forming a judgment about the revolutionary movement in the Ukraine, in comprehending the real nature of the hostility between the purely national Central Rada and the purely class Soviets, in understanding why the Ukrainian workers, who associated with the villagers, were more national, and why the non-Ukrainian petty bourgeoisie, who associated with the workers, was more international. In the same way the Ukrainian detachments[6] in Petrograd were noticeably revolutionary and internationalist, and when they returned to Kiev, they became nationalist and counterrevolutionary. "Why stick your noses into our business?" they said. "Go and play the master at home in Russia, and let us manage things in the Ukraine! We can take care of our own bourgeoisie."

In general terms, the division of democracy in this area into Ukrainian and non-Ukrainian was another manifestation of the hostility between an alien, non-Ukrainian city and our own Ukrainian village.

This division in the workers, with the alienation of the mass of the peasantry from the more advanced workers, was the fundamental and salient fact of the revolution. This split came to the surface in November, 1917–March, 1918.

The character and meaning of this split is best illustrated by one of the Ukrainian peasantry's most important demands—nationalization of the land and creation of a Ukrainian land fund, so as to bring it under the control of the Ukrainian democratic state. Comrade Kulyk states that the prosperous peasants did not want to share the land with the Russian peasants. This is true, and the prosperous peasants did not want to share their land with Ukrainian peasants either. Thus such a simple and easily understood explanation of the demand for a land fund is suited only to children of the first grades of the Katerynoslav seminary. If it is recalled that the Ukraine during the last two decades supplied the largest number of settlers in Siberia, Turkestan, and other regions, the peasantry should have wanted something else (following this "pickpocket" argumentation). Because if you demand your own land fund, not subject to alien management, you may be treated the same way yourself. Such considerations as Comrade Kulyk points out were probably present, but the gist of the matter was not in them. This demand is to be understood only within the framework of the general political, national, social, and economic demands of the Ukrainian masses. Then the demand for a land fund is seen to have the same meaning as all the other demands: the Ukraine does not want to be a foreign colony, a servant to the Russians and the Poles, but wants to live for itself.[7] The demand for a land fund was just one more link in the chain of Ukrainian efforts to constitute a nation, one more stage in the progress of the self-awareness of the Ukrainian spirit, enabling them finally to declare with Fichte: "I am I!" The Ukrainian land fund is that "not I" which leads eventually to "I"!

Thus the fight of the Ukrainian peasants (and workers), as the largest group in the Ukrainian movement, for their socioeconomic and national-political demands, which were aimed ultimately at creating a nation, a state-political organism, gave rise to language which always led ultimately to the Ukrainian Rome, that is, to Kiev. At the same time the most highly developed and influential segment of the Ukrainian workers of purely Russian origin (and also of the petty bourgeoisie, soldiers, and intelligentsia of purely Russian origin) was pursuing its own policy of stronger ties with Russia—differing from the landowners, capitalists, bureaucrats, shopkeepers, and intellectuals of purely Russian origin only in using words about the right of nations to self-determination, in being friendly to the Ukrainian movement when a common front against the counterrevolution was necessary, in being neutral when the Ukrainian movement remained confined to local matters, and in treating the movement with hostility when it seriously threatened the unity and indivisibility of the class struggle or the birthright.

One need only note that this discord was terribly harmful to revolutionary progress, and even fatal to it during the disaster of December, 1917–March, 1918. The Central Rada and its delegation[8] were not alone in seeing the German troops as liberators. And only the occupation and only occupation changed the feeling of the Ukrainian masses into its opposite. Only rule by an imperialist occupation army, the horrors of management by landowners, capitalists, bureaucrats, gendarmes, and Ukrainians of purely Russian origin, plunged the Ukrainian masses into that despair which is reflected in, among other things, the peasants' letters to the Marseille. And at this time, with the Entente's defeat of Germany and the establishment of Woodrow Wilson's hegemony, the Ukraine's objective position was such that her only course was union with Russia. The de facto situation impelled the Ukrainian masses to union with the Russian proletariat. We have discussed this de facto situation sufficiently in previous chapters, but our pamphlet has been delayed by printing difficulties, and in the meantime this de facto situation has disclosed still another interesting feature and some striking details on which we may dwell. This new feature is Poland's declared intention to include within its boundaries its own historic lands[9] of Galicia, part of Volyn (Volhynia), and Lithuania. The Allied counterrevolution will doubtless try to take advantage of the great-power dreams of the Polish, as well as the Russian, counterrevolutionaries. Suffice it to say that these intentions of Poland, added to the ancient historical hostility, are driving the Ukrainian masses to a union with the Russian proletariat.

Here are some details of the de facto international position of the Ukraine as outlined in the earlier chapters.

The December 20, 1918, issue of *Pravda* (No. 277) published the following telegrams from the representatives of the Entente (the "Allies"; the Anglo-French-American Capitalist Union) :*

1. To the President of the Directory, Vynnytsia (Vinnitsa), and Kiev. The Entente's aim is to fight the Bolsheviks. Consequently, first, the Volunteer Army detachments in Kiev should be considered as army detachments under the command of their officers and wear their military insignia; second, the Volunteer Army detachments should retain their arms—if they have been disarmed, their arms should be returned to them immediately; third, under these conditions the Volunteer Army detachments will preserve strict neutrality toward the Directory; fourth, I will come to Kiev after contacting the command of the allied troops now in transport; fifth, after my arrival the Volunteer Army detachments will take part in the fight against the Bolsheviks and will be sent to Odessa to join the army of General Denikin. I remind you that General Denikin's army enjoys the moral and material support of the Allied States (Entente). Please acknowledge receipt of this telegram and inform what measures have been taken. December 20, 1918. [signed—Ed.] Enno.[10]

2. Kiev. To the German High Command, copy to the Kiev Council of German Soldiers. Under the terms of the armistice you should, in behalf of the Entente states, secure and maintain

* "Pokhod soiuznicheskogo imperializma na Rosiiskuiu Revoliutsiiu," *Pravda*, No. 277 (December 20, 1918), p. 2.

order in the Russian territories under occupation by your troops. The new situation in Kiev will demand firmer measures than those used hitherto, in order to prevent killing, pillaging, and general disorder. Any failure to undertake such measures will be viewed as a serious offense on the part of yourselves and your government against the Entente states. Acknowledge receipt of this telegram and inform what measures have been taken. December 16, 1918. [signed—Ed.] Enno.

This is open and straightforward. The imperialists of the Anglo-French-American alliance need not concern themselves with anyone or anything. "Their hand is the lord." [Russian saying—Ed.]

Who will dare stand in their way? Where are those "enemies of humanity and civilization" against whom the democratic position must be defended? "The loser pays again and again!" says Lloyd George. The victors are not judged!

The Entente crushed Germany. Germany lost everything. The successor to all its conquests is the Entente.

From its victory over Russia and the Brest Litovsk peace Germany acquired an enormous indemnity. Before the money from Russia could be counted in the *Deutsche Bank* it had to be shipped on to Paris.

The victory over Russia gave Germany very large territories in the east that had formerly been part of the Russian Empire. These territories are now at the Entente's disposal. The troops who are preserving peace and order with fire and sword, who had formerly served their imperialist *Vaterland*, were to continue playing the role of executioners of the people in the occupied lands. While they formerly played this role for conscience sake, they now had to play it out of fear, because "any failure to undertake such measures will be viewed as a serious offense on the part of yourselves and your government."

The Entente imperialists not only stripped Germany bare, not only took from her the Rhineland, just as the German imperialists stripped Russia, but also forced the German troops to serve their interests. A rope has been placed around Germany's neck and is being gradually drawn tighter. Under the threat of strangulation the Entente imperialists want to maintain the German troops in their service. Thus the German troops must now strangle other peoples to postpone for a time the ultimate strangling of their own fatherland.

The Entente thinks that the German troops in the Ukraine have not yet had time to be "infected" by the revolutionary poison and that they will, for a mess of pottage and the mercy of the Entente, help it to hold the Ukraine in bondage until Mr. Enno "contacts the command of the allied troops now in transport."*

The Entente knows very well that a scoundrel can be turned into an executioner. But the executioner's neck is in a noose, and the rope must be held tight to prevent him from turning his ax against his masters. However thick-skinned the German troops in the Ukraine may be, of whatever conservative elements they may be composed, they must have been infected by the revolutionary virus, especially considering that, both there and at home, everything is boiling and struggling and that the Entente troops in Germany are starting to do the same things as the Germans did and are doing in the Ukraine. The Entente knows this full well and for that reason is not satisfied with the German troops but is sending its own, as yet untouched by the revolutionary virus.

In the meantime the German troops are to continue torturing the Ukrainian revolution because this was stipulated in the armistice between Germany and the Entente.

Everything is quite clear.

The attitude of the Entente toward the new power in the Ukraine, the Directory, is somewhat more complex.

Enno is also very solicitous about General Denikin's Volunteer Army. "General Denikin's army enjoys the moral and material support of the Allied States." Enno requests extraterritoriality for these troops in the Ukraine, asks that they not be molested before he comtacts the Entente troops on the way. If the Volunteer Army has already been disarmed, the arms should either be returned or . . . Enno does not say. Let the Directory guess.

Enno mentions only the fight against the Bolsheviks. It is true that the Bolsheviks are ugly people who offended the poor capitalists by refusing to pay back the blood money given to tsarist Russia: they say that Russia has already paid with the blood of her sons.

Well, the Directory does not much like the Bolsheviks either (nor did the Central Rada), and Enno thinks this will help to lure the Directory into the Entente's net. But what does the Entente offer the directory in return? Enno is silent.

They say that silence is golden.

But this silence is quite eloquent. On many occasions the Entente has declared itself in favor of regenerating the one and indivisible Russia. That is why General Denikin and his Volunteer Army were paid so much attention, and given so much moral and material

---

* [*Ibid.*—Ed.]

support, by the Entente. The Entente believed that he would regenerate the one and indivisible "not out of fear, but for conscience sake." This was no secret to anyone, including the Directory.

What, then, does Enno's declaration that the Entente has decided to fight the Bolsheviks mean for the Directory?

It means only this: *that, along with Bolshevik Soviet Russia, the independent Ukraine and its Directory will swing on the gallows of the one and indivisible.*

Is it possible that the Directory will again put its neck in the noose? Will it really return arms to the Volunteer Army which tomorrow will use them against it?

Is it possible that there has not been enough flogging? Or maybe there was, but the lesson did not sink in?

No, there was enough flogging, and the lesson was not lost.

When the Central Rada began to seek protection and help from the German imperialists in February–March, 1918, this was at least understandable because Germany was fighting the Entente. Germany was fighting the Bolsheviks. It was to Germany's advantage to use the Rada against both of them. It served to protect at least the shadow of Ukrainian "independence." Although they mocked the Central Rada and dispersed it, setting up the most noble puppet, Skoropadski, they still appeared to favor the independence of the Ukraine. At least the Central Rada could console itself with the thought that, even though it was being beaten and the Ukraine was being robbed and plundered by the liberators, the Ukrainian people were at least building their own home because the Germans "sincerely" favored Ukrainian independence.

But even these blasphemous consolations can no longer be entertained, because right now everything is clear.

The only logical outcome of this situation is the Directory's apparent proposal to negotiate with Soviet Russia.[11] We know this only as hearsay, but it is in no way unbelievable. It completely suits the de facto position of the Ukraine. Even the "hopeless" Kh. Rakovski learned in the Marseille that Petliura is not the hero of any Allied *roman*. In *Pravda* No. 3, of January 4, 1919, we find the following note: "The Ukraine and the Soviet Republic. We learn from the newspapers that the Directory has taken steps to approach the Soviet government and that during the stay of the Directory and Vynnychenko in Vynnytsia (Vinnitsa) there was a series of conferences between responsible representatives of the Directory and the Bolsheviks from Kharkiv (Kharkov). The subject under discussion was the question of the possibility of good-neighbor relations between the

Ukrainian People's Republic and Soviet Russia. According to rumor, the conferences succeeded in making clear that agreement with the Soviet government may be reached on the basis of: (1) unconditional recognition of the sovereignty of the Ukrainian People's Republic in exchange for recognition of the Soviet republic by the Ukraine; (2) complete noninterference in internal affairs; (3) legalization of the Bolshevik party and of the propaganda of Bolshevik ideas in the Ukraine; (4) the convocation of a Worker-Peasant Congress to decide the question of the form of the government.

"The Ukrainian Directory proposes to conduct negotiations with the Soviet government in the future, and, if agreement is reached, the possibility of a defensive-offensive alliance between Russia and the Ukraine against Russian and Western imperialists is not excluded."*

Whether or not this corresponds to reality is of little concern, since we only want again to underline the direction in which the Ukraine is now moving.

But even without such rumors, even before we heard of them, one could observe that the Ukrainian peasants and workers had different feelings than before the catastrophe of February–March, 1918. By calling in the Germans the Central Rada "internationalized" the Ukrainian peasantry.

This raises the question: what should be our attitude toward this feeling on the part of the Ukrainian peasants and workers?

We can adopt the same attitude as that taken already (according to all signs) by Soviet Russia and advocated by that "thorough expert," Kh. Rakovski. It even seems to us that Kh. Rakovski took the liberty to have an independent judgment mainly because the authorities permitted him. This attitude would be as follows: the Ukrainian masses, frightened by one occupation and threatened by a new Allied occupation, will surely throw themselves into our arms. "This will happen of itself in due course." Why should we usher in some kind of chauvinism or independence, when the Ukraine will be ours in any case? Kh. Rakovski states this quite frankly: "It would be foolish to think that the Ukrainian proletariat ('of purely Russian origin'!) and the Russian Soviet government will sell their birthright for a mess of pottage, even if this mess of pottage now takes the form of sugar and grain."†

* ["Polozhenie na Ukraine: Ukraina i Sovetskaia Respublika," *Pravda*, No. 3 (January 4, 1919), p. 2—Ed.]

† [Kh. Rakovski, "Beznadezhnoe delo: o Petliurovskoi avantiure," *Izvestiia*, No. 2 (554) (January 3, 1919), p. 1—Ed.]

Well, this is also a point of view, also a proletarian policy. But in accepting it one must reach the appropriate conclusions and be honest with oneself. One must then reject the hocus-pocus of a separate Soviet government of the Ukraine, reject all attempts to calm fears of russification, refuse to create a new Ukrainian culture with the left hand while destroying it with the right. If you drive the truth out by the door, it creeps in through the window. Secure for the Ukrainian peasants schools and an administration in the Ukrainian language (as the Ukrainian Soviet government of Kh. Rakovski is prepared to do), and tomorrow, when the independence of the Ukraine has been done away with, the peasants and workers will issue a new call for the independence of the Ukraine. Those Communists of the Ukraine who qualified as chauvinism the proposal of the writer of these lines that they use their spare time to learn the language of the people they were preparing to self-determine, revealed a far deeper understanding of the matter than is possessed by Kh. Rakovski. And here, to their own way of thinking, they were entirely consistent. The present situation is such that to learn the Ukrainian language and use it in one's daily work would only swell the stream which drives the mill of independence. One would be a *samostiinyk* against one's will. And the Communists of the Ukraine are consistent in greeting with ironic smiles the "white crow" among them who starts talking the "vulgar and naive" language of the people whose name they carry. When Kh. Rakovski wrote, and the Communists of the Ukraine read, that they would secure the use of Ukrainian in schools and government institutions better than any intellectuals, they must surely have laughed themselves to death, like the Roman pagan soothsayers. Introducing Ukrainian in schools and institutions at this time would mean that the same cursed intelligentsia would hold all sorts of offices—and where would that leave Kh. Rakovski and the Communists of the Ukraine? Who is an enemy to himself?

No, they will not secure it, but will destroy it so that not a trace of this accursed language will remain—this, in their view, is what should be done. And when the Communists of the Ukraine warn against the danger of the national and not the class movement in the Ukraine, in their own way they understand the matter well.

Kh. Rakovski states that "the struggle in the Ukraine, as in all of Russia, and as in the majority of European countries, is proceeding on the basis of a class, not a national, differentiation."

So much for Kh. Rakovski, who assures us that the Ukrainian workers are of purely Russian origin and that the peasants, whose ethnographic differences are so insignificant, do not even want to hear about the Ukrainian language, saying: "Not again? In Ukrainian?"

No, no! Not to secure, but to uproot completely and deprive of all influence, rivals of the "Shelukhyn type!"

One wants to do it . . . but it might be painful, and, in addition, the consequences might be unpleasant.

No, one cannot do this. "Believe me, it is the only course!" But to say that the Ukraine must become independent is too terrifying.

There is no Ukraine; there was Southern Russia, which became the "southern part of the eastern territories occupied by Germany"— but the Provisional Government of the Ukraine was formed: let it be called by that name.

There is no Ukraine, the Ukrainian workers are of purely Russian origin, but even so, let us call the party of the Communists of the Ukraine, Ukrainian.

We are told that the peasants do not even want to hear about Ukrainian culture—but why not secure their "vulgar and naive language" for them? Kh. Rakovski, however, speaks for others, "even when not asked by them to do so" (are we in error?) because, after all, the Communists of the Ukraine have not yet solved the morbid national problem, and maybe they will secure the language and maybe not.

On the above rumors about the Directory's proposal to negotiate with Soviet Russia *Pravda* writes that this proposal can be discussed in a "businesslike manner." What then happens to the Provisional Worker-Peasant Government of the Ukraine? Can there possibly have been no alliance with it even yet? Were we possibly correct in writing, about the Organizational Bureau's proposal (in its theses to the Russian Soviet government) to effect a close union with the People's Secretariat (resurrected in Moscow on the third day after its death in Tahanrih [Taganrog]) :

> *In vain, boy, you're coming,*
> *In vain your feet burn,*
> *You won't get anything,*
> *And, a fool, will home return!* [Russian folk song—Ed.]

Please excuse the word, *fool*, but you cannot throw it out of the song—this we heard from Comrade N. Lenin as far back as the Fourth Congress of Soviets.

Since the inventors of the Ukraine are court officials of the Shelukhyn variety, securing the Ukrainian language in schools and institutions means establishing there court officials of the Shelukhyn variety, as we do not speak it ourselves.

Street, street, why do you hide?
Tell me where is your right-left side! [Russian drinking song—Ed.]

No, the course proposed by Kh. Rakovski is too dangerous. Even if it is a success—if the eastern part of the Ukraine is annexed to Russia—both Russia and the Ukraine will have their Alsace, and both will for a long time remain in the "morbid state of having an unsolved national question."

And we are convinced by the facts—not only those occurring before the catastrophe of February–March, 1918, but current events as well—that this "morbid question" has played, now plays, and will continue to play an important role (it will not cease until solved). One has only to compare two facts: the permanent Provisional Soviet Government was doing just one thing the whole time—inciting to insurrection, and it twice declared that it would start one by itself if there was any further delay. Yet the leadership of the insurrection fell into the hands of the Directory, the successor to the same Central Rada which was so discredited by the events of February–March, 1918. King for a day, but why did the Permanent Government not become such a king for a day? What can one say? there is no stronger beast than a court official of the Shelukhyn variety, but you cannot ride far on a cat. If the Directory had been riding on court officials of the Shelukhyn variety and only on them, it would have been dead long since.

The Russian proletariat has open to it another possible attitude toward the Ukraine—to forget that it was a patrimony, a colony of Russia, to renounce forever their "birthright" in the Ukraine inherited from the tsarist regime of ill memory, to renounce it without any "mess of pottage in the form of sugar or grain" as compensation, but to adhere to the paragraph in its program which states (or formerly stated) that "nations have a right to self-determination." The left Socialist-Revolutionary insurrection ended a long time ago, and the time is now ripe to decide the morbid Ukrainian question fully —not the way the Katerynoslavians and the peace delegation in Kiev decided it and are still trying to decide it, but along the lines set out in the very valuable articles of Comrade N. Lenin. This way, of course, is more difficult and will not afford an opportunity of proclaiming victories with much rolling of drums *urbi et orbi*, or of confusing the German government with frightening questions from Kursk, excuse me, from "Poltava" (is it the name of a hotel, or what?) .[12]

By following the Katerynoslav way one can conquer Homel

(Gomel), Bilhorod (Belgorod), Sumy, Hlukhiv (Glukhov), Valu-
iky, Chernyhiv (Chernigov), Kharkiv (Kharkov), and other cities
and create a Russian-Ukrainian Alsace,[13] thus strengthening the
moral-political position of the Directory (the former Central Rada)
in the whole of the Ukraine. And this can be accomplished to the
thunder and clatter of international phrases and frightening "revolutionary manifestos."

To take the other course one will have to go to Kiev, not only to
the Marseille but to St. Sophia Square, and thence conquer the
Ukraine from the Don to the Carpathians—not for the sake of anyone's birthright, whether Russian, Polish, or Austrian, but for that of
the Ukraine itself. One will have to admit (may I here take a deep
sigh and add: "Believe me, this is the only course!") that the Ukraine
is the same kind of country as Russia, Germany, France, Italy, Norway, or England. Like them it not only has the right to exist but is in
reality as independent and sovereign as they are. It has the right and
the potential to live "by itself and for itself," just as these countries
do. The Ukrainian people are really a nation, not an invention of
court officials of the Shelukhyn variety, a nation which wants to live
its own free life and has all the necessary prerequisites, whether
geographic, ethnographic, economic, moral, physical, historical,
spiritual, or other. It is a people which had ceased being "khokhols"
and became "Ukrainians" long before the Katerynoslav daddies were
out of short pants and had stopped chasing their mammas.

When the Russian proletariat dares adopt this attitude toward
the Ukraine, and does so openly and sincerely, without ulterior motives or adaptation to local conditions, the sympathies of the Ukraine,
of worker-peasant Ukraine, will be with Russia forever. This will
lead to a much higher degree of proletarian unity than any Russian
proletarian dreams of a bygone birthright.

Nor should the following be forgotten. The same catastrophe of
February–March, 1918, which severed connections between the
Ukraine and Russia, which was so detrimental to both, which placed
Russia under the irritating scrutiny first of German and then of
Anglo-American imperialism, which threw the Ukraine into the same
tight clutches, had a further result. It completely routed the Ukrainian proletariat of purely Russian origin in causing the deaths of tens
of thousands of them in battle and forcing others to emigrate. Before
the catastrophe one could hope that the Ukraine would be one and
indivisible with Russia, but now either a Russian-Ukrainian Alsace
will have to be formed or *all* the Ukraine will have to be conquered

for itself, for its own sake, just as Russia and every other state exists and fights for itself, for its own sake.

If the first course is followed, it will be necessary every day to ponder: "Where is the right-left side?" Which is better: to form a Provisional Soviet Government of the Ukraine or to enter into an alliance with Petliura? And when a Ukrainian government is formed, it will be necessary to think again: "Should we have anything to do with the Directory?" It would be like the maiden who went down the garden path and started every time from the beginning.

If we follow the other course, we will have a free hand, unhindered by the Directory. We can discuss a coalition with Ukrainian democracy without paying any attention to the Directory. We will gain the support of the Ukrainian workers and peasants for the sake of their birthright, a birthright not only in name but in fact—the international solidarity of the workers.

Chapter XVII

The Stolypin Era

Not for nothing has the tsarist regime ruled over so many different peoples "from the cold Finnish rocks to the fiery Colchis."

It not only drained the country of wealth and destroyed its economy, but it also fostered its own culture and left a definite psychological heritage.

It enriched the Russian language with many slogans, proverbs, and anecdotes. Especially rich in these was the tsarist "constitutional" period.

Among the constitutional ministers greatest attention has always been, and will be, devoted to the colorful figure of Stolypin. Of all his slogans the most famous is the tsarist programmatic formula: "Stabilization first, reform afterwards."

The actual content of this formula was not identical with its grammatical content. The formula seems to indicate some measures which are to follow one another. But it only looks that way. As the clever "khokhol" son proposed to his father: "Either you, dad, will go to the forest for wood, and I will stay home; or I will stay home, and you will go to the forest for wood." [Ukrainian saying—Ed.] It looks like a choice, but actually there is none. Either way the son stays home and father goes to get wood. Logically and grammatically this is marking time. And so is the Stolypin formula. According to the rules of grammar and logic one "act," "stabilization," is followed by another, "reform." But it only looks that way, since reforms are necessary only as long as there is no stabilization. Reforms are needed precisely to preserve stability. When everything is stable, after all, why trouble or disturb the people with reforms. It was this very point that left uncle's house uncovered: the house should have a roof when it rains, but how can it be put on in the rain? And when it is not raining, why waste straw and effort, why worry? It's dry already! [Ukrainian folk tale—Ed.]

Thus the true meaning of the Stolypin formula was: stabilization first and then more stabilization—and don't think up any reforms. The tsarist house remained without a roof, and no one intended to cover it until the revolutionary rain inundated the whole place and drowned "uncle" himself.

Stolypin actually stole from a policeman on duty, Mymretsov,[1] his immortal "grab 'em and hold 'em!" He altered the form a little, gave it a constitutional look, and passed it out as his own creation. Mymretsov will be perfectly entitled in the next world to accuse Stolypin of plagiarism.

By this we do not imply that Stolypin plagiarized deliberately. On the contrary, we are convinced that Stolypin was subjectively honest with himself. It is just that both Stolypin and the policeman were in the same situation, and it led to the same response. The only difference is that the minister's response has a more scholarly and constitutional look, while that of the policeman is more purely authoritarian or purely nationalistic. But then their work is different, the policeman's technical and the minister's scientific. And while the policeman need not hesitate, but simply take a man by the scruff of the neck and "grab 'em and hold 'em" without paying attention to anyone or anything, the minister cannot do this. He has to prove that if the police "grab 'em" by the scruff of the neck and "hold 'em," it is done for the sake of reforms and benefit to the people.

The value of Mymretsov's formula lies in its classic clarity, being easily understood by all, even by those who have not studied in the Katerynoslav seminary. But Stolypin's formula is valuable because it hides its real meaning and offers much room for scholastic interpretation and exegesis of the words about the reforms following the stabilization. These interpretations and exegesis of words about future reforms obscure the present stabilization which is exclusively and entirely explained by the formula of "grab 'em and hold 'em."

And so we see that the situation which evoked the same actual response in policeman and minister gave rise to different verbal responses. This is customary in the ranks even though Voltairians from the Katerynoslav seminary may be indignant about this two-sided influence of the productive forces.

The value of the Stolypin formula, however, is not limited by its time or place of origin. It is such an absolute (or perhaps abstract?) formula that its meaning is the same for all peoples of the globe and for all periods in the history of humanity. It can take on a great variety of verbal colorings, change its form continually, or reject it entirely, while continually marking time with the identical content: "grab 'em and hold 'em."

The reader should not fear that we intend to regale him with a review of all the forms which this formula assumes. But it is worthwhile pausing over some aspects of this, especially when they are germane to the theme of our discussion.

For instance, at the First Ukrainian Military Congress in Kiev, in May, 1917, we heard the Ukrainian national liberals declare that the social problems can be solved only after the national problems. One need not dwell long on this declaration to perceive in it both the form and the content of Stolypin's formula. To resolve national problems it is first necessary to gather together and unite all classes of the population, to mollify their hostility. The class struggle must be halted because if the Ukrainian peasants demand not only a Ukrainian republic but also the immediate confiscation of all landowners' lands, then even Ukrainian landowners like Skoropadski will turn their backs on national affairs. What is to be done? Do not frighten Skoropadski—and this means "grab" and "hold" the peasant who is after the landowner's land. Everything should remain as it is until all shields are painted sky-blue and yellow.[2] Then we may discuss even the class struggle.

The Social Democratic variant of this formula was the thesis set forth by the Ukrainian Social Democrat, V. Vynnychenko, at the Second Military Congress—namely, in Russia the class struggle, but in the Ukraine a creative mutual effort on the part of all classes.

This is a variant of clerical socialism and the socialism of beautiful ladies: through nationalism we arrive at internationalism. First nationalism, then internationalism. Every beautiful lady is necessarily an angel and necessarily wants to get married; then she necessarily becomes a quarrelsome woman. Priests are only interested in performing the marriage ceremony; after all, not they, but the husbands, will later scratch their necks in exasperation. This is why beautiful ladies have the same consciousness as priests in various seminaries!

These are samples of national variants of Stolypin's formula. Here is its international variant:

1. "National problems will ultimately be solved under socialism." Until then . . . "national abstention," fast! Socialism implies a society based on the socialization of all the means of production. On this base will be erected a suitable superstructure about which past historical experience enables us to reason by analogy. For the time being we have only a negative response to the national question:

there will be *no* national oppression. To this it is sometimes added that under socialism there will be no Greeks and no Hebrews, that all nations will merge together. This is understood to mean that there will be no nations. And if there are no nations, there will be no national oppression. This means that . . . the trend of historical developments leads to a merging of nations, that no nationalities will exist, and that the only possibility will be internationalism.

First internationalism and then nationalism!

2. As a counterweight to the formula, national cause first and proletarian afterwards, is advanced the international formula: proletarian cause first and national afterwards.

In form and content this is the same as the Stolypin formula. This is quite obvious with regard to the form, but less obvious with regard to the content. But this is how it appears, and this appearance is the most characteristic feature of the Stolypin formula. The proletarian cause demands the complete unity and "amalgamation of the workers of all nationalities within a given state in unified proletarian organizations—political, trade-union, cooperative, educational, etc."* The outcome is the preservation by force of the unity and integrity of the state and the Katerynoslav practice of the national right to self-determination. But if the proletarian cause demands the amalgamation *now* of the workers of all nations to reach their common proletarian goals, why should there be any division among workers *after these goals have been reached?* We may be accused of putting different things in the same pile. We talk about the unity of the proletariat of all nations in a given state (which does not imply the maintenance by force of the state's unity and integrity) and about keeping the oppressed nations within its boundaries. The goal of proletarian unity in its common organizations is the "struggle against international capital and reaction, combating the propaganda and aspirations of the landowners, clergy, and bourgeois nationalists of all nations who usually conceal their anti-proletarian aspirations under the slogan of 'national culture'."† The question of the unity and integrity of the state, that is, of maintaining an oppressed nation within the boundaries of a given state, is answered by the nation's right to self-determination, that is, its right to become an independent country or to join some other state. It should be borne in mind that in opposing the separation of this nation or that, we do not use words about self-determination as the

* *Rezoliutsiia narady Ts. K. RSDRP v litku 1913r.*
† [*Ibid.*—Ed.]

Katerynoslavians do. The "nation's right to self-determination" (i.e., the constitutional guarantee of an absolutely free and democratic method of deciding the question of secession) must never be confused with the expediency of a given nation's secession. "The Social-Democratic Party must decide the latter question exclusively on its merits in each particular case in conformity with the interests of overall social development and with the interests of the proletarian class struggle for socialism."*

If this were really true, nothing could be said against it. But the reality is something far removed from it. No concrete analysis or solution has been based on it and, if this has been done, both the analysis and the solution bear the Katerynoslav character. "The interests of social development and the class struggle are always better served in a large state than in a small one," *ergo*, why separate? The productive forces will wax indignant. Thus it is better to leave them alone.

The formula for solving the national question proposed by Comrade N. Bukharin in his *Program of the Communist Party*,† that is, the right of the *working masses* of the oppressed[3] nation to separation (instead of that of the *nation*), only reveals a desire to avoid concrete analysis and to pass into the sphere of moral political postulates. The abstract formula of the right of a *nation* to self-determination demands concrete analysis, while the concrete formula of N. Bukharin does not demand such analysis. The working masses have common interests, and these can be attained and safeguarded only by uniting the working masses. *Ergo,* the working masses of all nations should not separate and should not differ from one another. And if the Constituent Assembly and the Soviets declare themselves for separation, then the Constituent Assembly and the Soviets are traitors to socialism. By following such excellent and often correct theses one can *reach* the conclusion: proletarian cause first and national afterwards. Comrade Bukharin's formula is the most perfect Stolypin kind of formula. Rather than stating directly and openly that separation is forbidden by the "writings and oral traditions of the church fathers" (to use the high style of the seminary where Comrade Zatonskii has studied), he speaks of the right of the working masses of the oppressed nation to separation. Either you, father, will go to the forest for wood, and I will stay home, or I will stay home, and you will go to the forest for wood!

* *Ibid.* Article 5 of the Resolution.
† [N. Bukharin, *Programma Kommunistov (Bol'shevikov)* (Petrograd, 1919), p. 55—Ed.]

3. "Let Comrade Shakh-Rai show us how the Ukraine can be independent. In view of the existence of the two camps: international imperialism and the international proletariat, how is it possible to separate from Soviet Russia? How is it possible to promote Ukrainian independence and thus sow disunity in the workers' ranks?" Such fearful arguments were thrown at us after our report. These questions were put not for the purpose of eliciting answers but "to kill" and . . . to prevent us from answering. We could reply to the *grammatical and logical* content of these arguments with further questions: how is it possible to advocate unity and indivisibility when right now there are two camps, international imperialism and the international proletariat, and when the first unanimously upholds the one and indivisible? How is it possible to answer "no" to the Ukraine's demand for independence when we hear resounding throughout the world this same *no! non! nein!* in all languages? Where is the line of demarcation between the two camps?

But we know beforehand that this argument will be inadequate. Because the trouble is not that the mare is grey, but that she won't pull. Because the root of the argument is the Stolypin formula: you are not to separate. *Da liegt der Hund begraben!*

4. "The struggle in the Ukraine, as in all of Russia and in most European countries, is already proceeding on the basis not of national, but of class, differentiation." *Ergo,* "the Ukrainian proletariat (of purely Russian origin) and the Russian Soviet government will not sell their birthright for a mess of pottage even if this mess of pottage now takes the form of sugar and grain" (Kh. Rakovski's "Hopeless Affair"[4]) *

5. "Petliura's proposals could be discussed in a businesslike manner. But the general line does not run where Petliura wants to draw it. The Ukrainian Republic should first of all be a *Soviet Republic.* The question of independence is less important, but every Soviet Republic naturally allies iself with Soviet Russia. The army of the Ukrainian Soviet Republic should be a *worker-peasant army,* not an army of petty bourgeois (peasant) ? blue Cossack mantles" [author's italics].† Thus comments the *Pravda* editorial (No. 3 of January 4, 1919) on the rumors, mentioned above, about the Directory's proposal to undertake negotiations with Soviet Russia. What is this?

"The question of independence is less important." This means

* [Kh. Rakovski, "Beznadezhnoe delo: o Petliurovskoi avantiure," *Izvestia,* No. 2 (554) (January 3, 1919), p. 1—Ed.]
† ["Direktoriia ili Sovety," *Pravda,* No. 3 (January 4, 1919), p. 1—Ed.]

that it is such a trifle, so minimal, that there can be no dispute about it? This means that *Pravda* has nothing against independence. *But* . . . Oh, immortal Shchedrin! oh immortal "but"! "But every Soviet Republic naturally allies itself with Soviet Russia!" But "your" army should be "ours." But the Soviet Ukraine must be "our" Ukraine! *Pravda* understands independence only on the stipulation that it alone delimits the content of that independence.

For the reader's information: (1) according to these rumors the Directory proposes an alliance with Soviet Russia in the fight with the Russian and world counterrevolutionaries; (2) we personally also advocate an alliance of the future Soviet Ukraine with Soviet Russia; (3) we also advocate a worker-peasant army.

But look at this wonderful argument. It fairly breathes the spirit of Stolypin.

Pravda does not object to the word independence! We also consider this label a trifle of such minimal importance as not to be worth a quarrel. But what is the use of such a label when independence is understood in the *Pravda* way? This is the fig leaf that hides the sinful body of the Stolypin formula.

6. "We will grant you the freedom to meet and express your views on unification [with Russia—Ed.]."

We think the above examples will suffice.

"It is our duty to teach the workers to be 'indifferent' to national distinctions. There is no doubt about that. But it must be the indifference of the *annexationists*. A member of an oppressor nation must be 'indifferent' to whether small nations belong to *his* state or *to a neighboring state,* or to themselves, according to where their sympathies lie. Without such 'indifference' he is *not* a Social-Democrat. To be an internationalist Social-Democrat one must *not* think only of one's own nation, but place *above* it the interests of all nations, their common liberty and equality. *Everyone accepts this in 'theory' but in practice manifests an annexationist indifference. There is the root of the evil."* "*The victorious proletariat can force no blessings of any kind upon any foreign nations without thereby undermining its own victory."*†

"Victorious socialism must necessarily establish full democracy and, consequntly, not only introduce the full equality of nations, but also *give effect* to the right of oppressed nations to self-determination,

* [V. I.] N. Lenin, "Itogi diskussii o samoopredelenii," *Sbornik Sotsial-Demokrata,* p. 23. [The last two sentences are stressed by Shakhrai—Ed.]

† Letter of F. Engels to K. Kautsky, in K. Kautsky, *Sozialismus und Kolonialpolitik* (Berlin, 1907), p. 79. [Engels' italics—Ed.]

i.e., to free political separation. The socialist parties which do not make clear in all their actions, *now, during the revolution, and after its victory,* that they will liberate the enslaved nations and build up relations with them on the basis of a free union—and free union is a false phrase without the right to secede—would be betraying socialism."*

But . . .

"The national cause comes first, and the proletarian cause second, say the bourgeois nationalists, and the Iurkeviches, Dontsovs, and such would-be Marxists repeat it after them. We say that the proletarian cause must come first because it protects not only the lasting and fundamental interests of labor and of humanity, but also those of democracy; and without democracy neither an autonomous nor an independent Ukraine is conceivable."†

Whose health should we toast, and to whom should we say, "Rest in peace"? [Ukrainian saying used in indicating a confusing state of affairs—Ed.] Do we have here more of the Stolypin formula or of Leninism? Let him decide who has studied in some seminary.

---

* [V. I. Lenin] "Sotsialisticheskaia revoliutsiia i pravo natsii na samoopredelenie: tezisy," *Sbornik Sotsial-Demokrata,* No. 1 [October, 1916, p. 1]. [Italics are Shakhrai's—Ed.]

† V. Il'in [Lenin], "Kriticheskie zametki po natsional'nomu voprosu," *Prosveshchenie,* Nos. 10–12 (1913).

Chapter XVIII

The Ukrainian Communist Party (Bolsheviks)

A handbill from the "Social Democracy of the Ukraine" to the Ukrainian workers, soldiers, and peasants was published in Kiev in November–December, 1917, at the time of the final break between the Central Rada and the Soviets, when the former, after allowing armed cossack troops to pass through its territory, began to disarm the "Bolshevik" Soviet troops on the eve of the First (Kiev) Congress of Soviets.

As was revealed at the Party conference held in Kiev in connection with the Congress, this proclamation was published by some members of the Russian Social-Democratic Party (Bolsheviks). To our regret, we have no copy of this proclamation, and did not even read it in its entirety, but we remember the beginning very well and what it contained (although not word for word). The proclamation began approximately as follows: "What? A new party? Haven't we enough of them yet?" Then the authors, admitting that there are already many parties, argued in favor of forming yet another—the party of Ukrainian Bolsheviks which made its appearance under the name of "Social Democracy of the Ukraine." This party was needed because no one was defending the interests of the Ukrainian workers and poor peasants, because the Ukrainian Social Democrats and Socialist-Revolutionaries were bound in with the bourgeoisie, and because the Russian Bolsheviks, although a fine revolutionary party, were still *katsaps*[1]—excuse the expression, the word used in the handbill was "Great Russian" or "Russian." At the conference this proclamation was protested as an antidisciplinary and antiparty act by some party members, although it is true that this protest was somewhat moderated by the conference's adoption of a resolution to establish an organization of Bolshevik party organizations and to name it the "Social Democracy of the Ukraine" as a subtitle to "Russian Social Democratic Workers' Party (Bolsheviks)."

We mention this little episode because it shows, first, when the concept of our "own" Ukrainian party first appeared and, second, because it reveals the evolution in the thinking of two persons. We think that this evolution is not accidental, not limited to personalities, but bears some social significance also.

One of the authors of this proclamation was Comrade Zatonskii. *At that time* V. Zatonskii publicly accused the Bolshevik party of lack of interest in the Ukrainian working masses. *Now* Comrade Zatonskii has the audacity to "inform comrades," but only in quotation marks, that the Ukrainian movement is not Hrushevsky's "invention," that the Ukrainian workers and peasants are really Ukrainian workers and peasants, that the Ukrainian peasant masses, "both kulaks and poor peasants," and "even" in the Katerynoslav and Kharkiv (Kharkov) regions, demand autonomy and a republic. Comrade Zatonskii reached this "chauvinist" and "nationalist" standpoint (in quotes) as a result of the following philosophical train of thought: "A Ukrainian nation? Oh yes!—and what is a nation?" It would be very interesting to know how he came to this change.

A very strong protest against this act, against the proclamation, was expressed by one man who attended both the conference and the congress—V. Shakh-Rai. At the time V. Shakh-Rai was opposed to a separate Ukrainian party and in favor of a one and indivisible Russian party. *Now* V. Shakh-Rai is a *samostiinyk* advocating an independent Ukraine and an independent party. The most fanatical nationalist and chauvinist. How did he come to make such a change? Did he suddenly become aware of a heightening of Ukrainian national feeling "in him and for him," or was it something else?

No, with regard to the Ukrainian feeling "in him and for him," he was always a nationalist and chauvinist.

And even at that conference, where he requested his protest to be recorded (regrettably the records have not yet been published, although much material is already lost), he took the part of a fanatical nationalist and chauvinist. As co-rapporteur on the Ukrainian national question against the superinternationalist point of view of the other rapporteur, he favored united Bolshevik committees, the creation of our own Ukrainian Central Committee (subordinate, in matters of all-Russian significance, to the Central Committee of the Russian Social-Democratic Workers' Party), and accepting the name Ukrainian Communist Party as a subtitle to the Russian Social-Democratic Workers' Party until such time as the Russian party also called itself communist. At that time Shakh-Rai opposed the appeal for a separate Ukrainian party. And at the Second (Katerynoslav) Congress he refused to undertake to establish the Ukrainian Organization of Bolsheviks proposed by Congress members registered in a Bolshevik section of the Party. What was the reason?

The reason was simple. At the decisive moment in the history of the Ukrainian and Russian revolutions, when the October overturn had thrown all socialists into the arms of reactionaries and counterrevolutionaries, when a terrible struggle was going on in every city, when even a small force could play a decisive role in the outcome of this struggle, it was impractical and foolish to create dissension among the Bolsheviks. At the time of the First (Kiev) and Second (Katerynoslav) Congresses it was necessary to maintain the closest organizational ties, as much in the interests of the struggle with the Russian (and Allied) counterrevolutionaries as in the interests of the struggle with Austro-German imperialism—with which Russia and the Ukraine were at war and with which peace had to be concluded. Maintaining the unity of the revolutionary front was in the interests of both the Russian and the Ukrainian revolutions. To be sure, it was felt that there were many Katerynoslavians among our members, but this was only a "little stiffness in the machinery" which would work itself out in the revolutionary process. The Party would recognize self-determination, would take the Ukrainian movement into consideration, and at a suitable time would implement article 5 of its resolution adopted at the 1913 Summer Conference.[2] The first step in this direction would be an all-Ukrainian organizational level within the party. In the worst possible case, that is, if the Katerynoslavians should get the upper hand, the Ukraine could still more easily free itself from this domination than from a counterrevolutionary victory. At the time, however, this opinion had not yet crystallized, because we were quite convinced that the party's internationalism was not merely verbal, Menshevik, and Katerynoslavian. In any case, if those days should return, V. Shakh-Rai would behave in the same way, despite his later experience. Things might have been different if there had been fewer Katerynoslavians, but this was secondary by comparison with the general historical content of the moment.

The revolutionary struggle from December, 1917, to April, 1918, provided much material on the party's attitude toward the Ukraine. The party lacked a definite line, and, what was more shocking, there were political intrigues. This is understandable. In the absence of a policy there can only be intrigue. People who until then had wondered if there was any Ukraine at all (and still wonder), who had always thought they were living in Southern Russia, could not have any policy, only intrigue. These intrigues occurred within their own circles as well as with respect to their Central Committee. The Central Committee sends its representatives (mind you, the Central Committee, itself; this means that another tune will be played henceforth). But the intrigues do not cease; on the contrary, they spread. Could it be that the Central Committee has no definite line? No, it is far away, unfamiliar with local conditions, and the information it gets is that everything is fine on the Shipka. The most striking examples of such intrigue were the proclamation of the Donets-Krivorih Republic (Donets-Krivoi Rog Republic) (the result of domestic intrigues) and the dispatch of the People's Secretariat delegation[3] to Moscow for peaceful negotiation of Ukrainian boundaries after Ukrainian independence had been declared at the Second (Katerynoslav) Congress (the result of Central Committee intrigues).

One's hair stood on end when this delegation was sent and the head of the Secretariat reported, after returning from Moscow, on how he had "fed nonsense" to his own party comrades. Why? He did not know himself—just for the sake of doing something.

The sending of the delegation was the culmination of intrigues on home [Ukrainian—Ed.] territory.

Next came the intrigues in connection with the liquidation of the Central Executive Committee and the "exile" intrigues, such as the Insurgent Nine, the chronic burial and resurrection of the Soviet Government of the Ukraine under various names (the People's Secretariat, the All-Ukrainian Executive Revolutionary Committee, the Provisional Workers and Peasants Government of the Ukraine), the proposed alliance with Soviet Russia, the creation of our own separate Ukrainian party, and The Communists of the Ukraine.

The reader should not retain the idea that we oppose these intrigues and the Communists of the Ukraine because of their Great-Russian, *katsap,* Russian character. On the contrary, we consider the strongest and most beneficial aspect of the Ukrainian party and government to be their connection with the Russian party.

The intrigues consist in the following:

As the noted historian, Kliuchevskii, characterized the empress Catherine II, she wanted to *seem,* but not to *be.*

Such is the case with this party and this government. They have nothing against seeming, but they do not want *to be* at any price. And what are they to be? There is no Ukraine, but there was Southern Russia, which became the southern part of the eastern territory occupied by Germany, and there was no Ukrainian movement, and there is none; there is "occupation and only occupation."

In the Ukraine they say, "if anything appears, cross yourself, and it will disappear."

Well, we cross ourselves and are spared these appearances. We see that this party is nothing but a regional committee of the Russian party. For us this has the following meaning: it *means* that the policy of the Katerynoslav party of the Communists of the Ukraine is the policy of the Russian party, that is, the policy of Soviet Russia, and it appears to be like the tattered sheet[4] which the housewife offered to the traveling boy and girl to cover themselves with when they stayed overnight in her house. What goes on underneath is shameful if seen. The Katerynoslavians feel very ashamed of themselves when told that to say they belong to the oppressed nation is clearly a lie.

Thus covering up with a sheet for the sake of appearance is also a part of the policy of Soviet Russia. We take a closer look at Soviet Russian policy—what an outrage. The Katerynoslav smell is quite distinct in Moscow as well.

The Peace delegation is in Kiev, and Kh. Rakovski is the darling of even the Black-Hundred public. What a wonder. It seems that terrible beasts are found in Kiev which cannot be seen anywhere else: court officials of the Shelukhyn variety. And these beasts think the Ukraine is, or ought to be, independent. And Kh. Rakovski declares that "the successor of the former Russian Empire is the Russian Soviet Federative Socialist Republic, and the former parts of the Russian Empire can become legal entities only when the R.S.F.S.R. agrees to it" (*Izvestiia Moskovskogo Soveta,* No. 113 (361) [June 6, 1918]). In *Kievskaya Mysl'* we find the argument made in one commission that a separating state should pay for all damages resulting from such separation (we lost our copy of this paper and cannot give the precise reference).

"Besides her *ethnographic and historical rights* to the riches of the Donets Basin Russia has other rights stemming from two well-known facts. The opening and exploitation of the Donets Basin was financed by the whole country, and, furthermore, it was mainly *migrant Russian workers* who were used *in the production of this concentrated wealth*"* (Kh. Rakovski, *Izvestiia Ts. I.K.,* No. 148 (412), [July 16, 1918]).

"At the conference table a stubborn fight is taking place over the Donets Basin. Referring to ethnographic rights, the Ukrainians demand a great part of it for themselves, leaving us with 12 percent

---

* ["K mirnym peregovoram s Ukrainoi: K voprosu o Donetskom Basseine (Rech tov. Rakovskogo)," *Izvestiia Ts. I.K.,* No. 148 (412) (July 16. 1918), p. 3. Italics are Shakhrai's—Ed.]

of the productive capacity and 30 percent of the coal beds. Of course we cannot agree to this. Besides, *a large percentage of the population of the Donets Basin is Great Russian;* we need only mention the fact that all the Donets industry—the blast furnaces, factories, mine installations—were built by the toil of *Great-Russian workers* from the central provinces who migrated to the Donets Basin in great numbers seeking employment"* (Kh. Rakovski, *Izvestiia Ts. I.K.*, No. 165 (429) [August 4, 1918] Italics ours).

What here is international and what national? What here is Soviet Russian policy and what is Rumanian diplomacy? What here reflects the struggle with the strongest beast in the world, the court officials of the Shelukhyn variety, and what is a service similar to that of the sincere friend who takes a stone to shoo away a fly from one's neck?

No one could answer us, and willy-nilly we had to turn to the writings and oral traditions of the Church Fathers where we found much that was instructive. For instance, Kh. Rakovski's assertion that the separate parts of the former Russian Empire may appear in the international arena only when they are allowed to do so by the Russian Federative Socialist Republic is the same as "joint determination of the future" of the oppressed nation by both the dominant and the oppressed nation. "All reactionaries and bourgeois grant, to the nations forcibly retained within the boundaries of a given state, the right to 'joint determination' of their fate in a common parliament. Wilhelm II also gives the Belgians the right to 'joint determination' of the fate of the German Empire in a common German Parliament."†

But we could not find a complete answer to our questions. One thing surprised us. Comrade N. Lenin recalls all sorts of events and questions and gives direct and straightforward answers. But why has he not said a word about the Ukrainian question? Could he possibly be in agreement with the Katerynoslav point of view, or Rumanian diplomacy? We notice the following in one of his 1913 articles on a dispute between the Bolsheviks and the liquidators[5] with respect to the nation's right to self-determination, the liquidators objecting to this formula as abstract and objectively foolish. On Semkovskii's[6] articles Lenin wrote:

* ["K mirnym peregovoram s Ukrainoi: Beseda s tov. Rakovskim," *Izvestiia Ts. I.K.*, No. 165 (429) (August 4, 1918), p. 2. Italics are Shakhrai's—Ed.]

† [V. I.] N. Lenin, "Itogi diskussii o samoopredelenii," *Sbornik Sotsial-Demokrata*, p. 12—Ed.]

"This is the sort of rubbish being published in the liquidators' organ of which Mr. L. Martov is one of the ideological leaders, the selfsame L. Martov who drafted the program and spoke in favor of its adoption in 1903, and even later wrote in favor of the right to secede. Apparently L. Martov now argues according to the rule:

> *No clever man is needed there;*
> *Better send Read,*
> *And I shall wait and see.*[7]

He sends Read-Semkovskii along and allows our program to be distorted and endlessly muddled up in a daily paper whose new readers are unacquainted with it!"*

And we—because of all these articles in the daily, weekly, bi-weekly, and monthly press, these diplomatic demarches and tattered sheets—were thinking:

"This is the sort of rubbish being published in the party organs, and stated at peace conferences in the name of that party, that government, that Russia, headed by Comrade N. Lenin, the selfsame Comrade N. Lenin who drafted the program and spoke in favor of its adoption in 1913, writing such magnificent articles as: 'Critical Notes on the National Question,' 'On the Right of Nations to Self-Determination,' 'Theses on Social Revolution and the Right of Nations to Self-Determination,' 'A Summing-Up of the Discussion on Self-Determination,' 'On the Pamphlet of "Junius."' Apparently, Comrade N. Lenin now argues according to the rule:

> *No clever man is needed here;*
> *Better send Read,*
> *And I shall wait and see.*

He sends Read—Katerynoslavians, Rakovskis—and permits people who know neither the program nor what they are talking about generally, to lie and confuse matters in the daily, weekly, monthly, and nonperiodical press, and at various peace conferences, before new readers and listeners who are not familiar with our program!"

Such was our opinion, and we thus came to the idea of relying on our own small abilities in treating this morbid question, of giving answers based on the writings and the oral tradition of the Church Fathers and on an analysis of trends in the development of national movements generally, and the Ukrainian in particular, in the given historical era, under the given concrete historical conditions, at the

* [V. I.] N. Lenin, "O prave natsii na samoopredelenie," *Prosveshchenie,* Nos. 4–6 (1914).

given historical moment. We have done the best we could. If anyone can do better, let him try.

And as a result of the "mind's cool observations and the heart's sorrowful notes" we have reached this conclusion:

"The Ukraine's only course is independence! Believe us, there is no other way." And there is nothing bad or harmful in that—for the Ukraine, of course, for the worker-peasant Ukraine. Nor, we think, for Soviet Russia. But, of course, not for the one and indivisible Russia of the Miliukovs and Rodziankos. You cannot satisfy everyone.

The surge of national consciousness and the intense will for a free, sovereign, and independent life revealed by the Ukrainian revolutionary national movement completely preclude the very thought of the Ukraine's return to the status of a colony of some other power. Sooner or later, through the difficult and bloody course of armed conflict or through agreement—the democratic way of resolving issues in dispute between neighboring countries—the Ukraine will be independent and sovereign not only in words but in reality. Either as the result of an extended diplomatic and armed struggle, by maneuvering among states, or through the revolutionary activity of its worker-peasant masses, the Ukraine will become independent. At best, the Ukraine will become completely free in the very near future thanks to the activity and consciousness of its national masses, and the more rapidly and fully this goal is reached the better it will be for the Ukraine and her neighbors. There will be fewer national quarrels and less hostility; the further progress of the Ukraine's economic, political, social, cultural, and spiritual life will be easier, and the Ukraine's contribution to the treasury of world culture will be greater. And on the other hand, the less strength and activity it manifests in the near future, the more drawn out is the independence process, the more the Ukraine has to rely on diplomacy or on external assistance—the longer will she remain in the morbid condition of an unsolved national question, and the more the poison of national hostility, quarrels, and incitement will hinder socioeconomic, sociopolitical, and spiritual-cultural progress. Revolutions not only reveal deeper springs and forces, not only reject all that is superficial and conventional, they are also the locomotives of history. Days in a revolutionary era are the equivalent of decades in more peaceful periods. What demands many long years in a peaceful era may be attained in a few months in a revolution. And just as steel is tempered in the conflagration of revolution, so peaceful development often rusts and corrodes it. If the Ukrainian national question is not settled now, during the revolutionary era, if it is handed on to posterity, like rust it will corrode the socioeconomic and cultural-political development of the Ukraine and its neighbors.

That is why it is so important that all the forces presently contending in the Ukraine, and because of the Ukraine, realize fully the importance of this decisive moment in history. This is especially true for the relations between the Ukraine and Russia. Many socioeconomic and cultural-spiritual links have been forged during the two and a half centuries of the Ukraine's confinement within the boundaries of tsarist and autocratic Russia, but, at the same time, so much filth has collected on these links that they have lost their elasticity and become stiff, incapable of bending with the turns of history. They crack and break, and the break is not clean; rails, beams, and ties point in different directions and intermingle in the most monstrous ways. This process is very painful for both sides of the break: rails and beams wound people; rocks, cement, and coal cover people; dust and chips are thrown in their faces, blinding them; and the crackling and roaring deafens them.

Instead of clearing away individual rails and beams and wasting energy attaching supports to walls which may fall in today or tomorrow, it is better to clear out the whole place, removing the old and installing new rafters.

The sooner this fact is realized, and the more clearly, the better it will be. Soviet Russia should realize this before all others. Kh. Rakovski spoke the truth when he said that the Russian Soviet Federative Socialist Republic is the heir to the Russian Empire. But the conclusion to be drawn from this is diametrically opposed to the one reached by Kh. Rakovski at the peace conference.[8] It should not be forgotten that Soviet Russia inherited not only a great state but also a lot of rottenness and dirt. One should inspect one's acquisitions with care; historical experience makes clear that some inheritances should be renounced in order not to ruin completely the possessions acquired through one's own efforts. Such is the case of the Ukraine. One should forget about the former Southern Russia and remember that the Ukraine rose in its place, forget about the former colony and remember that it is now a sovereign independent country—if not *im Sein* then *im Werden*—forget that workers came from Central Russia to work in the Donets Basin and will continue to come in the future, forget about the 2,100,000 Russians living among the 16,-500,000 Ukrainians and about the need, for their sake, to regain the birthright. Relations with the Ukraine must find a new set of foundations; they must be based on a real and alive—not a verbal—international unity. It is time to abandon the various scientific investigations demonstrating how insignificant are the ethnographic differences between Ukrainians and Russians, time to forget Valuevism, Stolypinism, and Mymretsovism, time to acknowledge sincerely the right of nations to self-determination, time, in short, to face the facts. It is time to implement Article 5 of the Resolution of the 1913 Summer Conference and reach the appropriate conclusion: either one way or the other. And this conclusion must be reached without fearing that others will differ. Forget about the pottage of lentils, sugar, coal, iron, or grain. These will take care of themselves. And when this is done you will have such an ally as cannot be acquired from any kind of one and indivisible.

The Ukrainian workers and peasants should also come to their senses. In the first place, this will help the Russian workers and peasants to their senses and, second, as the proverb states: Heaven helps those who help themselves.

For respect to develop it is not enough that all peoples be equal. It is still necessary that one have respect for oneself and that one compel others to respect one's will, one's language, one's person.

In the third place, a job once undertaken should be completed.

The Ukrainian workers and peasants were frightened by the occupation and the actions of the Central Rada. They burned their lips on hot milk, and some now even blow on cold water. Perhaps some are now repentant, but history cannot be turned back. The events of March, 1917, should not have been allowed to happen, but now only two courses lie before the Ukraine: to lie for decades like a rotten beam, poisoning the air with its sickness, or to season itself and forever be safe from all vermin and rottenness. It is better to be burnt to the ground than to lie like a rotten beam. Let even the ashes be scattered. One should be guided by the general, the total historical development, and not by a momentary aberration.

Up until recently we believed the proletariat would renounce various historical rights with relative ease, but the process is now seen to be much more difficult and complicated. We thought the historical process would quickly digest the warnings of the past and thus come to grips with it. We hoped, for instance, that the Communists of the Ukraine would face the facts, but now we see, at best, a strange breed of people whose heads are turned one way and bodies the other, whose heads, therefore, still look backwards. The process is much more difficult than we thought. We had hoped the Communists of the Ukraine would turn their faces forward on their own, but in vain.

> *It is useless to blunt even lead!*
> *Because where there is no good will*
> *There can never be any happiness!*[9]

And time does not wait, time flies.

Events follow upon one another with such extraordinary swiftness that the human brain can barely register them or gather their meaning. People live by old habits, guide themselves in their daily work by old habits of thought and action when the ground under their feet has already changed. They seize the torn shreds of olden times and try to sew them together, with one or two rails or beams they try to repair the dilapidated corners of an old building, by shoveling coal into a half-ruined oven they try to heat a fallen-down house. Such efforts must be either useless or injurious.

Such people cannot be convinced with words and polite notes in quotation marks. They can only be convinced by facts, because facts are stubborn things. Facts must be reckoned with.

Facts are taken into account even by the Russian landowners and capitalists who are familiar with the productive forces of the one and indivisible Russia and know them not in theory, not from reading, not abstractedly like the Katerynoslavians, but in reality, with every fiber of their being, with every empty pocket or empty purse. The Katerynoslavians have heard about productive forces from their uncle who was told by his uncle that he "saw how the *barin* dined." But the Russian landowners and capitalists have "dined" themselves, and their belching has not stopped yet. They have had to reckon with the facts. This may be because they are closer to these lower strata, these productive forces, and can see with their own eyes to what antagonizing the productive forces have led, what ties they have broken, where they lead, and what they really mean. Of course they cannot altogether forget the tasty productive forces of the one and indivisible—the soul rebels. It is absolutely necessary to regenerate the one and indivisible; it is the only one and indivisible way to get what remains for themselves. But they understand, even so, that one and indivisible is one and indivisible and that the old system cannot be completely restored. So they mumble about a federative status for the Ukraine, about guaranteeing it some rights on the basis of its national and state independence. To the extent they recognize the existence of the Ukraine and the Ukrainian people, they have faced the facts already.

This is not the case with the Katerynoslavians, mainly because they know the productive forces only in theory. For them these productive forces, finance capital, and combined enterprises are an abstraction and only an abstraction to which they cannot attach any real meaning because they know and use words they have read in fine books full of wisdom but do not know what's what, and it is therefore harder for them to face the facts. For them the real fact is their own shop, and this fact they can face. But the revolutionary storm tore the roof from the shop, shattered its walls, broke down the rafters; and now the Katerynoslav shopkeepers are gathering up bricks and pieces of iron and trying to rebuild their shop. They do not even realize that part of it is completely torn down and that their position is absolutely ridiculous. The *Svat* [matchmaker—Ed.] Kh. Rakovski appears with the *pidbrekhachi* [flatterers accompanying the matchmaker—Ed.] Katerynoslavians.

> MATCHMAKER: There is no independent Ukraine and will be none until the heirs of tsarist Russia agree to its independence.
> FLATTERERS: You bet, there is none! There was "Southern Russia," and now there is a southern part of the eastern territory under German occupation.
> MATCHMAKER: The Ukraine was invented by terrible beasts, "court officials of the Shelukhyn variety," because they want to be bureaucrats.
> FLATTERERS: They were not even beasts. It was just that some gentlemen suddenly became aware of Ukrainian feelings. The Ukraine exists only "in them and for them." In reality, there is "occupation and only occupation."
> MATCHMAKER: We are so generous that although you differ from us very little ethnographically and shun everything Ukrainian, even so we will guarantee you the Ukrainian language in schools and in governmental instituitons.
> FLATTERERS: Not quite! After all, we have hardly yet resolved the question—since the left Socialist-Revolutionaries prevented us. We will see later . . . this may breed chauvinism. . . .

This has happened once already. Do you know, dear reader, what the outcome was? The matchmaker and the flatterers were thrown out in contempt. The engagement fell through, and there was much shame and scorn.

This comedy should be made known to everyone. The Russian proletariat should be warned against such matchmakers and flatterers. The Ukrainian proletariat (including that portion of "Russian origin") should also be warned. It is a waste of effort to try and convince matchmakers and flatterers with words and respectful arguments for the comrades' information.[10] And these matchmakers and flatterers may even convince others that the Ukraine really does not exist, but has simply been invented by court officials of the Shelukhyn variety and other gentlemen who have feelings "in them and for them."

No, only facts can convince, because facts are stubborn things! Facts are to be reckoned with. Haven't we had enough of them so far? This means that we have to have more.

The most informative and convincing fact would be the birth of the *Ukrainian Communist Party (Bolsheviks)*.

This party must set itself the following objectives:

1. An energetic struggle with native Ukrainian, Russian, and world counterrevolutionaries, who have imperialist intentions of strangling the Ukraine. This is the easiest goal.

2. A struggle with those *samostiinyki* who will try to secure Ukrainian independence through diplomacy and orientation, if such a course leads to the danger of a new occupation or, more properly, indefinite prolongation of the present occupation. The seriousness of this danger is seen from Enno's telegram to the Directory and the German Council in Kiev. And the Directory's past gives no assurance that it will continue to reject the course followed by its proto-mother, the Central Rada, in February, 1918. *Ce n'est que le premier pas qui coute!*

3. To persuade the Russian proletariat, and the Ukrainian proletariat of Russian origin, by every step, every deed, every word, that the Ukraine exists, that there exists a Ukrainian people, and that the Ukrainian language in no way differs from international languages because it is unintelligible to those who do not know it. The more boldly this persuasion is undertaken the better it will be for the Ukraine and Russia and for the struggle with the world counter-revolution. The task will be difficult, especially at the outset, because there will be an immediate deluge of intimidating international words about nationalism and chauvinism. Fear deeds, but not words. Be alert against the deeds, not the words, and do what is appropriate. "Use a wedge to knock out a wedge!" [Russian saying—Ed.] And if you see the historical, ethnographic, and economic deeds done before your very eyes covered over and concealed by such international phrases as those of Kh. Rakovski or the Katerynoslavians—do not be afraid to be even a chauvinist or a nationalist. "Use a wedge to knock out a wedge!" *It is not only the historical right, but also the historical necessity and historical duty* of the Ukrainian worker and peasant to be a nationalist and a chauvinist at the present time.

Regrettably, even the most revolutionary and international section of the world proletariat, the Russian proletariat, gives evidence that the following were not empty words: "just because the proletariat has carried out a social revolution it will not become holy and immune to error and weakness."* Despite Marx's one-and-a-half or two-hour lectures on the necessity of independence for Ireland (even though it should later lead to federation), the English proletariat, even in the interests of its own liberation, has not yet managed to come out in favor of freedom for Ireland. And the German Social Democrats allowed themselves to be bound by their imperialists on August 4, 1914. To our regret we have seen facts and trends which confirm the well-known absolute truth that "it is much easier for a five-year-old girl than for a twenty-five-year-old maiden to preserve her virginity." [Ukrainian saying—Ed.]

Medical science informs us that it is better to anticipate sickness than to cure it after it has spread through the whole organism.

Therefore, it is better for the proletariat to anticipate possible errors than to wait for the time when possible errors (and selfish interests—attempts to saddle others) will lead it (the proletariat which has carried out a social revolution) inevitably to the realization that the "victorious proletariat cannot force happiness on an alien people without thereby undermining its own victory."†

4. To give effect to Petliura's thesis that the peasants and workers have become dominant all over the world. *Ergo*, we say, the peasants and workers should also become dominant in the Ukraine. *And this requires* the will to create Soviets of Worker and Peasant Deputies. To *safeguard this will* authority must be placed in the hands of these Soviets.

5. To implement, in fact and not in words or on paper, the independence and sovereignty of the Ukrainian Soviet Worker-Peasant Republic. This goal can be attained only by making the Ukrainian workers and peasants active and conscious and then relying on their strength.

"The Ukraine's only course is independence. Believe us, there is no other way." Whether through diplomacy and a common front with other states or through its own power and revolutionary consciousness, and the activity of its own workers and peasants, the Ukraine will be independent. For us, for the Ukraine (and for other countries generally) the latter way would be the best.

* [V. I. Lenin, "Itogi diskussii o samoopredelenii," *Sbornik Sotsial-Demokrata*, p. 25—Ed.]

† [*Ibid.*—Ed.]

Well, so be it; let us agree that "there is no other way." But why must the Ukraine defend its independence? Could the constitution of a one and indivisible Russia not include guarantees that the Ukraine has "rights based on its state and national identity"? An example from the Austrian constitution convinces us to the contrary. Paragraph 19 of the Austrian constitution reads:

> All nationalities of the state have equal rights, and every nationality has the indisputable right to preserve and develop its nationality and language.
>
> The state recognizes the equal right of every language used in the individual lands (*landesuebliche*) in schools, administration, and social life.
>
> In lands inhabited by several nationalities the state educational institutions shall be so organized that no nationality shall be forced to learn another local language (*Landessprache*) but shall be able to obtain all necessary education in its own language.*

One need only recall, for example, the red tape encountered by Ukrainian Galicia's every demand for a primary school, high school, or university for Ukrainians at precisely the time when this fine paragraph was in force to realize how great is the distance from fine words to fine deeds and how inadequate is a constitution for safeguarding in actuality the rights of small nationalities.

But this was bourgeois Austria, and the bourgeoisie draws up all sorts of constitutions to deceive people. This will not be so in a Soviet Ukraine united with Russia. We believed this up until recently, but our experience with the Katerynoslavians and some Soviet Russian diplomats has convinced us to the contrary. "O Lord, I believe; help thou mine unbelief!"

When Kh. Rakovski assures us that this Soviet government of the Ukraine will ensure a better use of the Ukrainian language in schools and governmental institutions, for the benefit of the Ukrainian workers and peasants, than those terrible beasts, the court officials of the Shelukhyn variety, we can say that Kh. Rakovski is a very fine man, and his words are friendly. But he is writing for the literate,[11] and literate Katerynoslavians have not yet solved this question in theory. As for the practice, the following trifle may shed some light.

---

* M. Ya. Lazerson, *Natsional'nost' i gosudarstvennyi stroi* (Petrograd: Kniga, 1918), p. 67.

At a gathering of the Communists of the Ukraine the question was raised of organizing courses for comrades preparing to go and work in the Ukraine. They had the spare time, and courses in administration were proposed to help fill this spare time. One of us, a "clever kho-khol,"[12] sincerely welcomed these preparations and proposed that the Ukrainian language and history, that is, the language and history of the people whom they were preparing to self-determine, be made compulsory subjects. Of course, the proposal was rejected, and this is not surprising since it happens to many proposals. But what is important is that the resolution was labeled chauvinistic and nationalistic. The gathering did not comprehend the proposal of the "clever khokhol," who just wanted to "poke an aching tooth" [Ukrainian saying—Ed.] and find out what kind of internationalism theirs was. Now this "clever khokhol" thinks that if the Ukrainian language is an expression of chauvinism and nationalism, and if the Communists of the Ukraine are afraid of being poisoned by this nationalism and chauvinism, may it not happen that, after having attended various instructive courses on the Cheka,[13] they will turn their talents to introducing nationalism and chauvinism in the Ukraine?

We believe your nice friendly words, dear Comrade Kh. Rakovski, but help thou our unbelief! Guarantee at least short-term courses in Ukrainian for the Communists of the Ukraine, at least in the beginning, at least in the way such short-term courses were organized for court officials of the Shelukhyn variety.[14]

Personally we are of the view that when the Ukrainian Communist Party (Bolsheviks) is organized, it will be a great historical service (and this, at least, will force the Communists of the Ukraine to attend short-term courses to learn Ukrainian, the language of the people whom they will self-determine). Because after two and a half centuries of colonial life the Ukraine is now in such a condition that it needs not only a guarantee of what it has already but also a revolutionary creation of a new school in the Ukrainian language. This demands more than just guarantee or permission; it demands that good will without which no happiness is possible.

Thus for an independent Soviet [Ukraine—Ed.]* not only is "independence the only course; believe us, there is no other way," but this is equally necessary in order to do away with the consequences of the tsarist administration.

* [The original reads "Soviet Russia," but it should logically read "Soviet Ukraine"—Ed.]

Therefore, a Ukrainian Communist Party (Bolsheviks) is needed not only because "there is no other way," but in order to anticipate "possible errors and selfish interests—attempts to saddle others," and to struggle for a truly independent and sovereign Ukraine in which the Ukrainian workers and peasants would be rulers, not only in the Directory's proclamations but also in reality.

The Ukrainian Communist Party (Bolsheviks) is also needed for the struggle at home, in the Ukraine, with its native nationalists and chauvinists, those who support the unity of the different classes of Ukrainian society.

"To all nationalist-socialists we say that there are two nations in every modern state, two national cultures in every national culture. There is the Great-Russian culture of Purishkevich, Guchkov, and Struve—and there is also the Great-Russian culture typified by the names of Chernyshevski and Plekhanov. The Ukraine has the *same two* cultures as Germany, France, England, the Jews, and so forth. While it is true that the majority of Ukrainian workers are under the influence of Great-Russian culture, it is equally true that the ideas of Great-Russian democracy and Social-Democracy offer a parallel to the Great-Russian clerical bourgeois culture. In fighting the latter kind of 'culture' the Ukrainian *Marxist* will always bring the former into focus and say to the workers: 'We must snatch at, make use of, and develop to the utmost every opportunity for intercourse with the class-conscious Great-Russian workers, their literature and their ideas, as the fundamental interests of *both* the Ukrainian and the Great-Russian working class movements demand it.'

"If the Ukrainian Marxist allows himself to be swayed by his *quite legitimate and natural* hatred of the Great-Russian oppressors *to such a degree* that he transfers even a particle of this hatred, if it be only estrangement, to the proletarian culture and proletarian cause of the Great-Russian workers, this Marxist will *ipso facto* get bogged down in bourgeois nationalism. Similarly, the Great-Russian Marxist will get bogged down not only in bourgeois, but also in Black-Hundred nationalism, if he loses sight for a moment of the Ukrainian demand for complete equality or for their *right* to form an independent state.

"The Great-Russian and Ukrainian workers must work together and, as long as they are living in a single state, act in the closest organizational unity and concert, toward a common or international proletarian culture, displaying absolute tolerance toward the language in which the propaganda is conducted and toward the purely local or purely national *details* of that propaganda. This is the im-

perative demand of Marxism. All advocacy of the segregation of workers of one nation from those of another, all attacks upon Marxist
'assimilation,' or attempts, where the proletariat is concerned, to set
up one national culture as a whole in opposition to another allegedly
integral national culture, and so forth, are *bourgeois* nationalism,
against which a ruthless struggle must be waged."*

This second part of every nation cannot avoid mistakes and cannot immediately rid itself of the influence of the first part of the
nation. The process is much more difficult and complicated than is
generally assumed.

In any given case we are confronted with the need to do everything possible to avoid the difficulties raised by possible errors.

The formation of a Ukrainian Communist Party (Bolsheviks)
will lead sooner to a genuine unity than will the hypocritical unity
of a tattered sheet or of "adaptation to the local situation." This is
an evil, but it is less of an evil than the internationalism of the
Katerynoslavian.

We view the formation of a Ukrainian Communist Party (Bolsheviks) as a *process* resulting from the everyday revolutionary
struggle in the Ukraine. The workers and peasants of the Ukraine
will soon become convinced of the absolute need for such a party
from their own experience, not from our arguments.

This party will cover both the former Russian and the former
Austrian Ukraine, that is, Galicia.[15]

It will be constructed on the territorial, not on the national,
principle. There are others in the Ukraine besides the Katerynoslavians. And the need for such a party has been felt not only by the
Ukrainian masses. Proclamations have been issued not only by the
"Social-Democracy of the Ukraine."[16] And it was not only Ukrainian
workers and peasants who asked one of us at the Katerynoslav Congress[17] to organize a Ukrainian Communist Party (Bolsheviks).

In Poltava between June and December, 1917, rather lively
negotiations were under way between the Ukrainian Social Democrats and the Bolshevik Committee.[18] The Poltava Ukrainian Social
Democrats made up the most revolutionary section of their own party,
and the Poltava Bolshevik committee was represented not by a "clever
khokhol," and in fact not by "khokhols" at all, but by non-Ukrainians. These negotiations, though never concluded, guaranteed the
party's unity and influence much better than the words of the Ka-

---

* [V. I.] N. Lenin, "Kriticheskie zametki po natsional'nomu voprosu,"
Prosveshchenie, Nos. 4–6. [Italics are Lenin's—Ed.]

terynoslavians which although revolutionary were only words. But the time was not yet ripe. The proper historical basis was absent.

Right now there is such a basis. It has been created by the occupation and only occupation.

Long live the Ukrainian Communist Party (Bolsheviks) !

Long live the Independent Worker-Peasant Soviet Ukraine!

Long live the Russian Socialist Federative Soviet Republic.

Chapter XIX

We Nationalists. We Chauvinists.

Police! Nationalists, chauvinists have been born! Already we hear these shouts too hastily directed at us.

Yes, we are nationalists, we are patriots, we are chauvinists. We, sinners, confess that there is such a "disease in us and for us." But we merit indulgence for our sincere confession and admission. And to convince the reader that our confession is really sincere, we will tell him everything that we intend to do. We confess to him that we want to infect with this disease the Russian and Ukrainian proletariat (that is, the Ukrainian proletariat of Russian origin, since that of Ukrainian origin has been infected long ago). We want to spread the virus of Ukrainian nationalism-chauvinism among the circles of Russian and Ukrainian (of Russian origin) workers, making them supporters of Ukrainian independence.

This is a serious sin, but . . . we confess it.

But everyone who confesses—and not only the nobleman on Tverskaya Street in Moscow (but, we think, not on the Friedrichstrasse) —is obliged to seek shelter in some authority, to quote someone in justification: "I certainly do confess, but this proves I am a good and sincere man, because I could have chosen not to confess."

And furthermore, every social-chauvinist, socialist-nationalist, social-patriot, not to mention every pure socialist, of necessity quotes "Marx." In introducing a genus of communist nationalists, communist chauvinists, communist patriots, we want at the same time to show that we are not just any kind of chauvinists, nationalists, or patriots, but real Marxists. The reader will of course see at once that this is some sort of imitation communism. We confess this also. But the reader must recall that we live in an era of wars of various kinds and that, for that reason, the sciences of war have become widespread. One need not have studied at the seminary to know about adaptation to local conditions. So, if others can use this approach, so can we. We will show you that ours is no worse than yours. The only difference is that we repent and tell in advance where and how we are going to adapt ourselves to local conditions. Of course, our adaptation is not identical with the adaptation of the Kateryno-slavians. Our tactics rather remind one of those of Sviatoslav[1] (and Caesar, as we have been assured by some good friends) who did not hide but openly declared: I march against you! We also tell the Russian and the Ukrainian (of Russian origin) proletariat that we will attack them with the disease of Ukrainian nationalism, that we want to infect them with the independence of the Ukraine. Is this, then, adaptation to local conditions? We will say no more. Thus we quote Marx to justify ourselves, to deceive you, and maybe for other reasons as well.

After all, do what you want, dear friend.
You're not a fool, think for yourself.[2]

W. Liebknecht (father of Karl Liebknecht) wrote memoirs about Marx. His book contains one chapter of great interest to us, and we think the reader will not take it amiss if we quote nearly all of it here. It will be a dessert after the Katerynoslav meal.

Here is the chapter:

PATRIOTISM AND ITS CONSEQUENCES*

"Even during the worst times of exile we often had a very merry life —of course, only those who were lucky enough not to die of starvation. We did not suffer from the blues. And if the world before us seemed shut off by a wooden wall, we adopted the motto of the Shef-field workingmen: A short life and a merry one. But who thought of dying? Never say die! Often we reveled madly—the worse off we were, the more reckless. There was only one remedy against the grinning misery: Laughter. Whoever gave way to somber thoughts was infected by the disease and swallowed up. But misery flies from a ringing merry peal of laughter like the devil from a cockcrow.

"And this is the remedy which I recommend to all, for it is good and will remain so as long as the world lasts. We never laughed more than when we were in the worst of circumstances.

"What did we not do in our reckless humor, sometimes even re-lapsing into our old student pranks. One evening Edgar Bauer, an

* V. Libknekht [W. Liebknecht], *Vospominaniia o Markse*, translated from the German by A. G. Gaplon (Petrograd: Rabochaia Biblioteka Ts. K. R.S.D.R.P., 1918), pp. 66–69.

acquaintance of Marx's from their Berlin days and not yet his personal enemy despite the Holy Family (*Die Heilige Familie*), had come to town from his hermitage in Highgate in order to make a beer trip—*Bierreise*. The problem was to take something in every pub from Oxford Street to Hampstead Road—even if one confined oneself to the minimum, taking this something was a very difficult task, considering the enormous number of pubs in that part of the city. But we went to work undaunted and managed to reach the end of Tottenham Court Road without accident. There loud singing issued from a public house; we entered and learned that a club of Odd Fellows were celebrating a festival. We met some of the men in the party, and they at once, with true English hospitality, invited us foreigners to go with them into one of the rooms. We followed them in the best of spirits, and the conversation naturally turned to politics—we had been easily recognized as German fugitives. The Englishmen, good old-fashioned people, who wanted to divert us a little, considered it their duty to revile thoroughly the German princes and Russian junkers. By Russian they meant Prussian junkers, as Russia and Prussia are frequently confounded in England, and not alone on account of the similarity of name. For a while everything went smoothly. We had to drink to the health of many and to propose, and listen to, many a toast.

"Then the unexpected suddenly happened.

"Patriotism is a disease which attacks sensible men only in foreign countries; for at home there are so many miserable defects that everyone not afflicted with paralysis of the brain or spinal meningitis is proof against the bacillus of this political 'vertigo' which is also called chauvinism or jingoism and which is most dangerous when those attacked by it sanctimoniously lower their eyes and bring God's name to their lips.

" 'In Saxony I praise Prussia, in Prussia I praise Saxony,' said Lessing. This is a sensible patriotism that tries to cure the defects of the home country by the example of the real or imagined good in foreign countries. I had benefited from this saying of Lessing's at an early age, and the only drubbing I have received since the days of my youth was due to an attack of patriotism I once had when abroad. It was in Switzerland. On an occasion when, in the Haefelei in Zurich, Germany was abused too violently, I jumped up and said to the gentlemen: Instead of abusing Germany, you should be glad of the German misery, for to it alone Switzerland owes her existence. Once the table is cleared in Germany, and out there in Italy and France also, Switzerland will cease to exist: German Switzerland will of itself revert to Germany, French Switzerland to France, and Italian Switzerland to Italy. It was really a silly political forecast that I kept on tap there, but it was a crazy time of life, and my patriotism had been aroused. My speech did not meet with pronounced approval— as I could gather from the frowning physiognomies of my hearers. There was violent opposition, but the conversation gradually slackened and, as it was becoming rather late, I turned homeward. On the landing place near my lodging several forms suddenly appeared before me, and, before I had become aware of it, I was tripped—I fell down and before I could get up I received several very hard blows, whereupon my assailants took to their heels. I never found out who they were, but I did not doubt for a moment that my patriotic speech in the Haefelei had procured this anonymous drubbing for me.

"And now in London, in the company of the kind old Odd Fellows, I and my two companions, 'without a country' got into quite a similar fix. Edgar Bauer, hurt by some chance remark, turned the tables and started ridiculing the English snobs.* Marx launched into an enthusiastic eulogy of German science and music—'No other country,' he said, 'could have produced such masters of music as Beethoven, Mozart, Handel, and Haydn, and the Englishmen who had no music were actually far below the Germans who had hitherto been prevented from any great practical achievements only by their miserable political and economic conditions, but who would yet outclass all other nations.' I have never heard him speak English so fluently. I, for my part, pointed out in strong terms that political conditions in England were not a bit better than in Germany (here Urquhart's pet phrases came very much in handy), the only difference being that we Germans realized that our public affairs were deplorable, while the English did not know it—whence it was apparent that we surpassed the English in political intelligence.

"Our hosts' brows began to cloud, just like that time in the Haefelei, and when Edgar Bauer brought up still heavier guns and began to allude to English hypocrisy, one could hear the expression 'damned foreigners' issue from the company, first in a low voice and then louder. Threatening words were uttered, brains began to be heated, fists were brandished in the air, and—we were sensible enough to choose the better part of valor and managed to effect, not entirely without difficulty, a passably dignified retreat."

* A snob, whom Thackeray describes in a very excellent satire, pretends to be a "brave, free brother" but actually grovels before titles, rank, and money.

We will soon show that our own patriotism has much in common with this Marxian patriotism (but not only with this).

First of all, these things happened in emigration. Are we not emigrants as well?

Then, with regard to laughter, the reader has probably noticed that we are not against it. He probably thinks that this laughter reveals our "khokhol humor," an upsurge of "in us and for us," of Ukrainian feeling. We confess to being guilty of this sin also. But look: Marx, Liebknecht, and their friends were not "khokhols" at all, but they laughed a lot and often. Hence our laughter contains something more than just "khokhol humor." First of all, laughter is the appropriate attitude to take toward something funny (Marx said it, too). And, again, laughter is the only help against the hypochondria which is sure to come over one after hearing the ideas of the Katerynoslavians.

To continue, we also became sick with patriotism while abroad. On the other hand, in our native land, the Ukraine, we were and will be sincere supporters of internationalism; we tried and will try to correct the defects of our fatherland by pointing to what is good abroad—what is really good and not just imagined so. We have said, and will say: native girls are very beautiful, real angels—I wonder where all the malicious wives come from?

But we are going to talk about "international" girls as well.

We know quite well that "just because the proletariat has carried out a social revolution it will not become holy and immune to error and weakness. But it will inevitably be led to realize this truth by possible errors (and selfish interest—attempts to saddle others)."*

The Russian proletariat made a social revolution, and praise and respect is therefore due it. But this does not mean that it did not inherit from tsarist Russia a bit of imperialism or of historical and ethnographic rights. On the contrary, our own experience convinces us that it did not rid itself of weaknesses and errors. If we succeed in this—through this pamphlet, for example—the better it will be both for you and for us. No?—what else can we do? Then you will have to convince yourselves later when the potential errors become actual. Then it will be more difficult, of course, but what can we do about it? You call us nationalists and chauvinists. We are not afraid of words and do not pursue them, leaving that to the Katerynoslavians, but we are willing to state openly and directly, without any

* [V. I.] N. Lenin, "Itogi diskussii o samoopredelenii," *Sbornik Sotsial-Demokrata*, p. 25.

words, that we would not fear even genuine chauvinism if that should be the only way. "Use a wedge to knock out a wedge!" Our nationalism and chauvinism are wholly and completely determined by your internationalism—as you do, we do too. The only difference is that you hide behind words, while we do not hide. We confess!

We think we have shown your internationalism has a strong Russian smell. And the very worst policy, in our opinion, would be "a sanctimonious lowering of the eyes with Marx's name on the lips."

And every time you send matchmakers (*svaty*) like Kh. Rakovski and flatterers like the Katerynoslavians, we will openly and directly warn against international ladies.

Dear and beautiful ladies, both native and international, please do not understand us as meaning that we do not respect you. By God, we like you very much, we love you ardently. We are ready to die for your kisses, your dark eyes, your most lovely conversation. But . . . why do you want to get married? Why do you love until . . . the marriage vows? You say that your marriage is so free that one can separate whenever one wants! If so, then why have a wedding? Let us rather love one another and sing the song:

> *I'll love when I want and stop when I want.*
> *My heart is free. Life is given us for enjoyment!*
> [Russian song—Ed.]

Furthermore, our patriotism, nationalism, and chauvinism were born in the Katerynoslav Odd Fellows Club. When we were in their club we saw that each of them considered it his duty to revile the Ukrainian nationalists, the Central Rada, the General Secretaries, the *Selospilka* (Village Associations) , and the Military Councils. This aroused "in us and for us," so to speak, the love for our borsch and our dumplings . . . and we were able to understand Heine's feelings when he was saying goodbye to Paris, the merry French people, and his wife, to return to Germany:

> *Painfully I long*
> *For the smell of turf, for the dear*
> *Sheep of the Lueneburger heath*
> *For sauerkraut and beets.*

> *I long for tobacco smoke,*
> *Court-counsellors and night-watchmen,*
> *For low-German, black bread, even for rudeness,*
> *And for blond vicars' daughters.*[3]

We cannot keep from remarking that the Katerynoslav Odd Fellows are very much mistaken when they act as if there were no Ukraine, but only Southern Russia which became the southern part of the eastern territory under German occupation, as if there were no Ukrainian movement, and as if there were just occupation and only occupation.

We do not think that those "speeches" (in quotation marks) of Comrade Zatonskii lead anywhere, just as nothing came of the applications to Alexander Ivanovich Khlestakov[4] by Peter Ivanovich Dobchynskii and Peter Ivanovich Bobchynskii. Bobchynskii wanted permission for his illegitimate son to bear his name, while Dobchynskii asked Khlestakov to inform various officials, ministers, and, if possible, the tsar, that in such-and-such a city lives Peter Ivanovich Dobchynskii. Comrade Zatonskii wants them to know that there are Ukrainian workers in Kherson, Katerynoslav, and Kharkiv (Kharkov) provinces. And so, he says please inform the comrades in Moscow that there are Ukrainian workers and peasants in Kharkiv (Kharkov) and Katerynoslav provinces, and that they have been self-determining themselves the way the Central Rada wanted only because we abandoned them to the Ukrainian social-patriots. Now there is not a drop of nationalism or chauvinism among them: both vanished with the Central Rada. We may be permitted to call them Ukrainians because they are the children of the Central Rada, even though bastards, born out of wedlock (of course, they were born the same way as in wedlock). "Let them be so called," answers the good Katerynoslavian, Alexander Ivanovich. "Good, I'll tell them. I will even tell the People's Commissars, if I see them."

We want to make an open and straightforward speech in praise of the Ukraine (because otherwise the analogy with Marx will not be complete). You say the Ukraine is this and that, but can you show us another country where such tasty borsch is cooked or such savory *varenyky* and dumplings? Where can you get a better drink? And the Little Russian hopak! And do you know the rich and beautiful literature of the Ukrainians? Do you know that we have our own poets, scholars, writers, singers, composers, and artists? And what sense of humor can match that of the "khokhol"? Who is as clever as a "khokhol"? You revile the Central Rada, but do you realize that it has performed a great historical service? Do you know that M. Hrushevsky,[5] who invented the Ukraine, is a great scholar? Do you know that V. Vynnychenko is an admirable and talented writer of whom any literature would be proud? Do you realize that one could learn a lot from M. Hrushevsky and V. Vynnychenko, while the wind whistles through the heads of the Katerynoslavians? One can learn a lot from the Katerynoslavians, not by listening to them, but by observing them. And do you know that . . .

"Damned khokhols!"— (we hear all around us). Good people! Enough of this analogy. Let us stop here. We will not continue according to Marx. What if he did come close to a beating, while Liebknecht himself was thrashed? Is it possible that we need a thrashing too?

If you want to continue the analogy in order to convince us, we declare ahead of time that we are already convinced.

During our whole chauvinistic period we have heard only one unanswerable argument. While in S.,[6] one of us read a report on the Ukrainian revolution and said that the Ukraine should be independent; at that one of the comrades present asked mysteriously: "And what does Lenin say to this?" When he was unable to find out what Lenin said "to this," in a private conversation he called the speaker a counterrevolutionary and recommended that he be reported to the Cheka. But it was a private conversation, and the comrade was talking about something very familiar—as he was from the Cheka himself.

The second time was when one of us, the same fellow in fact, happened to discuss Ukrainian independence with the People's Commissar for Nationality Affairs, Comrade Stalin. He also frightened us with the Cheka, but, noticing that we were scared, hastened to add: "No, no, I'm joking!" We confess that we are afraid of that joke, and we said that this was the sort of argument with which we could not help but agree. We cannot answer it. And we cannot but confess yet another sin. We are afraid of the Cheka, but not very much. Because we are "khokhols," and the "khokhols" are clever enough to outwit the devil. We knew that they would try to intimidate us with the Cheka, so we sent our own man to the Cheka quite early. It was M. Skrypnyk,[7] the former head of the former People's Secretariat. And this former head of the former People's Secretariat is a *samostiinyk*—it was after his own report at the Second (Katerynoslav) Congress of Soviets that the Soviet Worker-Peasant Ukraine was proclaimed independent. This resolution of the All-Ukrainian Congress of Soviets has not yet been repealed by anyone, and it can be repealed only by a new All-Ukrainian Congress of Soviets.

Is it possible that M. Skrypnyk will not dare

"To oblige his little native fellow"?

We must confess to still another sin: we are "afraid" of the following:

The "Manifesto of the Provisional Worker-Peasant Government of the Ukraine" states: "Anyone employing compulsion or persuasion to carry out the orders of the hetman or the Central Rada is liable to immediate execution by shooting." Petliura threatens to punish under martial law anyone who helps the hetman to flee or who urges the formation of an organization to seize the government. The hetman, God be praised, has already renounced his throne, but still threatens all who do not obey his legal authority.

We confess and declare to all three: We are peaceful people and only advise the Ukrainian workers and peasants to become the rulers at home because peasants and workers have already become the rulers throughout the world. Again, and finally, we advise the Congress of Soviets to declare the independence and sovereignty of the Ukrainian Worker-Peasant Soviet Republic.

But if our ideas are erroneous, pay no attention to them. Ah, yes, in hiding? Afraid? Are we confused? Why did we become infected with nationalism and chauvinism? Alas, you.

We again repent and apologize. We regard as the veriest truth the words of Lord (landowner!) Henry in Oscar Wilde's *The Picture of Dorian Gray*—"the only way to rid oneself of a temptation is to yield to it!" Well, we did yield, and we do not see that this is impermissible. But if it is not permissible, we will be further guided by the words of Kant (an intellectual!):

"No one can force me to say the opposite of what I think, but I will not dare to say all I think."

We will only alter the statement a little, as follows: No one can force us to say the opposite of what we think, but we will keep silent when forbidden to say all we think.

We say what we knew and know what we are talking about.

Who is there that only says what he knows? And who knows as much as he says?

Chapter xx

Questions for Comrade Lenin

Comrade Lenin, we would also confess to you. This pamphlet was written mainly for you. It was no accident that we often quoted from your articles. And we did so not only to quote an authority or to hide under your name (as if to imply that Lenin himself thinks this way), not only to be honest with ourselves, nor to pretend that what others have said is ours. In some few cases these motives were there, but this is not the point.

The point is this. We do not know who has more right to say about himself, *L'état, c'est moi*—Louis XIV in France or you in Soviet Russia. In any case, you could have said it many times within your party of Bolsheviks long before the October revolution of 1917. We have frequently noted during the revolution how skillfully you directed the mass movement, how accurately you used slogans, how correctly you took the pulse of the historical moment. Over and over we were convinced that you hold your position because you deserve to hold it. We watched diligently your every step, gesture, and word, and everywhere we have found balance and responsibility. For us, all your zigzags and turns merge into a single whole, each supplementing the other and clarifying it. To all this is given the name of Lenin, the great proletarian leader—great not only historically but also *morally-politically*.

This was our opinion. But we watched with diligence not only you, Comrade Lenin, but also the character and tendencies of the historical moment—the historical events, historical personages, and figures of lesser caliber which in one way or another comprise the content of that historical process about which you can say: *Tout cela, c'est moi!*

But for almost eight months we have been observing facts which seem to us altogether different from what is on the facade. What a mystery! Is there something we do not see? are we blinded by something "in us and for us," or does it just seem that way.

We happened to play a small part in the circles of your party (and ours) in the Ukraine. As we see it, the experience of the Ukrainian revolution proves that we were defeated not only by the arrival of the Germans, the occupation and only occupation. On the contrary, had there been no occupation and only occupation, we fear that our party would have been driven out of the Ukraine just the same and that it would not have been revived for a long time. One of us who was in the center in March and April, 1918, asked about this historical experience: What defeated us, was it something stronger than we were, or was it something "in us and for us"? Of course, it was both one and the other. But can that which was "in us and for us" be considered only a minor stiffness in the machinery?

Nobody could give us an answer. We did not actually try very hard to get an answer, since asking some would have been a waste of effort, while others had no time because of more important matters. We did not rely on anyone, but collected every possible bit of material on the history of the Ukrainian movement, compared it with other historical movements, and also examined and translated a few things into Ukrainian "word for word, omitting neither commas nor abbreviations."[1] In the meantime various things happened, facts poured in, and we considered the facts not only of the present, but of the past as well, not individually but in the common framework of the historical era, in the light of the general historical process of the socioeconomic, cultural-political, and spiritual development of humanity. Thus we came around to the independence of the Ukraine.

Of course, one could hardly help noticing this "white crow" in the party circles, and for a long time we were greeted at best with half-sympathetic shakes of the head: poor fellow, he is sick with a morbid question! And to the ironic question: are there many of you? for a long time we had to answer: One! Now our position is better: there are more of us than are given on the cover of our pamphlet. And the number has increased because of the existing facts; this assures us that soon there will be a great many of us. These are the facts of the Katerynoslavians and the Soviet Russian diplomats.

We happened to observe one sincere supporter of unity and enemy of Ukrainian independence, after reading your decree granting independence to Latvia and Lithuania and the further decision of the People's Commissariat for Foreign Affairs refusing independence to the Ukraine and Georgia, strike his sides and shout: "They make me a *samostiinyk*!"

While observing the facts of the Katerynoslavians and the diplomats and comparing them with the "writings and oral tradition of the Church Fathers," we frequently struck our sides in surprise (although by then we were already *samostiinyks*). How can such facts be perpetrated by a Soviet Russia headed by Comrade Lenin, who may be called the Jesus Christ of self-determination in Russia (excuse our use of this Katerynoslav seminary jargon: you become like the company you keep)? It is impossible to leave Lenin out and say that he knows nothing about it, that these things are happening against his will. It would be wrong to think that he is a Katerynoslavian or a Rumanian internationalist, and the writings and oral tradition stand in the way of such a deduction. What should one do? Go to Lenin himself and ask? Nothing would come of it: (1) he is too busy, (2) he will ask: How many of you are there? (and we answer: One!) And he will say he has no time to bother with petty intellectuals.

But the "khokhols" are clever. They ignore petty intellectuals and only consider the facts. Good! We have sweated over this thing for eight months in order to confront Comrade Lenin with the fact and make him say openly what he thinks, to dissipate all doubt.

Finally we were able to do this. We confront you with the fact, Comrade Lenin, with this pamphlet. Now we not only *request,* but *demand* a direct answer. You *must* answer, because the question is now being raised not by petty intellectuals, but by the facts. Not enough facts? There will be more to come.

> *Thou must! Thou must!*
> *and though my life it cost me!*[2]

Comrade Lenin, we must also confess to this.

We are not devoid of Ukrainian feelings. They are "in us and for us" (in one of us they may even take a "heightened" form).[3] They exist at least to the extent enabling us properly to understand the words of T. Shevchenko:

> *I love her, oh so very much,*
> *My poor Ukraine,*
> *That I will curse the holy God*
> *And lose my soul for her!*[4]

Yes, we love the Ukraine, love it as a live historical individual. This we confess. "In us and for us" the Ukraine is not only a geographical term, a word, or a name for the former Southern Russia.

But, leaving this aside, we must also confess that your answer will have much more meaning for us. "In us and for us" your answer on the Ukraine will serve as a verification of internationalism, a test of the pious words of international unity and solidarity of the working masses. Throughout its history humanity has heard so many fine words, and seen so many acts contradicting these words, that we have the right to suspect any fine word which leads . . . to some different deed. Comrade Lenin! Prove to us the necessity of uniting the Ukraine and Russia, but do not use the Katerynoslav arguments: show us where we are mistaken, in what way our analysis of the real conditions of life and development of the Ukrainian movement is incorrect; show us on the basis of this concrete example: how paragraph five of the 1913 resolution, that is, paragraph nine of the Communist Program, should be applied—and we will openly and publicly renounce the independence of the Ukraine and become the sincerest supporters of unification. Using the examples of the Ukraine, Georgia, Latvia, Lithuania, Byelorussia, and Estonia, show us how this principle of proletarian policy—the right of nations to self-determination—has been implemented. Because we do not understand your present policy, and, examining it, are apt to seize our heads and exclaim:

Why did we offer our silly cossack heads?

Or we feel like sitting down with that "half-dead Zaporozhian," Semen Palii, bowing our heads, and sighing:

> *Why was I born into this world,*
> *Why do I love my Ukraine?*[5]

Comrade Lenin, we have one more thing to confess to you.

No matter how desirable and important your answer is for us, no matter how much importance we attach to it, the world does not depend on it. And we will not stop believing beautiful words about the international unity and solidarity of the working masses. At the worst we will only repeat what we stated above: that it is much easier for a five-year-old girl, than for a twenty-five-year-old one, to preserve her virginity. So let's be on the alert.

Comrade Lenin. You may accuse us of hypocrisy when we state that your answer is of such great importance for us. If this were so, then we would "pause for a while, and stop spreading chauvinism and nationalism." We must confess to this also.

We believe that everything has its own logic. The road selected by Soviet Russia was not accidental. Everyone is influenced by this

road, the "children of the beggar and of the tsar," and this includes
you, Comrade Lenin. But we do not shut our eyes to the fact that
if anyone can avoid the influence of this road, you are that person,
Comrade Lenin. We express sincerely everything that has accumu-
lated "in us and for us" during the revolution.

For example, two reasons led us to advise the Ukrainian workers
and peasants to form a Ukrainian Communist Party (Bolsheviks).

First of all, we do not want to find ourselves in the position of
the very good man described by H. Heine:

> *By the sea, by the desert night-cover'd sea*
> *Standeth a youth,*
> *His breast full of sadness, his head full of doubtings,*
> *And with gloomy lips he asks of the billows:*
>
> *"O answer me life's hidden riddle,*
> *The riddle primeval and painful,*
> *Over which many a head has been poring,*
> *Heads in hieroglyphical nightcaps,*
> *Heads in turbans and swarthy bonnets,*
> *Heads in perukes, and a thousand other*
> *Poor and perspiring heads of us mortals—*
> *Tell me, what signifies man?*
> *From whence doth he come? And where doth he go?*
> *Who dwelleth amongst the golden stars yonder?*
>
> *The billows are murm'ring their murmur eternal,*
> *The wind is blowing, the clouds are flying,*
> *The stars are twinkling, all-listless and cold,*
> *And a fool is awaiting an answer.*[6]

Second, our proposal to the Ukrainian workers and peasants to
form a Ukrainian Communist party (Bolsheviks) is the logical outcome of our analysis of the present state of the Ukraine. We think
we show respect both to the Ukraine and to you, Comrade Lenin,
when we state that our sincerest wish is that the Ukraine have its own
Lenin.

In your speech on "the revolution and petty-bourgeois democrats," at the November 27, 1918, gathering of responsible communists, you, Comrade Lenin, stated, among other things: "They [the
petty bourgeoisie] attacked us with malice bordering on madness
because we were supposed to be offending their patriotic feelings, but
history has so changed the situation that patriotism is now on our

side."* It is true that we went against the patriotic feelings of the
petty bourgeoisie. This shows how difficult it is for human thought
to adapt itself to new objective conditions. And the objective position
of Russia throughout the whole revolution was such that the Bolshevik party was, and proved itself to be, the most patriotic party in
the best sense of the word. At the beginning of the revolution the
Cadet leader, P. Miliukov, tried to prove at a joint session of the
State Duma that the Russian revolution was a national revolution,
meaning, in his view, that Russia undertook its revolution in order
to carry the war to a victorious end—that is, endlessly. He should
have said that the Russian revolution was national mainly because
it reflected the desire to escape from the war at any price, in order
not to be totally ruined and plundered. The instinct of national
self-preservation pushed the country to revolution in February and
again in October. If not for the ill-fated offensive of June 18, if not
for the German threat to Petrograd in August, September, and October, 1917, it is doubtful that the Bolsheviks would have been able
to take over the leadership in Russia. The Paris proletariat took the
government into its own hands in 1871 only when the treachery of
the French bourgeoisie had become manifest. In order to disarm the
Paris proletariat General Trochu conducted the country's defense in
such a way as to let Paris fall into Prussian hands as soon as possible.
Is the analogous behavior of the Russian bourgeoisie an accident?
Just recall the behavior of General Kornilov at the Moscow Conference, the surrender of Riga, and Rodzianko's words: "Petrograd
is in danger. I think we should let it go . . . when Petrograd is taken
the fleet will be destroyed all the same . . . Some ships there have
become completely corrupt and appear to possess no combat potential. . . . It is feared that the central institutions (that is, the
Soviets, etc.) in Petrograd will be destroyed. My answer to this is that
I will be very glad to see them go, as they have given Russia nothing
but trouble."† In this there are many instructive analogies. The
malice of the petty bourgeoisie at the time can only be explained
by their inability, as a class, to understand this. Now they are convinced that the Bolsheviks, while doing international work, were
at the same time working for the national cause.

But the interesting part of this process is the following. The
petty bourgeoisie became convinced of Bolshevik patriotism and

* ["Revoliutsiia i melkaia burzhuaznaia demokratiia: rech tov. Lenina
na sobranii otvetstvennykh rabotnikov Kommunistov 27 noiabra, 1918 g.,"
Izvestiia Ts.I.K., No. 265 (529) (December 4, 1918), p. 2—Ed.]

† We quote from *Robitnycha Hazeta*, No. 161 (October 17, 1917).

rushed into the party and Soviet institutions. There is nothing wrong in this, and sabotage should actually have ended a long time ago. But the petty bourgeoisie always remains the petty bourgeoisie. They are subject to proletarian influence and influence the proletariat in return. And notice carefully how even the party press greets the enlargement of Soviet territory. Do we not hear, along with joy at the spreading of revolution, other notes such as that Russia is returning to her prewar boundaries? And when they discuss Russia and what it should be, listen carefully: they talk about Russia as it was drawn on Il'in's map before the war. Is this an accident? Oh, no! Internationalism is internationalism, and the fact that we regenerate Russia as Russia is beside the point. Of course, generally speaking, there is nothing wrong in this yet. Only, what will happen to self-determination? Why, for instance, is the Ukraine being united with Russia? Because it declared in favor of such unification (the facts prove the contrary) or because it is Southern Russia? And what kind of Ukraine is being unified? Is Galicia going to be included, that is, the Ukraine beyond the Volochyska? And where should we stop and say "enough, further on it is no longer 'ours'; they have not 'self-determined' themselves for us."

When one examines the spread of Soviet Russia and the practice of self-determination from this vantage point, it is very difficult to see to what extent your self-determination, Comrade Lenin, differs from that of Woodrow Wilson.

Comrade Lenin, please do not feel insulted. By God, we respect you as a proletarian fighter more than many of your flatterers do. And in order not to offend you, but to explain what we think, we will quote the following anecdote. We are usually "clever khokhols" and usually use "khokhol humor," but right now we do not feel like laughing. But why should we not laugh, even though we have a creepy feeling? Why should we not follow W. Liebknecht's advice: "a short life but a merry one?"

And so listen to the anecdote, Comrade Lenin.

One Saturday evening a priest had a hearty supper, kissed his wife, and sat down in his study to write the sermon for the next day's service. As usual, at home he wore an old cassock and an old pair of trousers (people think that priests do not wear trousers—we also confess to this). Having written the sermon, he put it into a pocket of the old trousers and went to sleep with his wife. We are not interested in how he slept. But in the morning, when church bells rang, he donned a new cassock and new trousers because it was a feast day and old clothes would not be becoming. When the time came for the sermon, the priest went up before the altar and faced his parishioners: "Brothers in Christ!" and searched in his pockets. "Brothers in Christ!"—feeling here, feeling there, and still no sermon. "Brothers in Christ! Do as it is written, as it is written in my old trousers, amen!"

That is all.

Comrade Lenin. We are sure you will agree with us when we say that priest's parishioners were completely abstracted from what they should really do. And it was not odd that later, outside the church, people should have commented on the sermon: "That funny *batiushka* [priest] speaks 'so unclearly' and gives an 'abstract formula.'"

Comrade Lenin! We think the priest could not deliver his sermon because he was completely abstracted from what he had written and put in his old trousers. And he wrote that sermon as it should have been written, according to the "writings and oral tradition of the Church Fathers."

But let it be. What is the point of this anecdote? The point is this. Those parishioners are not only the petty bourgeoisie but also your closest comrades. Read the articles in the official organ of the Communists of the Ukraine and remember what you wrote about "little boys in short pants" in such articles as: "Critical Notes on the National Question" and "On the Right of Nations to Self-Determination" on Saturday evening . . . excuse us . . . on the eve of war and revolution. These "little boys in short pants" are now dancing around you and not only are not ashamed but even smack their lips with relish and make obscene gestures.

Comrade Lenin, we will make a confession here too. We fear that you too are in the priest's position and have forgotten what was written and laid away in your old pants. There would be nothing odd in this. In his memoirs, published on the first anniversary of the October revolution in 1918, Comrade K. Radek relates that when he first came to Russia the first thing he noticed in your office was a pair of old trousers. K. Radek had bought these trousers for you himself in Stockholm, and he did not even recognize them they were so ragged and torn; it was shameful to look at.[7]

Alas, how we wish we were mistaken! How we wish you had not forgotten what was written in the old trousers.

Comrade Lenin, please forgive us this anecdote. Not because you are Chairman of the Council of People's Commissars, tsar and God of Soviet Russia, but because you are Lenin, because we consider you an honest political leader who can make mistakes but will not do an evil thing.

And, by God, it is not we who are your frightful enemies. Much more frightful are your friends, the Katerynoslavians, and the diplomats. You can settle accounts with us quickly: "Get him, I know who he is!" [Ukrainian saying] And not even a grease spot will remain. No, you will have to try to get out of the fix which you and Soviet Russia are in thanks to the various Katerynoslavians, and diplomats.

And when your "little boys in short pants" dance such a hopak, making fun of their own program and ridiculing self-determination, what will the petty bourgeoisie do then?

And what then will remain of your wonderful note to Wilson about his principle of self-determination? It will be just a "scrap of paper." And the sharp and venomous sarcasm of this note—will it not be turned against you and against Soviet Russia? When the Zaporozhian cossacks wrote their letter to the Sultan, they stated straight out: "Here it is the same day as where you are . . . For that you can kiss us someplace. . . ." Openly and directly. But you should not be the same as Wilson.

Show us how your self-determination differs from Wilson's.

Comrade Lenin, look around you, at how much political depravity there is. When "little boys in short pants" have their fun, when diplomats have conferences with court officials of the Shelukhyn variety, this is the result of the policy which Soviet Russia is following, which you are following, on the national question. This policy has neither rudder nor sails and is going nowhere.

Are we mistaken? In what? Just show us.

Comrade Lenin, we could say a lot more, but we had better wait for your answer.

And when we are *physically* and *technically* capable of saying everything we want to say, we think we will say it.

And with regard to the Ukraine, Comrade Lenin, we will say this. Now only two answers are possible: either, (1) an independent Ukraine (with our own government and our own party) , or (2) the Ukraine as Southern Russia (in which case you will have to curb the "little boys in short pants," or else they will spoil the business) .

Comrade Lenin, we ask you also to answer the following questions, which are of personal interest to us.

Can one remain a member of the Russian Communist Party and defend the independence of the Ukraine?

If it is not possible, why not. Is it because one is not supposed to defend Ukrainian independence, or because *the way we do it* is not permitted.

If the way we defend Ukrainian independence is not permitted,

how may one defend Ukrainian independence and be allowed to
remain in the Russian Communist Party?

Comrade Lenin, we await your answer! Facts have to be reckoned with. And your answer, just as your silence, will be facts of
great import.

We have said what we know, and said it as well as we could.
Let him who is able, say it better.
Comrade Lenin has the floor.

December 15, 1918 to January 14, 1919 (N.S.).
December 2, 1918 to January 1, 1919 (O.S.).

Notes

CHAPTER II

1. These lines are borrowed from Shevchenko's poem "Haidamaky," in a corrupted form. Shevchenko's lines are: "The days pass by, the summer flits away."

2. "Loser pays"—words allegedly spoken by David Lloyd George.

CHAPTER III

1. The words of the Ukrainian drinking song.

2. The Black Hundreds—a pejorative name given to two extreme right-wing Russian nationalist organizations implicated in pogroms against Jews and revolutionaries.

CHAPTER IV

1. It is also known as the July, 1917, offensive against the Austrians, toward Lvov in Galicia. The authors are using the Julian calendar; hence for them it is the June offensive. Hereafter in the notes the Julian calendar dates are in parentheses following the Gregorian calendar dates.

2. The port of Murmansk was built in 1915–16 when the Central Powers cut off the Russian Baltic and Black Sea supply routes. Allied forces occupied the Murmansk area in 1918–20. Archangel was the principal port of Russia until the foundation of St. Petersburg (Leningrad) in 1703. It too was occupied by Allied forces (including an American contingent) and the White Army from 1918 to 1920.

3. The reference here is to the Siberian government established on June 30, 1918. It had support among the officers; it suppressed the Soviets; it

sanctioned the formation of nonpolitical trade unions and undertook to raise an anti-Communist army by conscription.

4. The authors refer here to the events surrounding the activities of the Czechoslovak brigade which had fought in the World War on the Russian side, had survived the collapse of the front, and having been augmented after the February Revolution by volunteers from Austro-Hungarian prisoners of Czechoslovak origin, was being transported out of Russia via the Trans-Siberian Railroad.

5. The Ukrainian Central Rada was first formed on March 3 (17), 1917, by the Society of Ukrainian Progressives (TUP), later renamed the Ukrainian Party of Socialist Federalists. From April 4 to 9 (17 to 21), the Rada convened an All-Ukrainian National Congress, comprising delegates from various professional bodies, the town dumas, the zemstvos, and the peasant cooperatives. Drawing on the delegates to the various congresses of peasants', workers', and soldiers' deputies being held at this time, the Rada was gradually enlarged to about eight hundred members. In mid-June (old style) the Rada established a cabinet, the General Secretariat. In effect the Rada became a provisional Ukrainian parliament. It was overthrown in a coup on April 29, 1918, headed by General Skoropadski.

6. The official name was Vseukrainskyi Tsentralnyi Vykonavchyi Komitet (VUTSVK) (All-Ukrainian Central Executive Committee). The supreme executive organ of the Ukrainian Soviet Socialist Republic was elected on December 14 (27), 1917, in Kharkiv (Kharkov) by the First All-Ukrainian Congress of Soviets. Its name at that time was the Central Executive Committee of the Soviets of the Ukraine.

7. The Rada's delegation at Brest Litovsk had four representatives: Alexander Sevriuk, Nicholas Levytskii, Nicholas Liubynskii, and Vsevolod Holubovych. Later on S. Ostapenko replaced Holubovych. The Soviet Russian delegation headed by Trotsky did not turn against the Rada's delegation until it became obvious that a separate Ukrainian peace was in the making. Then on January 23, 1918, the Central Powers were informed that "the workers' and peasants' government of the Ukrainian Republic has decided to send two of its own delegates to Brest, but as a supplementary part of the Soviet Russian delegation." These two delegates were: E. Medvedev, chairman of the Central Executive Committee of the All-Ukrainian Soviet of Workers', Soldiers', and Peasants' Deputies, and V. Shakhrai, People's Secretary for Military Affairs and author of *Do Khvyli*.

8. The reference here is to the government of Soviet Russia.

9. Max Hoffman (1869–1927), German general in the First World War. As

the chief of staff on the eastern front he helped negotiate the Treaty of Brest Litovsk.

10. Sir John Picton Bagge, British representative in the Ukraine, who was then consul general in Odessa, proposed to organize financial and technical aid for the Ukraine. As a condition for accepting this aid, the Ukrainian government demanded the recognition of the Ukraine as an autonomous state by France and Britain. Later on, under the impact of the Bolshevik talks with the representatives of the Central Powers in Brest Litovsk and the presence there of the Ukrainian delegation, Bagge was appointed as the special representative of Great Britain in the Ukraine.

11. The reference here is to Alexander Shulhyn, who was appointed ambassador to Bulgaria.

CHAPTER V

1. The Octobrists intended to work with and develop the constitutional possibilities of the tsar's manifesto of October, 1905, ordaining that a duma participate in constitutional monarchy. They were strongly anti-revolutionary and anti-Marxist. Together with Cadets they dominated the first Provisional Government of Russia.

2. The Socialist-Revolutionary Party was founded by various Populist groups in 1901. It was primarily an agrarian party whose program called for the overthrow of the autocracy, the establishment of a classless society, and the socialization of the land. The reference in the text is to the Socialist-Revolutionary dominated government of the Committee of Members of the Constituent Assembly (*KOMUCH*) established in Samara.

CHAPTER V I

1. Paul P. Skoropadski (1873–1945), Hetman of the Ukraine (April–November, 1918). A descendant of Hetman Ivan Skoropadski, he was a Russian combat general who Ukrainianized the corps he commanded in 1917.

2. The reference here is to an appeal made to the Germans on February 12, 1918, by the Ukrainian delegates in Brest Litovsk. On February 23, the Rada government issued a statement in which it referred to the German troops as harbingers of "peace and order in our land."

3. The coup against the Central Rada took place on April 29, 1918, when a Farmers' Congress arranged by the Alliance of Landowners in the Ukraine proclaimed Skoropadski as Hetman of the Ukraine. The coup

took place with the knowledge and the support of the German army. He was, in turn, deposed by the uprising led by the Directory of the Ukrainian People's Republic.

4. Free Cossacks (*Vil'ne Kozatstvo*) was a spontaneous semi-military movement which had arisen during the summer of 1917 for the purpose of preventing banditry in the villages as a result of the disintegration of the regular police force. The Rada did not attempt to utilize this source of support, and by autumn it had come under the influence of Skoropadski. Some critics of the hetman have claimed that he refused to allow the Free Cossacks to defend the Rada in Kiev against the Bolsheviks. See John S. Reshetar, Jr., *The Ukrainian Revolution, 1917–1920: A Study in Nationalism* (Princeton: Princeton University Press, 1952), pp. 146–47.

5. F. A. Lyzohub (1851–1928), leader of the Poltava zemstvo: minister of internal affairs and premier under the hetman. He replaced N. Vasylenko in the premiership and resigned when, on November 17, 1918, the hetman published a declaration of a federative union with Russia. The new cabinet was now composed chiefly of Russian monarchists, including the Russians, Sergei Gerbel as premier and Georgii Afanasiev as minister of foreign affairs in place of Dmytro Doroshenko, a Ukrainian.

6. A. Shulhyn, a member of the Ukrainian Party of Socialists-Federalists (UPSF) and head of the faction of Ukrainian soldiers and workmen in the Petrograd Soviet of Workers' and Soldiers' Deputies, was the secretary for nationality affairs in the Secretariat of the Central Rada. He was then appointed the representative of the Ukraine in Bulgaria, and subsequently was a member of the Ukrainian delegation to the Paris Peace Conference and the head of an extraordinary mission to France.

7. The reference here is to Abishag, the Shunammite woman, David's attendant in his old age and the cause of Adonijah's murder. I Kings 1:2. The authors used Shevchenko's poem *The Kings* (*Tsari*) for the version. See M. Rylskii, ed., *Antolohiia Ukrains'koi poezii* (Kiev: Derzhlitvydav, 1958), I, pp. 282–83.

8. The reference here is to the Ukrainianization of the Cabinet following Lyzohub's conversation with Baron Mumm. It appears that the motive of the Germans in this case was prevention of the reunion of the Ukraine with Russia. See Reshetar, p. 170.

9. *Visnyk Ukrains'koho Viddilu Narodnoho Komisariatu Sprav Natsional'nykh*. Official organ of the Ukrainian section of Narkomnats. See A. V. Lykholat, *Zdiisnennia Leninskoi Natsional'noi Polityky na Ukraini, 1917–1920* (Kiev: Naukova Dumka, 1967), pp. 165–66.

10. The reference here is to the Congresses of the Russian Constitutional Democrats meeting with the approval and the participation of members of the hetman's administration. A congress of industrialists, bankers,

and landowners, which later formed the Union of Representatives of Industry, Commerce, Finance, and Agriculture (*Protofis*) was also held. Many of the Russians consistently demanded a restoration of the pre-revolutionary way of life and made overtures to the victorious Allies.

11. Reference to the various Ukrainian military formations that came into being as a result of the Ukrainianization in 1917 of detachments of the Russian army usually against the will of the Russian command. Only two such formations, Haidamatskyi Kish Slobids'koi Ukrainy and Haidamats' kyi kinnyi polk im. K. Hordienka, became, in February, 1918, units of the Regular Ukrainian army.

12. Fedor Keller (1857–1918), Russian general, known for his anti-Ukrainian sentiments. He participated in anti-Ukrainian pogroms in Galicia in 1914. In 1918 he became commander in chief of the hetmanate's forces. He sought to suppress the rebellion against the hetman but was defeated on November 18, 1918, in a battle near Motovylivka by the Sich Sharpshooters under the command of Colonel E. Konovalets. Keller was captured and executed by the Directory.

13. Baron Alfons Mumm von Schwarzenstein (1859–1924), the envoy of Germany to the Ukraine.

14. The reference here is to the Ukrainianized Cabinet of Lyzohub.

15. The reference is to Gerbel's cabinet, which was composed chiefly of Russian monarchists. The only person in the new cabinet who could pass as a Ukrainian nationalist was education minister V. P. Naumenko. The new premier, Sergei Gerbel, a landowner who had served as governor of Kharkiv (Kharkov) province under the tsar, had been minister of supply in Lyzohub's cabinet. The establishment of this cabinet was a vain effort on the part of the hetman to gain favor with the Allied powers. Its task was to implement the new policy of federation with a future non-Bolshevik Russia.

16. The new orientation was promulgated on November 14, 1918, in an edict which stated that "the former vigor and strength of the All-Russian state must be restored on the basis of the federative principle." This action hastened the outbreak of the mass uprising against the hetman's regime.

17. The reference here is to the delegation of May 2, 1918, to General Groener, Eichhorn's chief of staff, which was composed of Social-Democrats, Socialist-Revolutionaries, and Socialist-Federalists. They protested German involvement in the monarchist coup and followed this up with a note. It was he and not Mumm, as the authors claim, who responded with a laconic "too late."

18. The Directory's call to revolt against the hetmanate was issued on November 15, 1918. On December 14, 1918, the hetman abdicated.

19. The whole paragraph is an adaptation borrowed from Gogol's *Taras Bulba.*

1. The Directory came into existence on November 13 following a secret meeting of representatives of the Ukrainian National Union, an organization which had been seeking to Ukrainianize the hetmanate. The Cabinet of the Directory consisted first of three and later of five members: V. Vynnychenko (USD) as chairman, F. Shvets (Peasant Union), S. Petliura (USD), P. Andrievskii (Independent Socialists), and A. Makarenko (Independent, representative of the railwaymen's association). On December 26, 1918, the Directory formed a government (Rada Narodnykh Ministriv) with Volodymyr Chekhovskii as prime minister. The Directory ceased to exist as a collective body on May 21, 1920.

2. V. Vynnychenko (1880–1951), Ukrainian writer and statesman. He was one of the organizers of the Revolutionary Ukrainian Party (RUP), founded in 1900, member of the USDRP and its Central Committee following the demise of the RUP. He was editor of the party journal *Borot'ba,* and chief editor of the party's newspaper *Robitnycha Hazeta.* He was also vice-chairman of the Central Rada and the first premier of its General Secretariat—the autonomous Ukrainian government. He became head of the All-Ukrainian National Union at the time of the hetmanate, and participated in the rebellion against the regime. Politically, Vynnychenko vacillated between the program of the Social Democracy in behalf of a sovereign Ukraine and the Bolshevik conception of the Ukrainian Soviet Republic. In 1919 and again in 1920 he tried to negotiate with Lenin for an independent Ukrainian Soviet Republic but without success. In 1920 he returned to the Ukraine to become deputy premier of the Ukrainian S.S.R. and its People's Commissar of Foreign Affairs, but then resigned and returned to exile in Vienna. His *Rebirth of a Nation* (3 vols., 1920) deals with the history of the revolution (1917–20) in the Ukraine. After 1921 he resided in France where he died in 1951.

3. Symon V. Petliura (1877–1926), Ukrainian national-revolutionary leader. He played an important role in the establishment of an independent Ukrainian People's Republic in 1917. He was in charge of military affairs in the General Secretariat, and became commander in chief of the Directory's forces after the ousting of Hetman Skoropadski. He was assassinated in Paris by Samuel Schwartzbard.

4. The authors are incorrect in referring to Petliura's call to insurrection as the program of the Directory. The Directory did indeed issue a programmatic declaration on December 26, 1918, which was authored

by Vynnychenko who was then the head of the Directory. Petliura, who commanded the armed forces of the new government was not, in fact, in complete accord with the objectives as stated in the declaration. On the other hand, Vynnychenko felt that Petliura acted inappropriately in issuing his own summons to an uprising, thereby giving it a personal rather than a programmatic character. Petliura's proclamation was issued on November 15, 1918, under his and General Osetskii's signatures at the headquarters of the Ukrainian Republican forces in Konotop.

5. This Latin is incorrect. It should read *Amicus Platonis, sed magis amicus veritatis sum* (I am a friend to Plato but a greater friend to truth). The Latin in the text actually translates: "Plato is a friend, but truth is a greater friend."

6. V. Skorovstans'kyi is the pseudonym of V. Shakhrai. His brochure *Revolutsiia na Vkraini* was published in the Ukrainian language in 1918. The pamphlet appeared subsequently in two Russian language editions.

7. Skoropadski issued the *Hramota* upon assuming office on April 29, 1918. Some felt that the choice of the term *Hramota* was designed to break with the Rada's tradition of issuing Universals and was indicative of Muscovite influence in the new government. Reshetar, *op. cit.*, p. 148 n4.

8. The reference here is to the Ukrainian Party of Socialists-Federalists (UPSF). Its socialism was moderate advocating the transformation of Russia into a federation of free states. After the treaty of Brest Litovsk, however, it supported the Ukraine's independence. At its head were S. Iefremov, A. Nikovskii, E. Shrah, A. Lototskii, P. Stebnytskii, A. Viazlov, A. Shulhyn, and, at one time, D. Doroshenko and M. Hrushevsky. This party played a very important role in the political life of the Ukraine by supplying a large number of officials to the Rada, the Directory, and even to Skoropadski's government. The principal organ of the UPSF was *Nova Rada*.

9. The Ukrainian Social-Democratic Workers' Party (USDRP) had developed out of the old Revolutionary Ukrainian Party (RUP). The social basis of the party consisted of Ukrainian workers and a group of radical intelligentsia. In its political program and in its ideology the party was similar to the other Social-Democratic parties of Europe. Having first advocated an autonomous Ukraine in a federated Russia, it subsequently supported independence for the Ukraine. Among its leaders were L. Iurkevych-Rybalka, V. Vynnychenko, V. Chekhovskii, I. Mazepa, B. Martos, M. Porsh, L. Chykalenko, S. Petliura, and others. This party played a very important role in the government of the Rada and of the Directory.

10. The reference here is to the secret negotiations carried on between the hetman and the leadership of the Ukrainian National Union for the purpose of Ukrainianizing the hetman's cabinet. V. Vynnychenko was at the same time negotiating with the Bolshevik's "peace" delegation in

Kiev in order to obtain their support for the projected insurrection against Skoropadski.

11. The authors are inaccurate. Vynnychenko was negotiating with the hetmanate for the Ukrainianization of its cabinet.

12. The quotation comes from Petliura's summons to a rebellion against Skoropadski as published in "Vozzvanie Petliury," *Izvestiia VTsIK.*, No. 256 (520) (November 23, 1918), p. 2.

13. Peter Bolbochan (1883–1919). Colonel in the Army of the Ukrainian People's Republic, who fought against the Bolsheviks in 1917 when they invaded the Ukraine for the first time. Under the hetmanate, he won the Crimea for the Ukraine. Beginning with the fall of 1918, under the Directory, he was commander of the Ukrainian Republican Forces in Left Bank Ukraine. For his attempt to take over the command of the Zaporozhian Corps in Proskuriv in June 1919 he was arrested, court-martialed, and executed.

14. For Soviet reports of this event see: "Na Ukraine," *Pravda*, No. 268 (December 10, 1918), p. 1.

15. At this time the Rada was disarming Bolshevik-dominated Russian troops in the Ukraine because these troops were in the process of occupying Ukrainian territory in the name of Soviet power. Because of the confrontation between the Rada and the Bolsheviks, the Rada was permitting the passage through its territory of the Don Cossacks, who were returning from the front home to the Don, and with whom the Bolsheviks were already fighting.

16. The reference here is to an unsuccessful effort by the Rada to establish federal ties with the governments of the Don, the Kuban, the Caucasus and Siberia; as also with the autonomous administrations of Moldavia, of the Crimea, Bashkiria, and the Bolshevik government of Russia. One of the reasons for the failure of the effort was the refusal of the Don Cossacks to accept the Bolsheviks as the government of the Russian Republic.

17. The reference here is to Vynnychenko's speech at the First All-Ukrainian Congress of the Soviet of Workers' and Soldiers' Deputies on December 4, (17), 1917, in Kiev, protesting the ultimatum of the Russian Bolsheviks in Petrograd to the Ukrainian Central Rada in Kiev. In the ultimatum the Bolsheviks accused the Rada of "Carrying on a two-faced bourgeois policy . . . by disorganizing the front . . . disarming the Soviet troops in the Ukraine (and) . . . supporting the Cadet-Kaledin conspiracy . . . *in refusing to let through troops against Kaledin. (Izvestiia,* Dec. 6 (19), 1917.) The Ukrainian Bolsheviks were embarrassed by the ultimatum. Consequently, the author of *Do Khvyli,* one of their leaders, attempted to explain away the ultimatum as "a misunderstanding," assuring the Congress that the Ukrainian Bolsheviks, who "had just as much right to call themselves Ukrainians as the representatives of other

parties," would do their utmost to bring about a peaceful settlement between the Bolsheviks and the Rada.

18. Alexei M. Kaledin (1861–1918), Russian general and the Don Cossack *ataman.*

19. The reference here is to Vynnychenko's efforts to work out in his novels the conception of amorality, according to which honesty to oneself permitted the person to commit any crime as long as his feeling, reason, and will remained in harmony. Vynnychenko's novel *Honesty to Oneself* was published in 1911.

CHAPTER V I I I

1. According to the Ukrainian Soviet Encyclopedia the Manifesto of the Provisional Government of Ukraine was issued on November 29, 1918. See *Ukrains'ka Radians'ka Entsyklopedia,* VIII, p. 460, XIV, p. 401

2. The reference is to the Provisional Russian Government of Prince George Lvov.

3. The reference is to the First Coalition Government of Prince Lvov, formed on May 18, 1917.

4. The reference is to the Second Coalition Government with Kerenski succeeding Lvov as the premier.

5. The Directory formed by Kerenski on September 14 (September 1 O.S.), 1917, as a result of Kornilov's attempted coup. The Directory was in fact composed of five members.

6. Existed from the end of November, 1918, to the beginning of March, 1919. Established by the Central Committee of CP(b)U in Kursk. The following were members of the government: V. K. Averin, F. A. Sergeev (Artem), K. E. Voroshilov, V. P. Zatonskii, E. I. Kviring, Iu M. Kotsiubynskii, and others. Later on these individuals were added: M. I. Podvois'kii, O. H. Shlikhter, V. I. Mezhlauk, M. L. Rukhymovych, O. I. Khmel'nytskii, and others. On March 7, 1919, by a decision of the Third All-Ukrainian Congress of Soviets, the Provisional Government was renamed the Workers-Peasant Government of the Ukrainian Soviet Socialist Republic.

7.   *Ihr naht euch wieder, schwankende Gastalten,*
     Die früh sich einst dem trüben Blick gezeigt.
Cf. J. W. Goethe, *Die Faustdichtungen* (Zürich and Stuttgart, Artemis Verlag, 1962) , V, p. 141.

8. A Central Executive Committee (Tsentral'nyi Vykonavchyi Komitet, Ts. V. K.) was elected on December 25, 1917, by the First All-Ukrainian Congress of Soviets meeting in Kharkiv (Kharkov). Five days later (De-

cember 30) the CEC formed the first Soviet government of the Ukraine which was called the People's Secretariat of the Ukrainian People's Republic. It was composed of twelve People's Secretaries. These were: H. Kotsiubynskii, its head, M. Skrypnyk, V. Shakhrai, V. Zatonskii, H. Lapchynskii, E. Medvedev, G. Martianov, E. Bosh, S. Bakinskii, V. Aussem, V. Luksemburg, E. Luhanovskii. Five of the Secretaries were Ukrainians in an obvious attempt to give the new government as much of a national Ukrainian appearance as possible so that it would be better able to compete with the Central Rada.

The People's Secretariat existed until April, 1918, when it was abolished. Its place allegedly was taken by the Bureau which was to lead the guerilla war in the rear of German-Austrian armies in the Ukraine. Actually, most of the People's Secretaries resigned on February 24, 1918, protesting the proclamation of the Donets-Kryvoi Rog Republic (February 12, 1918) and Odessa Republic (January 30, 1918). V. Shakhrai went into opposition, criticizing the Russian Bolsheviks and Lenin personally for their hypocritical attitudes toward the Soviet Ukraine.

9. Tahanrih (Taganrog) Conference took place on April 19–20, 1918.

10. The "Insurgent Nine" comprised four Bolsheviks (Skrypnyk as the chairman of the nine, Piatakov, Bubnov, and Zatonskii, with S. Kossior, Kotsiubynskii, Hamarnyk, and Farbman as candidates), four left SR's., and one left SD.

11. The reference here is to the fact that the government of the Ukrainian Soviet Republic went on "being born" and "dying" in exile. Peasants' Government again returned to life and as early as May took part in Moscow in talks with the Sovnarkom on relations between the Ukraine and Russia. Then at the First Congress of the Communist Party of the Ukraine which took place in July 1918 (5–12 July) in Moscow it was resolved to dissolve the People's Secretariat of the Ukraine. Thus the Soviet Government in the Ukraine was dissolved for the second time. In its place was organized a Central Military Revolutionary Committee.

Then in August of 1918, this Committee again organized a "Workers' and Peasants' Government of the Ukraine." This government was, however, dissolved at the Second Congress of the CP(b)U, after an unsuccessful attempt at a rising in the Ukraine. The Bolsheviks themselves called this "CEC of the Ukraine playing at government." Iakovlev Epshtein, "O Sozdanii 'samostoiatel'noi' Kommunisticheskoi Partii Ukrainy," *Pravda*, No. 132 (June 30, 1918).

These attempts at forming a government reflect the unstable and often chaotic policy of the Russian Bolsheviks in the question of nationalities, particularly in the Ukrainian one.

12. Iakov Arkadievich Epshtein (1896–1939). Real name of Ia. A. Iakovlev. Member of the Party since 1913. From the spring of 1917 secretary of

the city committee of RSDRP (b), and a member of the Presidium of the City Council of Workers' and Soldiers' Deputies. Sent from Moscow into the Ukraine during the Civil War. In 1918 he was in Kiev and Kharkov where he was the head of the "Revkom" and one of the initiators of the so-called December Uprising (1918) against the Germans. During 1919 and 1920 he was the head of the Katerynoslav and Kiev Gubkom of the party, and the head of the political section of the 14th Army. Delegate of the I–III Congresses and the IVth Conference of CP(b)U. At the IInd Congress KP(b)U elected to the CC of CP(b)U. He can be considered one of the most important representatives of the Katerynoslav point of view opposing the creation of the independent Ukrainian Communist Party and even denying the existence of the Ukrainian nation.

13. The First Congress of the CP(b)U took place in Moscow on July 5–12, 1918.

14. This journal was published in Moscow during 1918. About eight numbers appeared at that time. It resumed publication in 1920–21 in Kharkiv (Kharkov) where another seven numbers appeared. Its language was Russian. It is not available outside the USSR.

15. Emanuil Kviring (1888–1939). Doctor of economic sciences. Member of the Party since 1912. Head of the so-called "right" or the Katerynoslav faction which stood for the incorporation of the Ukraine into RSFSR, or at least for the separation of Katerynoslav Gubernia from the Ukraine and its inclusion into *Donetsk-Krivoi Rog Soviet Republic.*

    Together with Iakovlev (Epshtein) defended at the Taganrog Party Conference and at the Ist Congress of the CP Ukraine the so-called Katerynoslav point of view which stood against the independence of the Communist Party of the Ukraine. During advance of the German armies in the Ukraine in 1918 he proposed the recognition of Central Rada by the Bolsheviks.

16. The All-Ukrainian Central Military Committee was organized in July, 1918, at the First Congress of CP(b)U. A. S. Bubnov was its head. V. P. Zatonskii, Iu. M. Kotsiubynskii, and others were members. The uprising referred to by the authors was planned for August 5, 1918, but it was a failure. As a result, F. A. Sergeev (Artem) was added to the Committee. The AUCMC went out of existence in November, 1918. At that time the Temporary Workers'-Peasants' Government of the Ukraine was established.

17. This quotation is taken from Griboedov's *Gore ot uma.*

18. The Second Congress of the CP(b)U took place 17–22 October, 1918, in Moscow. The call to uprising by the CC CP(b)U and of the Central Military Revolutionary Committee was labeled premature and as leading to the destruction of the party's organization in the Ukraine. This resolution was adopted with 62 votes against 37 with four abstentions.

19. The reference here is to the All-Ukrainian Congress of Workers', Soldiers', and Peasants' Soviets which was convened in Kiev on December 17, 1918. It proved a fiasco for the local Bolsheviks. Of the 2,500 delegates only about 80 were controlled by the Bolsheviks. Ministers of the Central Rada were elected as presiding officers of the Congress. Instead of censuring the Rada, the Congress protested the ultimatum of the Bolshevik government of Russia to Rada. The Bolsheviks then withdrew and proceeded to Kharkiv (Kharkov) where they called a new Ukrainian Congress of Soviets that is referred to in official sources as the First. V. Shakhrai participated in both meetings.

29. Ukrainian word *shakhrai* means swindler, cheat. It is partly for this reason that the author chose to spell his name as Shakh-Rai. The first part is equivalent to *Shah* and the second means "paradise."

21. The reference here is to the fact that he was one of the secretaries responsible for military affairs.

22. The reference here is to "an alliance" of the Russian Republic with the "Worker Peasant Government of the Ukraine."

23. This reference is completely obscure. In the absence of the author's papers or notes it is impossible to give even the title of the pamphlet in question. The author does not mention this pamphlet in his earlier work *Revolutsiia na Vkraini.*

24. On April 19–20, 1918, while retreating from Ukraine, the Ukrainian Bolsheviks assembled for a party conference in Taganrog. There on M. Skrypnyk's proposal but against the bitter opposition of the Russian Bolsheviks, led by E. I. Kviring, they founded the Communist Party (Bolsheviks) of the Ukraine (CP(b)U) as a wholly independent Ukrainian party, having relations with the RCP(b) only via the Communist International. At the same time, a group of Ukrainian Left SD's, led by P. Slynko and O. Butsenko, merged with the CP(b)U membership. The First Congress of the party declared CP(b)U an integral part and a provincial organization of the RCP (b).

25. The reference here is to the Conference of the South-Western Region, the so-called Kiev Conference of the party which took place on December 16–19, 1917, in Kiev. At the conference, creation of a single center for the Ukraine was hotly debated but with inconclusive results.

26. Shakhrai was a member of this committee.

27. The reference is to the C.E.C. elected on December 25, 1917, by the All-Ukrainian Congress of Soviets in Kharkiv (Kharkov).

28. The reference here is to the First Congress of CP(b)U.

29. The Second Congress of the CP(b)U took place in Moscow on October 17–22, 1918.

30. The Organizational Bureau which was elected at the Taganrog Conference in April, 1918, and which was given the task of convoking a Party Congress in Moscow on June 20, 1918, comprised of seven members: M. O. Skrypnyk, G. L. Piatakov, V. P. Zatonskii, J. Hamarnyk, I. M. Kreisberg, A. S. Bubnov, S. Kossior.

31. Ia. E. are the initials of Ia. A. Epshtein (Iakovlev). The authors refer here to Epshtein's article "O Sozdanii 'samostoiatel'noi' Kommunisticheskoi Partii Ukrainy," *Pravda*, No. 132 (June 30, 1918), p. 5.

32. The Katerynoslavians believed that Communist victory in the Ukraine would come through organizational work concentrated upon industrial laborers. They considered themselves an integral part of the Russian party and recognized no vital differences in the tasks facing the northern and southern sections of the party.

33. The full text of the Resolution is found in: *Komunistychna Partiia Ukrainy v Rezolutsiiakh, i Rishenniakh Zizdiv i Konferentsii, 1918–1956* (Kiev: Derzhpolitvydav, 1958), p. 10.

34. This motion, which was tabled by Kviring and was in the spirit of the one and indivisible Russia, was rejected. But, according to Ravich-Cherkasskii it represented the views of more than four-fifths of all the members of the Party in the Ukraine. He called this motion "russophil."

35. The reference here is to the joint proposal put forward by the "Leftists" or "Kievans" and the Ukrainian elements represented among others by Skrypnyk and Shakhrai. They wanted the Russian party to follow a policy of "hands off." This belief that a separate Communist party of the Ukraine could solve Ukrainian problems more successfully and more intelligently than Moscow is in fact the underlying reason for the appearance of *Do Khvyli*. The proposal of the Kievans was adopted by the Conference by 26 votes against 21. It was later condemned as a "deviation toward Ukrainian nationalism." Some, however, feared that it was also an attempt of the Left Communists to "secure themselves organizationally against the Leninist majority of the RCP(b)." According to Skrypnyk the resolution about the independence of the CP (b) U was approved also by the Russian Communist Party (RCP(b)) itself. See *Odinnadtsatyi S'ezd RKP(b): Mart-Aprel' 1922 Goda, Stenograficheskii Otchet* (Moscow: Gospolitizdat, 1961), p. 74.

36. Georgii Leonidovich Piatakov (1890–1938) was born near Kiev. Member of anarchist circles during his high-school days. While a student in Petersburg University during 1910 he became a member of the Social-Democratic Party. Arrested for his activity there, he was sent back to Kiev and expelled from the university. In Kiev, together with E. B. Bosh and others, he activized the local committee of the SD's. He was again arrested in 1912 and sent to Irkutsk in Siberia from where he escaped in October 1914. In 1917 he returned to Kiev, where he held

leading positions in the CP(b)U. At the Taganrog Conference and again at the First Congress of CP(b)U he defended the idea of a Ukrainian Communist Party independent from Moscow on the grounds that because of the closeness to Ukrainian events and intimate knowledge of Ukrainian affairs such a party could best make the necessary decisions and provide the most intelligent leadership. Piatakov was not moved by Ukrainian nationalism as, for example, V. Shakhrai was. In fact, his view was that self-determination of any sort was a false doctrine, that no revolutionary proletariat was capable of working out its own state order alone, and that each national proletariat within the Soviet federation should not be permitted to set up whatever political order it chose. Lenin considered Piatakov's approach imperialistic, pointing out that it would make RCP(b) an aggressor in all eyes.

37. The Leftists in the Ukraine were led by G. L. Piatakov, V. Zatonskii, E. Bosh, and others. There was also a close relationship between them and the left wing in the RCP(b). Both groups were opposed to Lenin's peace with the Germans and the growing centralization of authority.

38. This phrase is borrowed from *The Liberal*, a satirical fairytale by M. Saltykov-Shchedrin.

39. The fact is that at the Congress Skrypnyk did introduce a motion in defense of the independence of CP (B)U. This motion ran as follows: "The Communist organizations of the Ukraine are uniting in a separate Communist Party (Bolshevik) of the Ukraine (CP(b)U), with its own Central Committee and Congress, formally tied with the Russian Communist Party (RCP) through the International Commission of the Third International." See *Istoriia KP(b)U v Materiialakh Ta Dokumentakh: 1917–1920 rr.* 2d ed. by S. Barannyk (Kharkov, 1934) p. 356, note 1; see also: J. Borys, p. 140. Skrypnyk's motion was defeated and the countermotion, tabled by Kviring, was adopted.

   Kviring's motion said that since not a single one of the concrete questions which were before the communists of the Ukraine could be solved correctly "without reference to the tactics of the Russian Party, . . . the All-Ukrainian Congress of the Party resolved: 1. To unite the Communist Party Organizations of the Ukraine in an autonomous (as regards local matters) Communist Party of the Ukraine with its own Central Committee and Congresses; it shall, however, form part of a single Russian Communist Party subordinated in matters of programme to the general Congresses of the Russian Communist Party, and in general political matters to the CC RCP(b); 2. To charge the CC RCP(b) to put the CP(b)U organizationally and tactically into touch with the Communist Parties of Germany, Austria and the occupied countries." See *Komunistychna Partiia Ukrainy v Rezolutsiiakh i Rishenniakh Z'izdiv i Konferentsii, 1918–1956* (Kiev: Derzhpolitvydav, 1958), pp. 18–19; see also J. Borys, pp. 140–141. This resolution was adopted (by 33 votes against 5 with 16 abstentions) at a closed session after stormy debates.

40. Literally, "Moor."

41. A. V. Lunacharskii (1875–1933), Russian and Soviet writer and literary critic. He served in the high state and party positions, and was the People's Commissar of Education in the Russian Soviet regime.

42. The reference here is to the fact that the Provisional Government was composed primarily of the Leftists who were hostile to the idea of Ukrainian independence. The government was headed by G. L. Piatakov. Other members were V. K. Averin, Artem (F. A. Sergeev), K. E. Voroshilov, V. P. Zatonskii, E. I. Kviring, Iu. M. Kotsiubynskii, and some others. The authors refer to this government as a "coalition government" because it comprised the left, the right and the nationalist elements of the party.

43.   *... denn alles, was entsteht,*
                       Ist wert, dass es zugrunde geht;
    Cf. J. W. Goethe, *Goethes Werke,* ed. Karl Heinemann (Leipzig and Vienna: Bibliographisches Institut, n.d.), p. 69.

CHAPTER I X

1. The Sich Sharpshooters (Sichovi Stril'tsi) is the name of the Galician Battalion that was formed in November, 1917, from West Ukrainian prisoners of war formerly in the Austrian army.

2. The reference is to the events of April 26–27, 1918, when the Germans disarmed the First Ukrainian Division of "Blue Coats" (Syniezhupannyky) volunteers. This division was formed in Germany from Ukrainian war prisoners.

3. The reference here is to Premier Holubovych's statement to the Rada in which he distinguished between the German military in the Ukraine and the German government and incorrectly assumed that the former was pursuing its own policy under the influence of the Russian landowners in opposition to that of the latter. See also Hrushevsky's article quoted by Reshetar, p. 128, n. 49.

4. The reference here may be to the "Soviets" or councils which were organized rather spontaneously by the soldiers of some units in the German Army of Occupation in the Ukraine. It was impossible to determine what connection, if any, these councils had with the Spartacist groups that were very active in the Ukraine at that time.

5. The reference is probably to *Neue Preussische Zeitung,* the organ of the Prussian and German Conservative Party. It was founded in 1848. In

1911 its name was changed to *Neue Preussische (Kreuz-) Zeitung*. It was popularly known as the *Kreuz Zeitung*.

6. In the original: *iz poly v polu*.

CHAPTER X

1. The reference here is to the pronouncements of a special commission of functional and legal experts which was set up by the Russian Provisional Government in early April, 1917, in direct response to the Ukrainian demands for autonomy. The Ukrainian demands were communicated to the government by a ten-man delegation headed by V. Vynnychenko. These demands were rejected on the grounds that only the All-Russian Constituent Assembly has the right to pass on matters of such importance.

2. The Senate in the Russian Empire fulfilled both administrative and judicial functions, supervising the work of administration, hearing complaints against administrators, and serving as the highest administrative court and the highest court of appeal in the land.

3. The reference is to the democratic, liberal-minded zemstvo personnel—doctors, technicians, teachers, agriculturists—called the "third element" in a speech made in 1900 by the Samara Deputy Governor-General Kondoidi. The expression was subsequently used in literature to designate the zemstvo democratic intelligentsia.

4. These lines were borrowed by Shakhrai from a poem by V. A. Zhukovskii (1783–1852). See also Skorovstans'kyi, *Revoliutsiia na Ukraine*, 2d Russian ed., pp. 131–32.

5. "Mazepism" (Mazepynstvo). Ukrainian independence idea. The word derives from Ivan Mazepa (1632–1709), Hetman of the Ukraine. He was responsible for the renaissance of the Ukraine; under his direction churches, libraries, and universities were built. He formed an alliance with Charles XII of Sweden against Peter the Great of Russia. After the defeat at Poltava (1709) he fled to Bender, where he died.

6. The reference is to the first months of the war when the Russian forces of occupation in Austrian Ukraine (Galicia and Bukovina) began a merciless destruction of the various manifestations of Ukrainian national life there.

7. Numerous diverse congresses were held in Kiev during the spring. These included a Congress of Cooperatives of the Kiev region which met on March 14(27), 1917; the First All-Ukrainian Pedagogical Congress held during the third week in April; the First Ukrainian Military Congress (May 5 (18)–12 (25)); the First Ukrainian Peasant Congress (May 28 (June 10), 1917); the First Ukrainian Workers' Congress (July 11(24)–13

(26), 1917); and the Congresses of the Social Democratic and Social Revolutionary parties in April, 1917.

8. The Central Rada decided at its session on June 3(16), 1917, to prepare the Declaration to the Ukrainian People; and on June 10(23) such a Declaration was passed and was referred to as Universal. It was read at the Second Military Congress and welcomed enthusiastically by the delegates to the Congress. It was publicly proclaimed on June 11(24), 1917. The Universal recapitulated all of the requests of the Rada and declared that the Provisional Government had rejected them and had ignored the extended hand of the Ukrainian people.

9. The reference here is to the negotiations carried between the representatives of the Provisional Government and the General Secretariat of the Central Rada on June 28(July 11)–June 30(July 13), 1917. A. Kerenski, the minister of war, M. Tereshchenko, the minister of foreign affairs, and I. Tsereteli, the minister of post and telegraph represented the Provisional Government. Negotiators for the Ukrainians were Hrushevsky, Vynnychenko, and on military matters, Petliura. The result of these conversations was the Second Universal issued by the Rada on July 3(16), and acceded to by the three representatives of the Provisional Government.

10. The reference here is to the disastrous Russian offensive that began in Galicia on June 18 (July 1), 1917, and which soon turned into a retreat to the line of the River Zbruch.

11. The reference here is to disorder and violence that erupted on July 3–5 (July 16–18) as a result of a united-front manifestation organized by the Mensheviks and SR's in support of the government. The pent-up impatience of the Petrograd mob was spurred by the failure of the Galician offensive. In Kiev on July 4 (17) began the rebellion of the Polubotok Regiment. The soldiers disliked Vynnychenko and others in the Rada for their socialism and especially for their "pacifism" in dealing with Petrograd. The coup was liquidated on July 6 (19).

12. The Russian Provisional Government did not confirm the Statute. In its place it issued, on August 4 (17), a "Temporary Instruction" to the General Secretariat. (1) The General Secretariat was to be an organ not of the Central Rada but of the Provisional Government. (2) The number of Secretaries was reduced from fourteen to seven. (3) And its authority was to be confined to only five Guberniias—those of Kiev, Podolia, Poltava, Volyn' (Volynia), and Chernyhiv (Chernigov). Other Ukrainian areas could join the autonomous Ukraine should their provincial zemstvos express desire to do so.

13. Plural of *samostiinyk*. It refers to the supporter of an independent Ukraine. There is no really suitable translation of it in English. The proper French equivalent would be *independanciste*.

14. The authors allude here to Procrustean Legend.

15. The words of the First Universal.

16. The first Ukrainian Regiment of Bohdan Khmelnyts'kyi was organized on April 1, 1917, under the command of Lieutenant Colonel G. Kapkan from some of the Ukrainian soldiers temporarily stationed in Kiev. As the troops left Kiev to go to the front on July 26 (August 8) they were shot upon by the Russian troops, which had been conveniently deployed along the railroad tracks. A number of Ukrainians (16) were killed and about 30 wounded. No official investigation was made into this incident.

17. Reference to the adoption on November 7 (20), 1917, of the Third Universal, announcing the creation of the Ukrainian People's Republic. Despite the fact that the Universal contains the phrase "without breaking federative relations with Russia," this was a formal act creating a new Ukrainian state. It should be noted that the Rada in this Universal neither recognized nor rejected the Bolshevik government in Petrograd. It was willing to accept that government as the government of Great-Russia.

18. The reference is to the All-Ukrainian National Congress which was convened on April 6–8 (19–21), 1917, in Kiev. In its resolutions the Congress recognized the supreme authority of the Russian Constituent Assembly which was to be called soon in order to set up a new political order in the former Russian Empire. But it also demanded Ukrainian representation in the future peace conference, thus implying that it considered the Ukraine a separate body politic. This is the split that the authors talk about.

19. The paragraph 5 of the Resolution says the following:
    "The right of nations to self-determination (i.e., the constitutional guarantee of an absolutely free and democratic method of deciding the question of secession) must under no circumstances be confused with the expediency of a given nation's secession. The Social-Democratic Party must decide the latter question exclusively on its merits in each particular case in conformity with the interests of the proletarian class struggle for socialism.
    Social Democrats must moreover bear in mind that the landowners, the clergy and the bourgeoisie of the oppressed nations often cover up with nationalist slogans their efforts to divide the workers and dupe them by doing deals behind their backs with the landowners and bourgeoisie of the ruling nation to the detriment of the masses of the working people of all nations."
    "Resolutions of the Summer 1913, Joint Conference of the Central Committee of the RSDRP and Party Officials," in V. I. Lenin, *Collected Works.* 4th ed., Vol. 19, p. 429.
    The ninth paragraph of the Bolshevik Program reads as follows:

"With reference to the nationality question the All-Russian Communist Party is guided by the following theses:

(1) The principal aim is to bring into closer relations the proletarians and semi-proletarians of different nationalities, for the purpose of carrying on a general revolutionary struggle for the overthrow of the landlords and the bourgeoisie;

(2) In order to remove mistrust on the part of the working masses of the oppressed countries toward the proletariat of those states which formerly oppressed them, it is necessary to abolish all privileges of any national group, to proclaim the fullest equality of all nationalities and to recognize the rights of colonies and oppressed nations to political separation;

(3) For the same purpose, as a temporary measure toward achieving the unity of nations, the Party suggests a federative combination of all states organized on the Soviet basis;

(4) The All Russian Communist Party regards the question as to which class expresses the desire of a nation for separation, from a historical point of view, taking into consideration the level of historical development of the nation, i.e., whether the nation is passing from medievalism toward bourgeois democracy or from bourgeois democracy toward Soviet or proletarian democracy.

In any case, particular care and attention must be exercised by the proletariat of those nations which were oppressing nations, toward the prevailing national feelings of the working masses of the oppressed nations, or nations which are limited in their rights. Only by such a policy is it possible to create favourable conditions for a voluntary and real unity of different national elements of the international proletariat, as has been proved by the combination of different national Soviet republics around Soviet Russia.

The Program was adopted at the Eighth Party Congress March 18–23, 1919. This translation is taken from *Materials for the Study of the Soviet System*, edited by James H. Meisel and Edward S. Kozera (Ann Arbor, Michigan: The George Wahr Publishing Company, 1953), p. 108.

20. The reference here is to the appearance at Brest on January 23, 1918, of the two representatives of the Central Executive Committee of the All-Ukrainian Soviet of Workers', Soldiers', and Peasants' Deputies, but as a supplementary part of the Russian delegation. The two delegates were E. Medvedev, head of the executive committee, and V. Shakhrai, the commissar for military affairs. Thus Shakhrai speaks here as the participant in the negotiations.

21. The Fourth Universal proclaimed Ukrainian independence in the face of the Bolshevik invasion.—It was adopted at the second reading at the session of "Little Rada" on January 11 (24), and the final text was read

on January 12 (25) at 12:20 A.M. The date of the issuance of the Fourth Universal is usually incorrectly given as January 9 (22). The Ukrainian Independence Day celebrated by the Ukrainian communities outside of the Ukraine is always on January 22.

22. The authors refer to the Directory's leadership of the successful anti-Hetman uprising.

23. In the original *zagibaet salazki*. Reference here is to A. S. Salazkin, the millionaire merchant and president of the Nizhnyi-Novgorod Fair and Exchange Committee. He made a speech at a special meeting of the Committee held on August 16 (29), 1913, in connection with the visit to the fair of Prime Minister Kokovtsov. On behalf of all Russia's merchants Salazkin urged upon Kokovtsov the "vital necessity" of radical political reforms on the basis of the tsar's Manifesto of October 17, 1905, and expressed the desire of the commercial and industrial world "to take a direct part in the affairs of public self-government and state organization." His speech received a great deal of attention in the writings of the Social Democrats.

24. This ironic statement refers to the fact that the leadership of the CP(b)U was pretending to reside in Poltava, in the Ukraine, when in fact it was located within the borders of the Russian Republic.

25. A. V. Suvorov (1730–1800), Russian field marshal.

CHAPTER X I

1. Union for the Liberation of the Ukraine was organized on August 4, 1914, under Andrew Zhuk as a nonpartisan political representation of the Ukrainians of the Russian Empire living in Galicia, Austria-Hungary, and Germany. Its aim was to take advantage of the war in order to promote the idea of the Ukrainian independence. Its most active and influential members in addition to A. Zhuk were: V. Doroshenko, A. Skoropys-Ioltukhovskyi, and M. Melenevskyi.

2. The reference here is to:
   (a) The Ukrainian Socialist Radical Party which was founded in 1891 and in 1895 issued a call for the political independence of the Ukrainian people;
   (b) The National Democratic Party which came into being in 1899. It was composed of the most active members of the populist group and the right wing of the Radicals. In January, 1900, the National Committee of this party also proclaimed as its ultimate goal the establishment of an independent Ukraine.

3. The international socialist peace conference was to be held at Stockholm in 1917. The Petrograd Soviet was invited to send representatives to

this conference through a Danish socialist Borgbjerg. Lenin denounced Borgbjerg as an agent of the German bourgeoisie and the proposed conference as a comedy. The conference fell through when the British and French governments refused to allow British and French socialists to attend it.

4. Vynnychenko's statement at the Second Military Congress.

5. Graf Ottokar Czernin (1872–1932), Austro-Hungarian statesman. Served as foreign minister 1916–18. At Brest the Ukrainian delegation demanded, in fact, that the Kholm region, Galicia and Bukovina be united to the Ukraine. Czernin opposed these demands but in the end agreed to make a supplemental secret treaty separating these Western Ukrainian lands under Austria-Hungary into a special crown land.

6. The authors were entirely misinformed. No republic by that name was ever established.

On November 1, 1918, after the disintegration of Austria-Hungary, the Western Ukrainian People's Republic (ZUNR) was proclaimed in Galicia and Bukovina. From the very beginning the Western Ukraine tried to find ways of uniting with the Ukrainian People's Republic. Finally, the act of union was proclaimed on January 22, 1919, in Kiev and confirmed by the Labor Congress on January 28, 1919. The name of the Western Ukrainian People's Republic was changed to the Western Oblast of the Ukrainian People's Republic (ZOUNR).

CHAPTER X I I

1. A veiled allusion to the help received by Lenin.

2. The editor was unable to identify these lines. In the original:
   Kakoi by shum vy podniali druzia,
   Kogda by eto sdelal ia!

3. 1 pud = 36.07 lbs. = 16.38 kg.

4. Manilov is a character in Gogol's *Dead Souls,* whose name has become a synonym for unprincipled philistinism, sentimentality, and daydreaming.

5. This is a very common, somewhat vulgar, expression having to do with the wiping off of excrement.

CHAPTER X I I I

1. Ivan Iulianovych Kulyk (1897–1941). (Pseudonyms: R. Rolinato; Vasyl' Rolenko). Soviet Ukrainian writer and the Party and government activist. He joined the Communist Party in 1914. Born in Shpola (in the

Ukraine), in the family of a school teacher, he went in 1914 to the U.S.A. but in May, 1917, returned to the Ukraine. In December, 1917, at the Oblast' Conference of the RSDRP(b) of the South-Western region which took place in Kiev, he was made a member of the Main Committee of the Social Democracy of the Ukraine, and at the First All-Ukrainian Congress of Soviets he was elected to CEC of the Soviet Ukraine. He was a member of the *Narkomnats* in Moscow, and from 1919 worked in the People's Commissariat of Foreign Affairs. In 1924–26 he was appointed Consul General of the USSR in Canada. He opposed the Independent Communist Party for the Ukraine and the independence of the Soviet Ukraine. During Stalin's purges he was arrested, and accused of nationalism. He died in 1941.

2. Kulyk in Ukrainian is the name of a bird *(Numenius Arguata)*, in English: curlew, common curlew, Eurasian curlew.

3. A corrupted version of the following: "If you give me six sentences written by the most innocent of men, I will find something in them with which to hang him." By Armand Jean du Plessis, Duc de Richelieu (1585–1642), French Cardinal and statesman.

4. The editor was unable to identify the verse.

CHAPTER XIV

1. The reference is to I. Kotliarevskyi (1769–1838), the founder of the new Ukrainian literature in the vernacular. He chose for his subject Virgil's *Aeneid*, a traditional material for travesties in many languages. Kotliarevskyi transformed the heroes of the *Aeneid* into Ukrainian Cossacks and thus was able to make use in his work of ethnographic material, to enrich the language, and to produce a valuable collection of linguistic material.

2. Taras H. Shevchenko (1814–61), Ukrainian poet and artist. The son of a serf, his freedom was purchased by a group of intellectuals. In his writings he bitterly attacked serfdom, Russian autocracy, and Russian domination of non-Russian lands. He was made a soldier and banished to Central Asia for his political ideas. Shevchenko had tremendous influence on Ukrainian literature and political thought.

3. The reference here is to the edict of the minister of the Interior, Count Peter Valuev, on June 8, 1863 (O.S.). In it he asserted: "The majority of the Little Russians (official name for the Ukrainians) themselves thoroughly prove that there has not been, is not, and never can be any Little Russian language, and that their dialect, used by the common people, is the same Russian language, but corrupted by the influence

upon it of Poland; that the general Russian language is comprehensible to the Little Russians and even more understandable than the so-called Ukrainian language now being formed for them by some Little Russians, and especially by Poles; the circle of those persons who try to prove the opposite are accused by the majority of the Little Russians themselves of having separatist plans, hostile to Russia and disastrous for Little Russia."

4. These lines seem to be from Gogol's *Taras Bulba.*

5. Reference here is again to Valuev's edict.

6. This expression was used by the Russian writer Gleb Uspenski to describe police tyranny.

7. This reference is primarily to Kh. Rakovski. It is possible, however, that the authors had in mind the leadership of both the "Leftist Kievans" and the "Rightists Katerynoslavians," the majority of whom were hostile to the Ukrainian national aspirations.

8. The first line of the poem called "Ridna mova" by Sydir Vorobkevych (1836–1903).

9. The reference here is to the use of Ukrainian Cossacks in the Russian campaigns in the Baltic area, and especially in building of new fortifications and cities. There are estimates claiming that nearly 30,000 Ukrainians died in building St. Petersburg.

10. The reference here is to the sixteenth and seventeenth centuries when with the help of the Kievan (Mohyla) Academy the cultural influences of the Ukraine spread throughout the entire Russian empire.

11. These words come from one of Shevchenko's poems popularly known as "Poslanie."

12. The reference here is to the declaration of the Central Rada which was addressed to the Provisional Government as well as to the Petrograd Soviet which shared authority with the government in Petrograd. It was delivered to the government at the end of May, 1917, by a ten-man delegation headed by V. Vynnychenko. The full text of the declaration is to be found in P. Khrystiuk, *Zamitky: Materialy do Istorii Ukrains'koi Revolutsii, 1917–1920* (Vienna: 1921–22), 1, 55 ff.

13. The reference here is to an article on the Irish rebellion entitled "Their Song Is Over" in the *Berner Tagwacht*, the organ of the Zimmerwald group, signed with the initials K. R. [Karl Radek—Ed.] It described the Irish rebellion as a putsch, for, as the author argued, "the Irish question was an agrarian one," the peasants had been pacified by reforms, and the nationalist movement remained only a "purely urban, petty bourgeois movement, which, notwithstanding the sensation it caused, had not much social backing." This assessment of the rebellion was similar with that of a Russian national-liberal Cadet, A. Kulisher who in his article

"The Dublin Putsch," *Rech*, No. 102 (April 15, 1916), used the same phraseology.

CHAPTER X V

1. This expression originated during the Russo-Turkish War, 1877–78. There was heavy fighting in the Shipka Pass (mountain pass through Balkan mountains in central Bulgaria) but the headquarters of the Russian Army issued communiques stating "All quiet on Shipka." The expression was used ironically in respect of those who tried to hide the true state of affairs.

2. Volodymyr Zatonskii (1888–1937), since 1917 member of the Kiev organization of the Bolsheviks. One of the founders of the CP(B)U. Secretary of Education in the first Ukrainian Soviet Government, and in 1918 a representative of the Ukraine to the RSFSR government. He also served (from March 1918) as the Chairman of VUTsVK. Arrested and executed in 1937.

3. The reference is to the "Donetsk-Kryvyi Rih Soviet Republic" which was proclaimed with the approval of the Soviet Russian government in February, 1918, at Kharkiv (Kharkov) by the Fourth Oblast' Congress of Soviets of the Donetsk and Kryvyi Rih (Krivoi Rog) regions. Similarly, on January 30, 1918, the "Soviet Odessa Republic" proclaimed its independence. However, on March 7, 1918, Skrypnyk's government unilaterally proclaimed the restoration of these republics to the Soviet Ukraine.

4. These lines are borrowed from the poem "Baba v Tserkvi," by S. V. Rudanskyi (1833–73), Ukrainian satirical writer.

5. The reference here is to attempts to put into practice the federal principles which were made in the spring of 1918, when the government of the RSFSR ordered the formation of Tatar-Bashkir and Turkestan Republics.

6. The Organizational Bureau and the "insurgent nine" were located in Hotel Lux on Tverskii Boulevard, now Gorkii Street.

7. In the original *"Uchredilka."* The All-Russian Constituent Assembly was forcibly dissolved by the Bolsheviks on January 6 (19), 1918, just one day after its convocation on January 5 (18), 1918.

8. The reference here is to the "Temporary Instruction" of the Russian Provisional Government of August 17, 1917, in which it acknowledged under the Kievan administration only five gubernias—those of Kiev, Volhynia, Podillia (Podolia), Poltava, and Chernyhiv (Chernigov). The Katerynoslav, Kherson, and Kharkiv (Kharkov) regions were placed outside the jurisdiction of the General Secretariat of the Central Rada.

9. Lev Iurkevych (1885–1918), editor of *Borot'ba* and financial backer of *Dzvin*. Member of the USDRP. Wrote several articles on the national question.

10. A monthly of the Social-Democratic trend, published in the Ukrainian language in Kiev from January 1913 to the middle of 1914.

11. Dmytro Dontsov (b. 1883), Ukrainian journalist and political writer. Member of the RUP and USDRP, he is a well-known ideologist of the Ukrainian brand of integral nationalism.

12. The authors refer here to the killing of Mirbach by the left SR's and the Declaration of the First Congress of the CP(B)U. See *Komunistychna Partiia Ukrainy v Rezoliutsiiakh, op. cit.*, pp. 20–22.

13. In the original: "Russkii um i russkii dukh, zady tverdit i lzhet za dvukh!" The editor was unable to identify the source of this quotation.

14. "Khokhol"—a derogatory term, which Russians employed in referring to Ukrainians, derived from the name for the long lock of hair which adorned the shaved heads of the Zaporozhian Cossacks of the Dnieper.

15. The authors refer here to a ten-man delegation headed by V. Vynny- chenko.

16. The reference here is to the Second All-Ukrainian Congress of Soviets (March 17–19, 1918) at Katerynoslav which declared the secession of the Soviet Ukraine from Russia.

17. The reference is to Rada's invitation of Germans into the Ukraine.

18. The Soviet Russian government immediately recognized the indepen- dence of the Soviet Ukraine.

19. The reference is to a decision of the German Socialists to support the war effort.

20. This quotation was borrowed from one of Shevchenko's poems.

21. The reference here is to Miliukov's newspaper interview of April 5, 1917, in which he spelled out the war aims which he as foreign minister was pursuing; he mentioned among other things the annexation of Constantinople and the "Red Rus'" (historical name for Galicia), as an "immemorial" national objective.

22. V. M. Purishkevich (1870–1920), Russian political leader and founder of the reactionary "Union of the Russian People" and the "Union of Michael Archangel" which are known as Black Hundreds.

23. The authors are referring here to the phrase employed by Miliukov in his May 1 note to the Allies. The phrase "war to decisive victory" served as a signal for demonstrations in front of the Marinsky Palace. Miliukov was forced to resign his post two days later.

24. The Cadet party in the Ukraine had the same program as the All-

Russian party under Miliukov's leadership. Its attitude to the Ukrainian demands for self-determination vaccilated between total hostility and some concessions in cultural questions.

25. This party (RSDRP—the Mensheviks) concentrated its activity mainly in the big cities and in the industrial regions of the country. The Mensheviks were willing to support Ukrainian demands for autonomy, but not independence. Kost' Kononenko (died in the USA) was one of the leaders of this party in the Ukraine.

26. The party (RPSR) in the Ukraine was just a section of the All-Russian Party of the SR's. It was in favor of an autonomous Ukraine within the Russian federation. It opposed independence for the Ukraine.

27. There were, however, open instances of hostility to Ukrainian demands for autonomy. On the eve of the Ukrainian National Congress (April 19–21, 1917), the head of the Soviet of Workers' Deputies in Kiev, P. Nezlobin, described the Ukrainian demand for autonomy as "a stab in the back of the Revolution."

28. The reference here is made to the Resolution of November 24, 1917, of the Poltava Committee of the Party in which a demand was made for the convocation of the All-Ukrainian Party Congress. A little earlier, on November 12, the Poltava Committee in its letter to the CC RSDRP(b) requested that "in connection with the proclamation of the Ukrainian People's Republic" it was necessary "to convoke a Congress of all Party organizations of the Ukrainian Republic. . . ." Both Shakhrai and Mazlakh belonged to the Committee and probably influenced its decision. See *Bol'shevitskie Organizatsii Ukrainy v period Ustanovleniia i Ukrepleniia Sovetskoi Vlasti: Noiabr' 1917–Aprel' 1918* (Kiev: Gospolitizdat, 1962), pp. 482–83.

29. The armed clashes began in late December, 1917. The beginning of the war between Soviet Russia and the Ukraine is dated December 4 (17), 1917, when the Soviet government in Petrograd sent the Ukrainian government an ultimatum, which was promptly rejected.

30. The reference here is to the resolutions of the First (Kharkiv) All-Ukrainian Congress of Soviets (December 11–12 (24–25), 1917), and of the Second (Katerynoslav) All-Ukrainian Congress of Soviets (March 17–19, 1918).

31. The reference here is to the Don, the Kuban, and Siberian regions.

32. Serhii Shelukhyn (1864–1938), noted Ukrainian jurist and the head of the Ukrainian delegation to negotiate peace treaty with the Bolsheviks. As a result of his labors an official armistice was signed on June 12, 1918, containing a recognition by the Soviets of the Ukrainian State and agreement as to an exchange of consular representatives; but the formal peace treaty was not signed.

33. The reference here is to one of Krylov's fables, *Pustynnik i Medved*. The line in the fable, of course, is "an obliging fool is worse than an enemy."

34. An obvious allusion to Ia. A. Epshtein (Iakovlev).

35. The authors refer to Kh. Rakovski.

CHAPTER X V I

1. The All-Ukrainian Council of Peasants' Deputies sent about 212 delegates to the Central Rada. The All-Ukrainian Council of Soldiers' Deputies had about 158 delegates, and the All-Ukrainian Council of Workers' Deputies had 100 delegates. See Ia. Zozulia, *Velyka Ukrains'ka Revoliutsiia* (New York: UVAN, 1967), 2d ed., pp. 98–111.

2. The reference here is to the statement by M. Porsh that the Census had very strong Russian bias. See M. Porsh, "Iz statystyky Ukrainy," *Ukraina*, III (July–August, 1907), p. 27.

3. Among patriotic Ukrainians the term "Little Russian" had a very definite derogatory meaning.

4. This refers to Vynnychenko's statement that Ukrainians still lack national consciousness and have some way to go before their political development is fully completed.

5. "Koronet" in the original. This reference is probably to M. G. Kornfeld, editor-in-chief of the *Satirikon*. It is either a spelling error in the original or it might refer to Kornfeld's military rank, i.e., junior officer.

6. The reference here is to the Volhynian Regiment which supported the revolution and which in the majority was composed of Ukrainians.

7. This quotation is borrowed from the Ukrainian protest song "Ne pora, Ne pora," which quite often was used as an unofficial national anthem.

8. The reference here is to Rada's delegation to Brest Litovsk.

9. The reference here might be to the declaration made on November 13, 1918, by a Polish National Committee to the Paris Peace Conference. Roman Dmowski, its head, employed the historical argument pointing out that Eastern Galicia had been a part of Poland since the fourteenth century.

10. Emile Enno (Henno), a minor diplomat representing the Allied powers in the Ukraine.

    There is considerable disagreement regarding the spelling of this surname. Some scholars refer to this man as "Hainnot," "Hennot," "Aynaud," and "Henno." See Reshetar, *op. cit.*, p. 235n.

11. The reference here probably is to the exchange of the telegrams be-

tween the Directory and Chicherin, the People's Commissar for Foreign Affairs, and the sending of a small delegation, headed by S. Mazurenko (in January 1919), with instructions "to seek a settlement (with the Bolsheviks) even at the price of accepting the soviet form of government in the Ukraine." Reshetar, *op. cit.*, p. 227.

12. The seat of the Soviet Ukrainian government was in Kursk in Russia. Evidently the telegrams were being signed as if originating in Poltava, in the Ukraine, to confuse the Germans.

13. The authors probably borrowed this phrase from the statement by B. Martos at the meeting of the Little Rada that discussed a need to convene the Ukrainian Constituent Assembly. See *Informator (Radio Liberty)*, No. 20 (90) (October 1967), p. 12.

CHAPTER X V I I

1. A character from Uspenskii's *Budka*. A typical representative of the autocratic police regime.

2. Sky-blue and yellow are the Ukrainian national colors.

3. This criticism appears unwarranted. Bukharin does not use the phrase "the working masses of the oppressed nation." See N. Bukharin, *Programma Kommunistov (Bol'shevikov)* (Petrograd: 1919), p. 54–56. The decision "to limit the principle of free self-determination of nations, by granting it to the toilers and refusing it to the bourgeoisie" was made by Stalin in January, 1918, as Commissar of Nationalities.

4. The reference here is to Rakovski's article "Beznadezhnoe delo: o Petliurovskoi avantiure," *Izvestiia*, No. 2 (554) (January 3, 1919), p. 1.

CHAPTER X V I I I

1. "Katsaps"—Ukrainian "Katsapy." Derogatory name used by the Ukrainians for the Russians. It is supposedly made up of two Russian words "kak" and "tsap," meaning "as goat" in allusion to the fact that many Russians were bearded.

2. The reference here is to the *Joint Conference of the RSDRP Central Committee and Party Officials*, held in village of Poronin from September 23 to October 1 (October 6–14), 1913, and called, for reasons of secrecy, the "August" ("Summer") Conference.

3. The reference here is to a delegation composed of Skrypnyk, Iu. Kotsiubynskii, and N. E. Vrublevskii (left USD) which attended a meeting of

the Sovnarkom on April 3, 1918. See *Bolshevitskie Organizatsii Ukrainy, op. cit.* (Kiev: Gospolitizdat, 1962), pp. 72–73, 706–7.

4. In Ukrainian folklore the tattered sheet represents a rather crude attempt to hide things.

5. The reference here is to the radical right wing of the RSDRP which came into existence after the Russian Revolution of 1905, and of which P. Akselrod, F. Dan, and A. Potresov were leaders. This group was expelled from the party by the January, 1912, Conference of the RSDRP.

6. S. Semkovskii (S. Iu. Bronshtein) (b. 1882). He was a member of the RSDRP (Mensheviks) until 1920, when he joined the Bolsheviks. He became a member of the editorial board of Trotsky's *Pravda* (appeared in Vienna), and contributor to various publications of the "liquidators." He was severely criticized by Lenin for his stand on the nationality question. After the revolution he taught in the Ukraine. In 1931 he was accused of being a follower of Bukharin in his interpretations of historical materialism. He was arrested and probably died in jail.

7. Lenin quotes the words of a Sevastopol soldiers' song written by Leo Tolstoi. The song is about the unsuccessful operation of the Russian troops at the Chornaia River on August 4, 1855, during the Crimean War. In that action General Read commanded two divisions.

8. The reference here is to peace talks in Kiev between the Soviets and the hetman's regime.

9. The editor was unable to trace the source of this verse. It may have been borrowed from one of Shevchenko's poems.

10. Reference to Zatonskii's article.

11. The meaning here is that what the Katerynoslavians have to say is much more important than what Rakovski can promise. The Katerynoslavians by that time had the full backing of Lenin.

12. "Clever khokhol" is an epithet given by Russians to Ukrainians. Shakhrai refers here to himself. Mazlakh was of Jewish origin and therefore this epithet would not fit him.

13. Refers to Chrezvychainaia Kommissiia, the Soviet Secret Police.

14. Reference to the hetman's attempts to Ukrainianize his bureaucracy.

15. In fact, a separate party was created for Galicia; at first, under the name of the Communist Party of Eastern Galicia, which was formally set up in February, 1919, and then renamed the Communist Party of the Western Ukraine (KPZU) in 1923.

16. Reference to the Party Conference of the South-Western Region in Kiev and an attempt to organize a separate party for the Ukraine.

17. The authors here refer to the Second All-Ukrainian Congress of Soviets which met on March 17–19, 1918, in Katerynoslav.

18. The attitude of the Poltava Bolsheviks to this question is well reflected in the two recently published documents. See *Bol'shevitskie organizatsii Ukrainy v period ustanovleniia i ukrepleniia Sovetskoi vlasti, op. cit.* (Kiev: Gospolitizdat, 1962), pp. 482–83. The attitude of the Central Committee of the RSDRP is shown best in the note by Ia. M. Sverdlov, *ibid.*, p. 419.

CHAPTER X I X

1. Sviatoslav (920–972), duke of Kiev. His reign, spent in conquests, ushered in the most glorious period of the Kievan State. He had the habit of forewarning his enemies about his war plans.

2. The editor was unable to trace the source of this quotation.

3. These verses are found in the original introductory chapter to Winter-maerchen "Deutschland" in the book *Letzte Gedichte und Gedanken von Heinrich Heine*, p. 61. Cf. Heinrich Heine, *Saemtliche Werke*, ed. Dr. Ernst Elster (Leipzig and Vienna: Bibliographisches Institut, n.d.), II, p. 540. ed." . . . mit Schmerzen sehne ich mich nach Torfgeruch, nach den lieben Heidschnuken der Lüneburger Heide, Nach Sauerkraut und Rüben. Ich sehne mich nach Tabaksqualm, Hofräten und Nachtwächtern, Nach Plattdeutsch, Schwarzbrot, Grobheit sogar, Nach blönden Predigerstöchtern."

4. Characters in Gogol's comedy *The Inspector-General*. Khlestakov typifies a reckless braggart and liar.

5. M. S. Hrushevsky (1886–1934), Ukrainian historian and statesman. He became head of Central Rada and president of the Ukrainian People's Republic on its proclamation in January, 1918. After German occupation of the Ukraine he went to Austria but returned in 1924. In 1930 he was exiled from Kiev by the Soviet authorities and died in exile in 1934.

6. Refers to Saratov, Russia, a place of our authors' exile.

7. M. O. Skrypnyk (1872–1933), Soviet Ukrainian statesman and party leader. Member of the RSDRP and an active member of the Bolshevik wing both in Russia and in the Ukraine. One of the founders of the CP(b)U, the head of the Organizational Bureau for the Convocation of the First Congress of the CP(b)U in Moscow. In March, 1918, he was appointed head of the Soviet Ukrainian government. Later on, in 1918, he became a member of the Cheka where he headed the section for combatting the counterrevolution. From 1921 he served in the various ministerial positions in the Soviet Ukrainian government. Committed suicide in 1933.

CHAPTER XX

1. The authors borrowed this line from one of Shevchenko's poems.

2. In the original: "Du musst! du musst! und kostet' es mein leben!" Goethe's *Faust*.

3. Reference is probably to S. Mazlakh, who was of Jewish origin.

4. This verse was borrowed from Shevchenko's poem "Son."

5. The authors refer to Shevchenko's *"Chernets'."*

6. English translation by Edgar Alfred Bowing, *The Poems of Heine* (London: George Bell and Sons, 1901), pp. 260–61. Cf. Heinrich Heine, *Sämtliche Werke*, ed. Dr. Ernst Elster (Leipzig and Vienna: Bibliographisches Institut, n.d.), I, p. 190.

7. The last part of the sentence is taken from Kotliarevskyi's *Aeneid*.

Abbreviations

AUCMC	All-Ukrainian Central Military Committee
CC	Central Committee
Cheka	Soviet Secret Police
CEC	(See Ts.V.K.U.)
CIK	Central Executive Committee
CIKU	(See Ts.V.K.U.)
CP (b) U	(See CP (B) U)
CP (B) U	Communist Party (Bolsheviks) of the Ukraine
Chrezvychaika	(See Cheka)
CVKU	(See Ts.V.K.U.)
KP (B) U	(See CP (B) U)
KP (b) U	(See CP (B) U)
KPZU	Communist Party of Western Ukraine
PC	People's Commissars
PUR	Political Board of the Republic
RCP (B)	Russian Communist Party (Bolsheviks)
RKP (B)	(See RCP (B))
RKP (b)	(See RCP (B))
RNK	Council of Peoples' Commissars (in Ukrainian)
RPSR	Russian Party of the Socialist Revolutionaries
RSDLP	(See RSDRP)
RSDRP	Russian Social Democratic Workers Party
RSDRP (b)	Russian Social Democratic Workers Party (Bolshevik)
RSDWP	(See RSDRP)
RSFSR	Russian Soviet Federative Socialist Republic

RSP	(See RPSR)
RSR	Soviet Socialist Republic (in Ukrainian)
RUP	Ukrainian Revolutionary Party
RVS	(See RVSR)
RVSR	Revolutionary Military Council of the Republic
SD (SD's)	Social Democrat
SDPL	Social Democracy of Poland and Lithuania
SF	Socialist Federalist
SKRKD	Soviet of Workers' Peasants' and Cossack Deputies
SRKD	Soviet of Workers' and Peasant Deputies
SRSD	Soviet of Workers' and Peasant Deputies (in Ukrainian)
SRKSD	Soviet of Workers', Peasants' and Soldiers' Deputies
SNK	Council of Peoples' Commissars
Sovdepy	Soviet Deputies
Sovnarkom	(See SNK)
SPC	(See SNK)
SR (SR's)	Socialist Revolutionary
STO	Council of Labor and Defense
Ts.V.K.U.	Central Executive Committee of the Ukraine
TUP	Association of the Ukrainian Progressives
UCP	Ukrainian Communist Party
UCP (Bor.)	Ukrainian Communist Party (Borot'bists)
UCP (B)	Ukrainian Communist Party (Bolsheviks)
UKP	(See UCP)
UKP (B)	(See UCP (B))
UKP (Bor.)	(See UCP (Bor.))
UNR	Ukrainian People's Republic
UPS-F	Ukrainian Party of Socialists-Federalists
UPS-R	Ukrainian Party of the Socialist-Revolutionaries
URDP	Ukrainian Radical Democratic Party
URSR	Ukrainian Soviet Socialist Republic (in Ukrainian)
USDRP	Ukrainian Social Democratic Workers Party
USDWP	(See USDRP)
USR	(See UPS-R)
USSR	Union of the Soviet Socialist Republics

VCIK	All-Russian Central Executive Committee
	All-Union Central Executive Committee
VCP (B)	All-Union Communist Party
VKP (b)	(See VCP (B))
VTs.IK	(See VCIK)
VTs.VRK	(See AUCMC)
VUCIK	(See VUTs.VK)
VUTs.IK	(See VUTs.VK)
VUTs.VK	All-Ukrainian Central Executive Committee
ZOUNR	Western Oblast of the Ukrainian People's Republic
ZUNR	Western Ukrainian People's Republic

Bibliography of the Works Used

Bukharin, N. *Programma Kommunistov (Bol'shevikov)* [The Program of Communists (Bolsheviks)]. Petrograd, 1919.

"Deistviia i rasporiazheniia Pravitel'stva" [Acts and Orders of the Government] *Izvestiia V. Ts. I. K.*, No. 282 (546) (December 24, 1918).

"Direktoriia ili sovety" [The Directory of the Soviets], *Pravda*, No. 3 (January 4, 1919).

Ia. E. "O sozdanii 'samostoiatelnoi' Kommunisticheskoi Partii Ukrainy" [On the Creation of an "Independent" Communist Party of the Ukraine]. *Pravda*, No. 132 (June 30, 1918).

Il'in, V. (Lenin, V. I.). "Kriticheskie zametki po natsional'nomu voprosu" [Critical Notes on the National Question]. *Prosveshchenie*, Nos. 10–12 (1913).

"Itogi s'ezda" [Summary of the Congress]. *Kommunist*, No. 5 (August 15, 1918).

Iurchenko, V. "Na rozdorizhzhi" [At the Crossroad], *Vistnyk Ukrains'koho Viddilu Narkomnats*, No. 5 (1919).

Izveshchenie o sozyve konferentsii partiinykh organizatsii (Bol'shevikov) Ukrainy [The Announcement of the Convocation of a Conference of Party Organizations of Communists (Bolsheviks) of the Ukraine]. Moscow, 1918.

"K mirnym peregovoram s Ukrainoi: Beseda s tov. Kh. G. Rakovskim" [Toward Peace Negotiations with the Ukraine: A Talk with Comrade Kh. G. Rakovski]. *Izvestiia V. Ts. I. K.*, No. 165 (429) (August 4, 1918).

Kautsky, K. *Nationalstaat, Imperialistischer Staat und Staatenbund.* Nurnberg, 1915.

Kautsky, K. *Natsional'nye problemy* [Nationality Problems]. Moscow, 1918.

Kautsky, K. *Sozialismus und Kolonialpolitik* [Socialism and the Colonial Policy]. Berlin, 1907.

Kulyk, I. "Istoriia revoliutsii na Ukraini" [History of the Revolution in the Ukraine] *Visnyk Ukrains'koho Viddilu Narkomnats*, No. 8 (1918).

Lazerson, M. Ia. *Natsional'nost' i gosudarstvennyi stroi* [Nationality and the State Structure]. Petrograd: Kniga, 1918.

Lenin, V. I. "Itogi diskussii o samoopredelenii" [Discussion on Self-determination Summed Up]. *Sbornik Sotsial-Demokrata*, No. 1 (October, 1916).

Lenin, V. I. "O prave natsii na samoopredelenie" [On the Right of Nations to Self-determination]. *Prosveshchenie*, No. 4–6 (1914).

Lenin, V. I. "Sotsialisticheskaia revoliutsiia i pravo natsii na samoopredel-enie" [The Socialist Revolution and the Right of Nations to Self-determination]. *Sbornik Sotsial-Demokrata*, No. 1 (October, 1916).

Liebknecht, W. *Vospominaniia o Markse* [Reminiscences of Marx]. Petrograd, 1918.

"Manifest Vremennogo Raboche-Krestianskogo Pravitel'stva Ukrainy" [A Manifesto of the Temporary Worker-Peasant Government of the Ukraine]. *Izvestiia V. Ts. I. K.*, December 1, 1918.

"Natsional'nyi vopros v programme Kommunisticheskoi Partii Ukrainy" [The National Ouestion in the Program of the Communist Party of the Ukraine]. *Pravda*, No. 132 (June 30, 1918).

Piatakov, G. L. "Nadgrobnoe slovo tezisam Skrypnika" [Funeral Oration Over Skrypnk's Theses]. *Kommunist*, Nos. 3–4 (1918).

"Pokhod soiuznicheskogo imperializma na Rossiiskuiu revoliutsiiu" [The Attack of the Allied Imperialism Against the Russian Revolution]. *Pravda*, No. 227 (December 20, 1918).

"Polozhenie na Ukraine: Ukraina i Sovetskaia Respublika" [The Situation in the Ukraine: the Ukraine and the Soviet Republic]. *Pravda*, No. 3 (January 4, 1919).

Rakovski, Kh. "Beznadezhnoe delo; O Petliurovskoi avantiure" [The Hopeless Cause: About the Petliura's Adventure]. *Izvestiia V. Ts. I. K.*, No. 2 (554) (January 3, 1919).

"Revoliutsiia i melkaia burzhuaznaia demokratiia: Rech tov. Lenina na sobranii otvetstvennykh rabotnikov kommunistov 27 Noiabria, 1918g" [Revolution and Petty Bourgeois Democracy: Speech of Comrade Lenin at the Meeting of the Leading Workers' Communists of November 27, 1918]. *Izvestiia V. Ts. I. K.*, No. 265 (529) (December 4, 1918).

Rudnitskii, S. "Ocherk geografii Ukrainy" [A Description of the Geography of the Ukraine], *Ukrainskii narod v ego proshlom i nastoiashchem* [Ukrainian People in their Past and Present]. Vol. II, ed. F. K. Volkov. Petrograd, 1916.

Rusov, A. "Statistika ukrainskogo naseleniia evropeiskoi Rossii" [Statistics of the Ukrainian Population of European Russia]. *Ukrainskii narod v ego proshlom i nastoiashchem*. Petrograd, 1916.

Shakhrai, V. An unidentified pamphlet.

Shul'hyn, O. *Polityka* [Politics]. Kiev, 1918.

Skorovstans'kyi, V. [Shakhrai]. *Revoliutsiia na Vkraini* [Revolution in the Ukraine]. Saratov, 1918.

"Ukraina" [The Ukraine]. *Pravda*, June 28 (15 O.S.), 1917.

"Vozzvanie Petliury" [Petliura's Call]. *Izvestiia V. Ts. I. K.* No. 256 (520) (November 23, 1918).

Zatonskii, V. "Iz nedavnogo proshlogo" [From the Recent Past]. *Kommunist*, Nos. 3–4 (1918).

Selected List of Useful Sources

Adams, A. *Bolsheviks in the Ukraine*. New Haven, 1963.

Bol'shaia Sovetskaia Entsiklopediia [Large Soviet Encyclopedia]. 2d ed. 52 vols. Moscow, 1949–58.

Bol'shevitskie Organizatsii Ukrainy v Period Ustanovleniia i Ukrepleniia Sovetskoi Vlasti, Noiabr' 1917–Aprel' 1918 [Bolshevik Organizations of the Ukraine in the Period of the Establishment and Strengthening of Soviet Power, November 1917–April 1918]. Kiev, 1962.

Borys, Jurij. *The Russian Communist Party and the Sovietization of the Ukraine*. Stockholm, 1960.

Deiateli Soiuza Sovetskikh Sotsialisticheskikh Respublik i Oktiabr'skoi Revoliutsii etc. [Leaders of the Union of Soviet Socialist Republics and of the October Revolution] /Entsyklopedicheskii Slovar Russkogo Bibliograficheskogo Instituta Granat, Vol. 41, No. 1–3, Moscow, 1929?/. 3 vols. Photocopy (Ann Arbor, Michigan: University Microfilms, 1964).

Grazhdanskaia Voina na Ukraine, 1918–1920. 4 vols. Kiev, 1967.

Entsyklopediia Ukrainoznavstva [Encyclopedia of the Things Ukrainian]. Munich, 1949.

Doroshenko, Dmytro. *A Survey of Ukrainian Historiography*. New York, 1957.

Dzyuba, I. *Internationalism or Russification?* London and New York, 1968.

Khrystiuk, P. *Zamitky i Materialy do Istorii Ukrains'koi Revoliutsii, 1917–1920* [Notes and Materials for the History of the Ukrainian Revolution, 1917–1920]. 4 vols. Vienna, 1921–22.

Komunistychna Partiia Ukrainy v Rezolutsiiakh i Rishenniakh Zizdiv i Konferentsii, 1918–1956 [The Communist Party of the Ukraine in Resolutions and Decisions of Its Congresses and Conferences, 1918–1956]. Kiev, 1958.

Lawrynenko, J. *Ukrainian Communism and Soviet Russian Policy Toward the Ukraine. An Annotated Bibliography*. New York, 1953.

Luckyj, G. S. N. *Literary Policies in the Soviet Ukraine, 1917–1934*. New York, 1956.

Lykholat, A. *Zdiisnennia Lenins'koi Natsional'noi Polityky na Ukraini, 1917–1920* [The Realization of the Leninist Nationality Policy in the Ukraine, 1917–1920]. Kiev, 1967.

Majstrenko, I. *Borot-bism. A Chapter in the History of Ukrainian Commu-nism.* New York, 1954.

Mazepa, I. *Ukraina v Ohni i Buri Revoliutsii, 1917–1921* [Ukraine in Flames and Storm of the Revolution, 1917–1921]. 2d ed. 3 vols. Munich, 1950–51.

Peremoha Velykoi Zhovtnevoi Sotsialistychnoi Revoliutsii na Ukraini [Victory of the Great October Socialist Revolution in the Ukraine]. 2 vols. Kiev, 1967.

Reshetar, John S., Jr. *The Ukrainian Revolution, 1917–1920. A Study in Nationalism.* Princeton, 1952.

Ukraine: a Concise Encyclopaedia. Vol. I. Toronto, 1963.

Ukrains'ka Radians'ka Entsyklopediia [The Ukrainian Soviet Encyclopedia]. 17 vols. Kiev, 1959–65.

Ukrains'ka Zahal'na Entsyklopediia [The Ukrainian General Encyclo-pedia]. 3 vols. Lviv, 1934.

Ukrains'kyi Radians'kyi Entsyklopedychnyi Slovnyk [The Ukrainian Encyclopedic Dictionary]. 3 vols. Kiev, 1966–68.

Vynnychenko, V. *Vidrodzhennia Natsii. Istoriia Ukrains'koi Revoliutsii, Marets' 1917–Hruden' 1919* [Rebirth of the Nation. History of the Ukrainian Revolution, March 1917–December 1919]. 3 vols. Kiev-Vienna, 1920.

Zozulia, Ia. *Velyka Ukrains'ka Revoliutsiia* [The Great Ukrainian Revolu-tion]. New York, n.d.

Index